Irrationality

Irrationality

AN ESSAY ON AKRASIA, SELF-DECEPTION, AND SELF-CONTROL

Alfred R. Mele

New York   Oxford

OXFORD UNIVERSITY PRESS

1987

Oxford University Press

Oxford   New York   Toronto
Delhi   Bombay   Calcutta   Madras   Karachi
Petaling Jaya   Singapore   Hong Kong   Tokyo
Nairobi   Dar es Salaam   Cape Town
Melbourne   Auckland

and associated companies in
Beirut   Berlin   Ibadan   Nicosia

Library of Congress Cataloging-in-Publication Data
Mele, Alfred R., 1951–
Irrationality: an essay on akrasia,
self-deception, self-control.
Bibliography: p.   Includes index.
1. Irrationalism (Philosophy)   2. Act (Philosophy)
3. Self-deception.   4. Self-control.   I. Title.   II. Title: Akrasia.
B824.2.M45   1987   128'.4   86-23608
ISBN 0-19-504321-9 (alk. paper)

1 3 5 7 9 8 6 4 2

Printed in the United States of America
on acid-free paper

*To my mother and father and
to Connie and our children,
Al, Nick, and Angela.*

§

Preface

If the popularity of self-help manuals and therapies is any indication, irrational behavior is remarkably common. People eat, spend, smoke, and so on more (or less) than they think they should, and they expend much time and effort attempting to bring their behavior into line with their better judgments. Yet certain garden-variety forms of irrationality—most notably, incontinent action and self-deception—pose such difficult theoretical problems that some philosophers have rejected them as logically or psychologically impossible.[1] Moreover, when the possibility of these species of irrationality is admitted, the phenomena tend either to be diluted or to be explained by means of relatively drastic hypotheses.

Part of the problem—a large part of it, I believe—is that philosophical models for the explanation of action and belief are typically designed specifically for rational behavior. When irrational behaviors cannot be stretched or cut to fit a favored model, their very existence may be denied. And when they are made to fit, they often look more rational than one should have thought.

Sometimes, of course, the *models* bend; but not far enough, or not in the right places. Thus, Donald Davidson, in his important and influential paper, "How Is Weakness of the Will Possible?" (1970a), countenances incontinent action against an all-things-considered better judgment, but his conception of action-explanation commits him to denying that we can act incontinently against an "unconditional" judgment (i.e., an intention). In a later paper (1982), rather than not bending far enough, Davidson expands his model in an unpromising direction, insisting that incontinent action depends upon a problematic form of mental partitioning.

This tendency is prevalent as well in the literature on self-deception. Some who admit that the phenomenon is possible will not allow the self-deceiver to go so far as to *believe* the proposition that he would like to be true, limiting him to sincere avowals of the proposition or to avoiding the thought of a proposition that he would like to be false. Others attempt to make room for the favored belief by locating a competing false belief outside of consciousness, or by dividing the mind into a deceiving agent and a deceived patient who is unaware of the agent's machinations.

In this book, rather than attempting to make incontinent action and self-deception fit popular philosophical preconceptions about action and belief, I start with a blank slate, inquiring at times about the implications of motivated irrationality for traditional theories of the mind. I employ a traditional conception of incontinent action and focus on the theoretically most challenging species—akratic action against an intention to perform an action of a particular type here and now. In the case of self-deception, I reject a common, interpersonal approach to characterizing the phenomenon and defend an account that is much more adequate to the examples treated in the philosophical and psychological literature on the topic.

The primary purpose of this study is to show that and *how* incontinent action and self-deception are possible. In both cases, drawing upon recent experimental work in the psychology of action and inference, I advance naturalized explanations of the phenomena while resolving the paradoxes around which the philosophical literature on motivated irrationality revolves.

This book has two secondary goals as well. One concerns self-control, a prophylaxis of sorts against motivated irrationality. I explain what self-control is, resolve a collection of intriguing and little-discussed paradoxes about its exercise, and illuminate the role of self-control in explanations of human behavior. Another objective of this essay is to clarify the etiology of intentional action in general. I show that what I call strict akratic action is an insurmountable obstacle for traditional belief-desire models of action-explanation and I explain how a considerably modified belief-desire model may accommodate action of this sort and, more generally, intentional action performed in the face of competing motivation.

Initially, the centerpiece of this book was to have been a full-scale account of intentional action that took incontinent action seriously from the start. I had worked out an interpretation of Aristotle's theory of human action which seemed to me to accommodate most types of incontinent action,[2] and I wanted to advance an improved, quasi-Aristotelian theory of my own. However, I could not resist tantalizing problems posed by the hypothesis that *akrasia* (variously translated as 'incontinence,' 'weakness of will,' or 'lack of self-control') is manifested in belief as well as action and by the related paradoxes of self-deception. The focus of the book consequently shifted to motivated irrationality in general. Rational behavior had to take a back seat.

On some conceptions of the philosophical enterprise, I venture well outside my province in this book, especially in Chapters 6 and 10. I agree that armchair explanations of behavior are bound to be deficient. But I believe that philosophy is continuous with science; and in my effort to understand incontinent action, self-deception, and self-control, I reap substantial rewards from the literature of experimental psychology.

Acknowledgments

This book incorporates, in revised form, some previously published work of mine, as follows. Chapter 2.1: "Pears on *Akrasia,* and Defeated Intentions," *Philosophia* 14(1984):145–152. Chapter 2.2: "Is Akratic Action Unfree?" *Philosophy and Phenomenological Research* 46(1986):673-679; Chapter 3: "*Akrasia,* Reasons, and Causes," *Philosophical Studies* 44(1983):345–368 (© 1983 by D. Reidel Publishing Company); Chapter 4.1–2: "Self-Control, Action, and Belief," *American Philosophical Quarterly* 22(1985):169–175; Chapter 8: "Incontinent Believing," *Philosophical Quarterly* 36(1986): 212–222. Chapter 9.1,2,4–6: "Self-Deception," *Philosophical Quarterly* 33(1983):365–377. I am grateful to the editors and publishers for permission to reprint material from these articles.

I am indebted to many friends and colleagues for their helpful comments on one or another ancestor of various chapters and sections. Thanks are due to George Abernethy, Fred Adams, Robert Audi, Joe Beatty, Norman Dahl, Irwin Goldstein, John Heil, Brian McLaughlin, Earl MacCormac, Bob Maydole, Jim Montmarquet, Paul Moser, George Quattrone, Richard Reilly, Ed Sankowski, Michael Smith, Ronald de Sousa, Lance Stell, Irving Thalberg, and Michael White.

I am grateful also to the National Endowment for the Humanities for supporting my work on this book with a 1985/86 Fellowship for College Teachers and to Davidson College for a sabbatical leave during the same academic year. Lee French did a thoroughly professional job of typing the manuscript. Michele Miller helped with the typing of revisions and with numerous other tasks.

I would like to express my gratitude, finally, to Connie and to our children, Al, Nick, and Angela—for everything. Al, at the age of fourteen, not only introduced me to the world of computers and word processing, but also wrote an excellent alphabetizing program for my bibliography.

NOTES

1. I suggest in Chapter 8 that not all instances of self-deception need be irrational.
2. See, especially, Mele (1985a). See also, Mele (1984a), (1984c), (1984d), (1981a), (1981b), (1981c).

Davidson, N.C.   A. R. M.
July 1986

§

Contents

Irrationality

1

Akratic Action: Some Theoretical Difficulties

The earliest detailed philosophical treatment of *akrasia* or weakness of will is found in Plato's *Protagoras,* where Socrates defends the thesis (352aff.) that "no one willingly does wrong." The notion of *akrasia* finds expression earlier, however, in Greek literature (e.g., in Euripides' "Hippolytus," 380ff.,[1] and in his "Medea," 1078ff.). Homer, much earlier yet, makes it painfully evident how hunger and greed can pull reason from her throne, but he does not leave his audience feeling that reason is a slave of the appetites and passions. Odysseus's having himself lashed to the mast in order that he may safely hear the Sirens' song shows what a little foresight can do (*Odyssey,* Bk. 12).

Akrasia is obviously a practical problem. It is an impediment to the achievement of certain of our goals, to the execution of certain of our projects and intentions. It is also a theoretical problem, as Socrates' denial of its very possibility suggests. In the first two sections of this chapter, I define a central species of akratic action and delineate a range of theoretical difficulties raised by the phenomenon—difficulties that an adequate explanation of the nature and possibility of akratic behavior must resolve. Attention to early philosophical work on the topic will facilitate both tasks, and for this reason I have chosen to introduce this nonhistorical study with a semihistorical chapter. The third and final section addresses a question about motivation and relative motivational strength.

1. Akrasia and Akratic Action

Akrasia, strictly speaking, is not a type of action but a trait of character. It is a lack of, or deficiency in, a certain kind of power or strength (*kratos*), namely, the power of self-control. Aristotle tells us that self-control and incontinence (*enkrateia* and *akrasia*) "are concerned with that which is in excess of the state characteristic of most men; for the continent man abides by his resolutions more and the incontinent man less than most men can" (*Nicomachean Ethics* 1152a25–27). This is at least roughly correct. We do not restrict our use of these terms to people who are perfectly possessed of, or wholly lacking in, self-control. *Akrasia* is, in this sense, relativistic.

Given our relativistic understanding of *akrasia* or weakness of will, not every instance of incontinent action is a manifestation of this trait. Even someone who is very self-controlled with respect to the temptations of extramarital sex may, in a particularly stimulating situation, incontinently fail to live up to his standards. In acting incontinently, such a person shows, not that he is *deficient* in self-control, but only that his powers of self-control are less than perfect.

It should also be observed that *akrasia* and self-control need not be *global* traits of character. Many people who are adept at resisting certain kinds of temptation make a poor showing against other kinds. Someone who exhibits a great deal of self-control in his professional life, for example, may be quite weak-willed about eating or smoking. Perhaps, as Amelie Rorty has put it (1980a, p. 205), *akrasia* is "characteristically regional."

My concern in the present section is less with the *trait* of *akrasia* than with akratic *action*. Standardly conceived, akratic or incontinent action is *free, intentional* action contrary to the agent's *better judgment*. Not everyone would admit that there are such actions, of course; but the question of their reality cannot properly be broached until the notion of akratic action itself has been clarified.

Not all intentional action against one's better judgment is incontinent. We distinguish the heroin addict's injecting the drug against his better judgment from the thrillseeker's experimenting with the drug contrary to what he judges best. The former action, unlike the latter, is compelled, or so we are inclined to say; and compelled action, on the standard view, is importantly different from incontinent action. These are the intuitions that lie behind the common conception of akratic action as *free* action. This conception has been challenged, of course. The challenge is taken up in Chapter 2.

A note of caution is in order about the intentionality of incontinent action. Properly understood, the assertion that incontinent action is intentional action does not entail that the agent of an akratic action intends to act *akratically*. Just as a woman (intentionally) walking down a snowy sidewalk may know that in doing so she is getting her shoes wet without intending to get her shoes wet, a man (intentionally) eating a large helping of dessert may know that in doing so he is acting akratically without intending to act akratically. Actions intended under one description (e.g., 'eating some pie') may not be intended under another (e.g., 'acting akratically'). Or alternatively, for those who favor a finer-grained method of act-individuation, an action level-generated by an intended action need not itself be intended (cf. Goldman, 1970, Ch. 3.3). If akratic action is intentional action, then the person who akratically eats the pie, intentionally *eats the pie,* and (typically) intends to eat the pie;[2] but the stronger claim, that he intends to act akratically, does not follow.

The third and last characteristic of akratic action, traditionally conceived, is that it is contrary to the agent's better judgment. A number of observations are in order. First, some have mistakenly identified *akrasia* with *moral* weakness (e.g., Hare, 1963, Ch. 5). The better judgment against which the akratic agent acts is not necessarily a judgment of the morally better. A person who judges that, morally speaking, it is better to do A than B (both of which competing actions he recognizes to be open to him) may freely and intentionally do B without acting akratically; for he may have judged that *all things considered* (moral and otherwise) his doing B would be better than his doing A. Surely, moral considerations are not always regarded as overriding, even by agents who take morality seriously.

We must distinguish, in this connection, between two types of first-person practical judgments, namely, judgments that commit the agent to action (provided that the judgment is retained) and judgments that do not. Suppose that S judges that, from the perspective of his own aesthetic values, it would be better to do A than B at t. Unless he takes aesthetic considerations to be overriding, he is not thereby committed to doing A in preference to B (i.e., to doing A at t, if he does either A or B at t). But, we are inclined to say, some judgments do commit agents to action; that is, some judgments are such that if, while we hold them, we do not act in accordance with them, we open ourselves up to the charge of irrationality. When an agent intentionally and freely performs B while holding the judgment that, *all things considered,* it is best not to do B, what he does is *subjectively* irrational. It is irrational from his *own* point of view, the point of view reflected in that judgment.[3] Of course, a judgment need not actually have been made on the basis of a *consideration* of *all* of the agent's relevant values and beliefs in order for a failure to act on it to exhibit irrationality. When, for example, there is time only for brief deliberation, a person may consider only what he takes to be his strongest reasons for and against his imagined options. If, on the basis of a consideration of such reasons, he judges that it is best to do A at t, which judgment he retains at t, he is surely committed to doing A at t and is open to the charge of irrationality if he fails to do A at t.[4]

I shall use the term *decisive better judgment* for judgments that commit the agent to action in the sense explained. The rare judgment that is based on (and supported by) a consideration of the totality of the agent's pertinent beliefs and values (including desires, fears, principles, etc.) qualifies as a 'decisive better judgment' in my sense. So do judgments made from the perspective of a segment of this totality which the agent takes to be overriding. More generally, any judgment that, in the agent's opinion, constitutes sufficient reason for action is a decisive better judgment. Decisive better judgments are importantly different from better judgments made only from the point of view of some segment of the agent's system of values which is not taken by him to be overriding; for, the latter do not settle for the agent the question what it is better or best to do at t, but only what it *would* be better or best to do if the agent *were* to regard certain of his values as being overriding. (In the remainder of this chapter, 'better judgment' should be understood as 'decisive better judgment' unless otherwise indicated.)

The philosophical literature on incontinent action tends to concentrate on the incontinent agent's decisive better judgment about a specific (type of) action to be performed or avoided in his present situation. However, an agent may act incontinently against decisive better judgments of other types. For example, someone who holds the judgment that he should never risk endangering his professional advancement for the sake of sensory gratification, may, due to *akrasia,* be temporarily blinded to the fact that his attempting to seduce his boss's voluptuous daughter may well be detrimental to his career. He may consequently fail to judge that it would be best not to make an attempt at seduction. If, in his blindness, he makes an attempt, he is not acting contrary to a specific better judgment about that attempt, but he is acting contrary to the more general judgment. And if his temporary blindness, which (*ex hypothesi*) is itself an instance of incontinence, prepares the way for the attempt, his efforts at seduction may be derivatively incontinent. In the same vein, an agent may act incontinently against a specific judgment of the better which he does not *explicitly* make or endorse. He may, for example, act incontinently against a judgment of the better which, other things being equal, he *would have made* at the time if his thinking had not been clouded by certain of his desires. Here, *akrasia* is exhibited in his thinking itself, and his action is derivatively akratic.[5] (We may count certain 'implicit' better judgments as decisive in a derivative sense if they *would* constitute sufficient reason for action in the agent's opinion, provided they *were* explicitly made or endorsed.)

In a very useful paper (1980c), Amelie Rorty distinguishes among four points at which an "akratic break" may occur. Her schema is Aristotelian. For Aristotle, the generation of intentional action is roughly divisible into four stages: (1) assent to the "major" premise of a practical syllogism; (2) assent to a pertinent "minor" premise; (3) assent to a conclusion; (4) action.[6] Rorty argues that *akrasia* may defeat the process at any of these junctures. *Akrasia* can manifest itself in an agent's failure to commit himself to the value specified in the major premise, in his interpretation of his particular situation (the "minor premise"), in his not drawing the conclusion warranted by his premises, or in his failing to act on a correct conclusion that he draws.

Debates about the possibility and explanation of incontinent action typically focus on what I shall call *strict incontinent action,* that is, incontinent action against a consciously held better judgment about something to be done *here and now.* Strict incontinent action may be characterized more precisely as follows:

> An action *A* is a *strict incontinent action* if and only if it is performed intentionally and freely and, at the time at which it is performed, its agent consciously holds a judgment to the effect that there is good and sufficient reason for his not performing an *A* at that time.

It is with strict incontinent action that I shall primarily be concerned in the remainder of this chapter.

The traditional conception of akratic action that I have been elaborating requires revision on one point. Akratic action, traditionally conceived, is free, intentional action contrary to the agent's (decisive) better judgment. However, it certainly looks as though an agent can exhibit 'weakness of will' in cases in which what he freely and intentionally does is *in accordance with* his decisive better judgment (cf. Jackson, 1984, p. 41). Consider the following example, Rocky, who has promised his mother that he would never play tackle football, has just been invited by some older boys to play in tomorrow's pick-up game. He believes that his promise evaluatively defeats his reasons for playing and consequently judges that it would be best not to play; but he decides to play anyway. However, when the time comes, he suffers a failure of nerve. He does not show up for the game—not because he judges it best not to play, but rather because he is afraid. He would not have played even if he had decisively judged it best to do so.

Rocky's failure to play in the football game may exhibit weakness of will even though he judges it best not to play. The traditional conception of akratic action should be broadened to accommodate such cases.

However, free, intentional action contrary to one's decisive better judgment remains an important and historically central species of akratic action; and this is the species on which I shall focus in this book. *Strict incontinent action*, as I have defined it, is a subspecies of akratic action of the traditional sort. But what I say in subsequent chapters about its possibility and explanation may be applied, with some minor adjustments, to nontraditional cases.

2. Theoretical Problems

Incontinent action is generally discussed only in connection with a favored thesis for which it constitutes a problem. Because of the tendentiousness of the program, the typical result is that *akrasia* is allowed to extend only as far as the favored thesis permits. In some cases, strict akratic action as a whole is rejected as illusory, as it is, most notably, by Socrates and R. M. Hare. I shall take up the question of the possibility of the phenomenon in subsequent chapters. The purpose of the present section is to identify some of the more important questions that a satisfactory explanation of the possibility of strict akratic action must address.

Socrates' denial of the possibility of strict akratic action in Plato's *Protagoras* seems to rest on the idea that it is not "in human nature" (see 358d) to pursue freely what one takes to be the lesser good (or greater evil). If this impression is correct, Socrates accepts what I shall call the thesis of *natural practical rationality:*

> *NPR*. Human beings are psychologically so constituted that they freely do *A* at *t* only if they do not, at *t*, take some competing action to be better.

The *Protagoras* does not make clear the grounds on which *NPR* is held. One possibility is that Socrates accepted a version of the thesis that whenever we act freely we do what we are most motivated to do, while making no distinction between our *assessments* or *rankings* of the objects of our desires on the one hand and the *motivational force* of our desires on the other (cf. Santas, 1966, pp. 27, 29). Another is that he accepted the motivational thesis in question while also thinking that when the strength of a desire is out of line with the agent's assessment of the desired object, the agent lacks control over his conative condition and therefore does not *freely* act on the desires that move him to action (Santas, pp. 30–33). In either case, Socrates presents us with a worthy challenge. If strict akratic action depends upon a lack of alignment between motivational strength and evaluation, the distinction must be articulated and defended. Moreover, it must be made and defended in such a way as to allow for *free* action contrary to one's better judgment.

Plato's own (or later) position is not, for present purposes, significantly different from the Socratic one. Although he explicitly admits the possibility of action against one's better judgment (*Republic* IV 439e–440b; *Laws* III 689a–b, IX 863a–e), he retains the Socratic view that no one *freely* does wrong (*Laws* IX 860c–863e). Like his mentor, Plato leaves us with an important question: Is human psychology such as to permit strict akratic action?

The idea that what seems to be strict akratic action is really unfree action is by no means a mere archaic oddity. A version of this view is defended by R. M. Hare in *Freedom and Reason* (1963, Ch. 5) and, more recently, by Gary Watson (1977) and David Pugmire (1982). Their arguments are examined in the following chapter. It will suffice to notice at this point that whereas Socrates' view seems to rest on his conception of human nature, Hare appeals to an alleged logical connection between judgment and action (1963, p. 79), while Watson and Pugmire focus on the notion of resistance, contending that if the *akrates* could have resisted his offending desire he would have done so. Thus, we are faced with two additional questions: Is strict akratic action *logically* possible? And can someone who judges it best not to do A and who is able to resist (successfully) his desire to do A nevertheless succumb to temptation? (We might also ask whether someone who is unable to resist a certain desire can nevertheless freely act to satisfy that desire.)

Aristotle is much more latitudinarian about akratic action, or so I have argued elsewhere (1981c; 1985a). However, some interpretations of his work on the topic have the result that he also rules strict akratic action out of court. Brief attention to one such interpretation will prove instructive.

In a number of texts, Aristotle seeks to explain intentional action by means of what has come to be called the "practical syllogism."[7] On one interpretation of the syllogism, its conclusion *is* an action.[8] The upshot, of course, is that akratic action against the conclusion of a practical syllogism is impossible: To conclude a syllogism *is* to act. However, as another interpretation has it, the conclusion is a choice, decision, or intention to do an A here and now, or a judgment that it would be best to do an A straightaway. Does this leave room for strict akratic action? Not if the relationship between conclusions of practical syllogisms and actions is such that were the *akrates* to draw a conclusion concerning immediate action he would act accordingly. "When a single opinion results" from one's practical premises, Aristotle contends, "the man who can act and is not prevented must immediately act accordingly" (*NE* VII.3,

1147a26-31); and, one might suggest, the qualifications leave room for unfree action that violates the agent's better judgment, but not for akratic action.

The philosophical thesis in the last sentence is open to two different interpretations, a causal and a logical one. The causal interpretation gives us what I shall call the *thesis of causal sufficiency:*

> CS. *S*'s judging it best (or intending, deciding, choosing)[9] at *t*, to do *A* at *t* is causally sufficient for his doing *A* at *t*, provided that he is physically and psychologically able to do so.

The corresponding logical thesis—the *thesis of logical sufficiency*—is as follows:

> LS. Necessarily, if *S* judges it best (or intends, decides, chooses) at *t* to do *A* at *t* and is physically and psychologically able to do *A* at *t,* then *S* does *A* at *t*.

The two theses share a common core. The same conditions are deemed sufficient for intentional action; and both theses exclude the possibility of strict akratic action, if the freedom of an akratic action depends upon the agent's being physically and psychologically able to perform the action judged best. The difference lies in the type of sufficiency urged—causal or logical—and, correspondingly, in the type of impossibility that is supposed to be involved in strict akratic action.

It is noteworthy that Hare propounds a version of the logical thesis while Donald Davidson embraces a close relative of the causal thesis. Hare contends (1963, p. 79) that an agent who assents to the judgment that he ought to do *X* "must also assent to the command 'Let me do *X*'." Further, "it is a tautology to say that we cannot sincerely assent to a command addressed to ourselves, and *at the same time* not perform it, if now is the occasion for performing it, and it is in our (physical and psychological) power to do so." Davidson, in his influential paper "How Is Weakness of the Will Possible?", accepts a pair of principles that jointly imply the following: If an agent judges that it would be better to do *x* than to do *y*, then he will intentionally do *x* if he does either *x* or *y* intentionally (1970a, p. 95). And the principles rest, for him, on a "very persuasive" *causal* "view of the nature of intentional action and practical reasoning" (p. 102).

The causal thesis presents us with yet another important question: Is the truth of a causal theory of action incompatible with the occurrence of strict akratic action? More specifically, is the causal connection between better judgments and action such as to preclude the occurrence of strict akratic action? Most plausible philosophical theories of action give important explanatory roles to practical judgments, decisions, intentions, and the like. However, if our free, intentional actions are sometimes at odds with what we decisively judge best, and even with what we decide or intend to do on the basis of such a judgment, then the bearing that intentions, decisions, and judgments have upon action becomes problematic. The problem is obvious if one holds, as I do, that these psychological items play a *causal* role in action. If practical judgments, decisions, or intentions result in appropriate actions in some cases but not in others, some explanation is required. And if we resist the temptation to write off ostensibly akratic action as the product of irresistible desires, a satisfactory explanation may seem unattainable.

The broader causal questions will be taken up in Chapter 3. I shall argue there that a causal theory of action leaves room even for strict akratic action against an intention to do an *A* here and now. The other questions identified here—questions about the logical and psychological possibility of strict akratic action, particularly as regards its being free—are addressed in Chapter 2.

3. Motivation and Motivational Strength

In the preceding section, I alluded to a distinction that is central to much of this book. This is a distinction between an agent's assessments or rankings of the objects of his wants and the motivational force of those wants.[10] The distinction is articulated and defended in Chapter 3 below; and it is fruitfully employed in several chapters. The present section addresses a related and more fundamental issue.

In a challenging, provocative article, Irving Thalberg finds fault with an earlier suggestion of mine (Mele, 1983a) about the explanation of strict akratic action (Thalberg, 1985). The suggestion depends upon a common notion of motivation and, more specifically, on the idea that some motivations (or wants, very broadly conceived) have more motivational force or strength than others.[11] It is the latter that Thalberg calls into question. When I first read his paper, I thought that if one had to reject the notion of relative motivational strength to refute my suggestion about *akrasia,* then my suggestion must be very well-grounded indeed. I still think so, and in this section I shall explain why. Or, rather, I shall make a case for the inclusion of a notion of motivation, and of motivational strength, in an intentionalistic psychological model of action-explanation.[12]

Thalberg is well aware of the intuitive appeal of the idea that wants vary in motivational strength and of the lengthy tradition of the idea in both philosophical and psychological work on human action. But he finds it difficult to understand what can be meant by the claim that S is most strongly motivated at t to A at t, if not simply that he does A at t. And, he asks, if this *is* what is meant, how can we *explain* an agent's A-ing at t by pointing out that he was most motivated to do so at the time? Moreover, if actions cannot be explained in terms of motivational strength, the notion may seem to lack application entirely.

Thalberg's challenge should be met. I shall start with a question about motivation and work my way up to motivational strength.

In his recent book, *Intending and Acting,* Myles Brand asks the reader to imagine an agent who now has "the opportunity to jump up and touch the ceiling" and who focuses his attention upon doing so—even "to the extent that [his] attending to this course of action fully occupies [his] consciousness" (1984, p. 45). Will the agent jump? Only, Brand observes, if he is "moved" to jump. "Representing to oneself a future course of action, no matter the centrality and persistence of this representation, will not by itself initiate action. There must also be a noncognitive feature—a *conative* feature, to revive some old style terminology—to the mental event initiating action" (p. 45). Brand's point, in short, is this: Cognition without motivation will not issue in intentional action.

Another example of Brand's is worth considering. A high school friend of mine—I shall call him Enzo—used to do precisely the sort of thing that Brand imagines (pp. 238ff.), and I shall embellish his example a bit to bring it into line with Enzo's behavior. Enzo was fond of constructing elaborate plans of action for robbing local banks. He would gather information about a bank's security system, draw up plans for breaking in, identify the safest time for the robbery, and so on. He also seemed quite confident about his ability to execute his plans. But Enzo never robbed a bank, and I doubt that he was even tempted to do so. For him, the planning was simply a very stimulating intellectual exercise.

Why didn't Enzo rob banks? A natural answer is that he had no desire to do so (or that he was more motivated to refrain from robbing banks than to rob them; the notion of relative motivational strength is addressed shortly). The idea that an agent's intentionally A-ing depends upon his being motivated to A is not the Humean one, that reason is a slave of the passions (*Treatise,* p. 415). Indeed, it is compatible even with Plato's contention that reason has a motivational reservoir of its own (e.g., *Phaedrus,* 237d9-238a2; cf. Reid, 1788, Essay 3, Ch. 2). The idea is compatible as well with an agent's A-ing because he believes that he has a moral obligation to do so, or for some other similarly lofty reason. The motivational thesis at issue is simply that cognition—however intense, complete, and so forth it may be—will not initiate an intentional *A*-ing unless the agent is motivated to *A*, and that there is nothing else to turn the trick either: Intentional action is motivated action.

Can someone who is not at all motivated to *A* nevertheless *A* intentionally? Of course, no one would claim that we are always *intrinsically* motivated to do what we intentionally do, that is, that all of our intentional actions are desired as ends in themselves. Many intentional actions are *extrinsically* motivated—motivated by a concern for something the agent thinks will (or might) be achieved or promoted by his performing the action at issue. But what about intentional byproducts of intentional actions? Suppose, for example, that *S* wants to bail out his overflowing bathtub as quickly as possible and believes that he may do this by throwing the water through his open bathroom window. *S* knows that his daughter's empty wading pool is beneath the window and that he will fill the pool if he empties the bath water in the envisaged way; but he has no desire (motivation) whatsoever to fill the pool. Nevertheless, in order to empty the tub, he throws the water through the window, thereby filling the pool.

My inclination is to say that *S* did not *intentionally* fill the pool.[13] But suppose that I am wrong. Then, granted the stated circumstances, *S* intentionally did something that he had no motivation to do. Nevertheless, the initiation of *S*'s filling the pool is not motivation independent. *S* filled the pool *by* dumping the water out the window, and he was motivated to do the latter. *S*'s filling the pool, we might say, was *motivated by* his desire to empty the tub. And, in this sense of the quoted phrase, we may plausibly say that *S* 'was motivated to fill the pool' even though he *had no motivation* (desire) to fill it.[14]

This illustration suggests a gloss on the claim above that an agent does not intentionally do *A* unless he is motivated to do *A*—that, as I put it, intentional action is motivated action. The thesis need not be construed as entailing that agents have motivation to do everything that they intentionally do. It may be given a more modest reading: Everything that we intentionally do we are motivated to do. What motivates an intentional *A*-ing may be, not motivation to *A*, but rather motivation to do something, *B*, which one knows or believes will (or might) result in one's *A*-ing.

If intentional action is motivated action, what happens when an agent has conflicting motivations? It is at this juncture that a notion of motivational strength is typically introduced into models of action-explanation that give an explanatory role to motivation. A common answer—with the required qualifications about ability, skill, opportunity, the cooperation of the world, and the like—is that the agent will intentionally do at *t* what he is most motivated at *t* to do at *t*. Now, as I shall argue later, to say that *S* *A*-ed because he was most motivated to *A* is not to *explain* his *A*-ing. Rather, it is to provide a point of departure for one who is seeking an explanation of *S*'s *A*-ing. One can explain *S*'s *A*-ing, in significant part, by explaining his motivational condition at the time of action, or so I shall argue.

One who accepts the thesis that intentional actions are motivated actions will find it very difficult to reject the idea that motivations vary in strength. This is not to say that in accepting the thesis in question one commits oneself to explaining actions in terms of relative motivational *strength*, or even to giving motivation itself a role in one's explanations of actions. One may think, for example, that the notion of motivation is too crude and unwieldy to function in a useful model of action-explanation and opt for a purely neurophysiological model without attempting to link the physical states or events to motivation. Rather, the point is this. If there is such a thing as motivation to act, it is a matter of degree. If human beings have any motivation at all, they are often *more* motivated to do some things than others.

It will prove instructive to ask whether one who rejects the notion of motivational strength as spurious can construct an adequate *motivational* model of action-explanation. Suppose that *S* has at *t* a desire to eat an extra helping of dessert at *t* and that he also has at *t* a desire not to violate his New Year's resolution against eating second helpings of dessert. If what he does at *t* is in no way a function of the relative strengths of these desires (or others), how should a motivational explanation of what he proceeds to do be constructed? One might claim that *S* will do whatever he judges best (in light of his evaluations of the objects of his competing desires). But if there are strict akratic actions, as I shall argue later, better judgments are sometimes rendered ineffective by opposing wants (motivations). One might suggest instead that desires (motivations) are hierarchically or-dered—not on the basis of relative motivational strength, of course—and that the agent will act on the higher-ranking desire. This reduces to the previous suggestion if the position of a desire in the hierarchy is determined by the agent's evaluations. But one might advance a hierar-chical framework whose structure is not determined by the agent's evaluations of the objects of wants (nor by motivational strength). It may be suggested, for example, that the hierarchy is a function of habit or character. This, however, is a very dubious bit of psychologizing; for, many competing desires are not related to habitual patterns of behavior in the requisite way, and a wealth of experimental data indicate that 'character' is not a reliable predictor of behavior.[15]

Why should one who accepts the thesis that intentional action is motivated action reject the notion of relative motivational strength? Thalberg (1985) voices an important concern when he asks what it means to say that *S* is most motivated at *t* to *A* at *t*, if not that he *A*-s at *t*. If *the sole criterion* of relative motivational strength is what the agent does, how can the motivational strength of his wants *explain* what he does?

It is worth noting that there are indicators of motivational strength other than subsequent action. An agent's own reports on the matter are relevant, as are past effective choices among options similar to those with which he is now presented. Moreover, the relative motivational strengths of an agent's present desires for competing *future* actions (e.g., buying a house before his infant daughter starts kindergarten versus buying a yacht within five years) cannot *now* be gauged on the basis of which future action he performs; but present goal-directed behavior of his can be quite telling. Indeed, an agent's present behavior concerning temporally distant action-goals is generally a better indication of the relative strength of his *present* motivation to perform the future actions than is his subsequent performance of one of the competing future actions.

Another point merits greater emphasis, however. As I mentioned earlier, I shall be claiming, not that the relative motivational strength of competing items explains an agent's intentional behavior, but only that it provides a point of departure for explanation. Even if an agent's intentionally *A*-ing at *t* were the sole criterion of the relative strength of his motivation at *t* to *A* at *t*, an *explanation* of his motivational condition may help us understand why he acted as he did.

2

The Possibility
of Strict Akratic Action:
Self-Contradiction and Compulsion

The contention that strict akratic action is impossible seems to fly in the face of experience. Philosophers who defend the contention are well aware of this; here, they claim, appearances are deceiving. Nor are they likely to be impressed by alleged examples of strict akratic action, such as those that fill the literature on the topic. What they rightly demand is that their arguments be met head on. Mere refutation, however, is not sufficient. Stalemates are rarely satisfying, and it is not obvious that when their arguments have been defeated 'experience' must carry the day. What is needed is an adequate explanation of the possibility of strict akratic action. The purpose of the present chapter is to prepare the way for such an explanation by defusing some of the more challenging arguments for the impossibility of strict *akrasia*.

1. Better Judgments and Defeated Intentions

A recent paper by David Pears (1982a) is, in significant part, a refutation of an argument for the impossibility of strict akratic action.[1] The argument, which Pears attributes to Donald Davidson, runs as follows:

ARGUMENT A

1. "If an agent does an action intentionally and avoidably, then he must judge it best to do that action" (p. 38).
2. Hence, if the reasoning against which an agent acted incontinently were complete—that is, if it issued in a judgment of 'the best'—the

16

incontinent agent would contradict himself (unless he merely changed his mind, in which case we do not have *akrasia*). For, he would judge that A, the action which he does perform, is best and that B, the action which he incontinently fails to perform, is best (p. 42).

3. But self-contradiction of this sort is impossible (p. 40).

4. There can, therefore, be no akratic actions against a complete process of reasoning.

This argument is nowhere explicitly advanced by Davidson; but its basic elements are present in his paper (1970a), where Pears takes himself to have found it.

In the present section, drawing upon a claim of Davidson's about intending, I shall construct a stronger argument than *Argument A* and show that even this stronger argument fails. I shall here follow Pears in restricting the discussion to the question whether strict akratic action must involve self-contradiction. Other claims against the possibility of strict akratic action are addressed in Section 2 below and in Chapter 3.

Pears objects to premise (1) above. What we intentionally do, he insists, is not always what we judge it best to do; indeed, sometimes we act without making any 'judgment of the best' (p. 41). Unless 'judgment' is given a special, technical sense, Pears is surely right. When, upon coming to the end of a page that one is reading, one intentionally turns to the next page, one typically is not aware of making or holding a judgment that it is best to turn the page. And there is no evident need to suppose that this judgment is present in some nonconscious form in order to explain our ordinary intentional page-turnings. However, 'judgment' *is* a technical term for Davidson.[2] And in a later paper (1978) he makes its meaning clearer. A certain kind of "unconditional" or "all out" judgment, Davidson informs us, "a judgment that something I think I can do—that I think I see my way clear to doing—a judgment that such an action is desirable not only for one or another reason, but in the light of all my reasons, a judgment like this is . . . an *intention*" (1978, p. 58). Whether or not such judgments are properly identified with intentions, Davidson's claim is suggestive of an intuitively plausible replacement for (1), namely,

1′. If, at *t*, an agent intentionally *A*-ed, then he must have intended at *t* to *A* at *t*.

Now if a person's practical reasoning yields an intention to do an *A* in the nonimmediate future and, when the time comes, the agent intentionally does *B*, a competing action,[3] nothing as interesting as self-contradiction need have occurred. The agent may simply have changed his mind. He may, for example, have decided, on the basis of information acquired in the interim, that it would be better to do *B* than *A* at the time in question and so have abandoned his earlier intention. This may still be a case of *akrasia*; for a change of mind may manifest one's 'weakness of will' or 'deficiency in self-control.' But the resulting action, *B,* would be at most derivatively akratic; and our concern is with strict akratic action.

If we want to concentrate, as Pears does, on cases in which akratic action is theoretically most perplexing, we should restrict ourselves to akratic actions against intentions to do an *A* here and now (i.e., if there are any such actions). Here-and-now intentions may derive in either of two ways from practical reasoning. One's practical reasoning may issue *directly* in a here-and-now intention, or one's reasoning may issue in an intention for the nonimmediate future which, roughly speaking, is retained at the time of action. It will be helpful further to restrict our discussion for a short while to cases in which the here-and-now intention against which an *akrates* may be supposed to act is a *direct* result of practical reasoning.[4] This reasoning will be, at least typically, reasoning with a view to action in the immediate future. We may refer to it as 'here-and-now reasoning' and modify *Argument A* as follows:

ARGUMENT B

1′. If, at *t,* an agent intentionally *A*-ed, then he must have intended at *t* to *A* at t.

2′. Hence, if the here-and-now reasoning against which an agent acted incontinently at *t* were complete—that is, if it issued in an intention to do a *B* here and now—the agent would, in a sense, contradict himself (unless he merely changed his mind, in which case we have at most akratic action of a derivative sort). For, it would be true of him both that he intended at *t* to do a *B* at *t* and that he intended at *t* to do an *A* at *t,* even though he knew that he could not do both at *t.*

3′. This kind of self-contradiction is impossible.

4′. There can, therefore, be no underivative actions against a complete process of reasoning.

This argument avoids Pears's objection to premise 1 of the original 'Davidsonian' argument; for *judging A best* is no longer being claimed to be a necessary condition of doing *A* intentionally. It also presents us with an interesting puzzle. Must akratic action against a here-and-now intention involve the agent's having, at one and the same time, competing here-and-now intentions, that is, here-and-now intentions such that he knows that he cannot perform both (or all) the intended actions at the same time? If so, is it possible for a person to have competing intentions of the sort in question?

Premise 1' has recently been attacked (Bratman, 1984), and premise 3' is not beyond question. However, it is premise 2' on which I shall focus here; for, its falsity is particularly revealing in an examination of the alleged impossibility of akratic action. I shall argue that akratic action against a here-and-now intention need not involve the agent's having competing intentions of the sort at issue, *even if* doing X intentionally entails intending to do X.

It is obvious, setting *akrasia* aside for a moment, that not all here-and-now intentions need be executed, even by a subject who is both physically and psychologically able to execute them. Suppose, for example, that, upon having lit a cigar in my study, I recall my promise to my wife not to poison the atmosphere of our home with my cigar smoke, and not only decide to put it out but intend to do so at once (here and now). However, as I move the lit end of the cigar toward the ashtray at my right elbow, I hear the telephone ring and get up to answer it, absentmindedly resting the lit cigar on the rim of the ashtray. There is nothing paradoxical about this. There is time even for here-and-now intentions to be overridden, as it were, by subsequent intentions.

Unless I *decided* to postpone putting out the cigar until I had dealt with the phone call, or *judged* that it would be best to answer the phone before putting out the cigar, it would be odd to describe this as a case of 'changing my mind'; but a person who intends to A here and now does have time to change his mind. For example, a football quarterback, upon forming (or acquiring) an intention to throw the ball here and now to a certain receiver, may see a defender dart in front of his target and stop his arm during its forward motion. Here, it is natural to say that he changed his mind about throwing it to him. If there is time for this, there is also time for an *incontinent* change of mind. A man who, after careful deliberation, forms the here-and-now intention to shoot his injured horse, may, while taking aim at its head, catch a glimpse of its doleful eyes and decide, due to weakness of will, that it would be best after all to save it. His refraining from shooting the horse would, however, be a case of derivative akratic action, and, again, our concern is with strict akratic action.

Let us modify the last case as follows. The man, after careful deliberation, judges it best to put the horse out of its misery and intends to shoot it in the head here and now. While aiming at its head, he notices the sad expression in its eyes and, *still thinking that it would be best to shoot it,* he intentionally refrains from doing so. In this case, the man does not reverse his opinion about what it is best to do. As in the cigar example, the agent's intentional behavior (i.e., his intentionally not shooting the horse) is not attributable to a change in judgment. If this is right, and if the agent *freely* refrains from shooting the horse, we have here an instance of strict akratic action. Furthermore, and most importantly, it is not necessary that our agent have competing intentions of the kind at issue. Just as when I set the lit cigar on the rim of the ashtray I am no longer intending to put it out here and now, our man, when he intentionally refrains from shooting the horse, would seem no longer to have the here-and-now intention to shoot it.

If matters are as I have suggested, then the dissolution of an agent's intention to do an *A* is compatible with his retaining the decisive judgment that it is best to do an *A*. This implies, of course, that decisive better judgments are not intentions. But why should we think otherwise? Davidson's notion of an "unconditional" or "all out" judgment, it should be noted, is stronger than my notion of a decisive better judgment. For Davidson, *S*'s judgment that, *all things considered,* it would be best to do *A* is not an unconditional judgment (1970a, p. 110); for, expressions of unconditional judgments make no reference to the considerations on the basis of which they are formed (p. 110). All-things-considered judgments are, however, *decisive* judgments, in my sense. And, just as Davidson maintains that there is a "step" between all-things-considered judgments and unconditional judgments, it is open to me to postulate a step between *decisive* better judgments and intentions (an idea to which I shall return later). Moreover, if it is insisted, contrary to ordinary usage, that there is some notion of better judgment according to which such a judgment *is* an intention, an obvious reply (in light of the preceding discussion) is that it is not *this* notion that enters into the definition of strict akratic action.

Other important questions remain to be answered of course. Can our agent's refraining from shooting the horse really have been a free action? And how is it possible for someone to judge that his reasons for doing *A* are better than his reasons for doing *B* and yet act, freely and intentionally, in accordance with the latter? The former question is addressed in the following section. The latter—a question bound up closely with the "forward," *causal* connection between judging best and doing which Pears declines to discuss in his essay (see, e.g., p. 47)—is investigated at length in Chapter 3. Thus far, the purpose of the present section has been simply to display a fatal weakness in the strengthened 'Davidsonian' argument for the impossibility of strict akratic action.

A brief comment on Hare's denial of the possibility of akratic action is in order before we move on. Hare, it will be recalled, maintains that sincere assent to an ought-judgment entails sincere assent to a corresponding self-command and that it is tautologous that "we cannot sincerely assent to a command addressed to ourselves, and *at the same time* not perform it, if now is the occasion for performing it, and it is in our (physical and psychological) power to do so" (1963, p. 79). Not only is the latter claim not tautologous, it is false (even if we qualify the antecedent with the stipulation that the agent is aware that now is the time and believes that it is in his power to perform the commanded action). A basketball player who sinks ninety percent of his free throws may, on a particular occasion, command himself (or intend) to sink the one that he is about to shoot and yet fail to sink it even though he is both physically and psychologically able to do so. He is no less able than usual, we may suppose, to make the shot; he simply misses. Hare's claim may be modified to accommodate this point by the insertion of 'attempt to' between 'not' and 'perform' in the statement just quoted. And it may be suggested accordingly that an agent cannot intentionally refrain from doing A (or intentionally do B, recognizing this to be incompatible with his doing A) *while attempting* to do A. But we have already seen that, even if this is true, it does not show that strict akratic action is impossible. Even action against a here-and-now intention to A need not involve the agent's simultaneously attempting to do A and intentionally refraining from doing A.

It is worth noting that the example of the basketball player falsifies not only the *thesis of logical sufficiency* (LS) but also the *thesis of causal sufficiency* (CS) (both formulated in Ch. 1.2). Judging an action best, in conjunction with the physical and psychological ability to perform that action, is neither a logically nor a causally sufficient condition of the performance of that action. Of course, there is an important difference between an akratic failure to act as one judges best and the basketball player's failure to sink the free throw: The action that the akratic agent performs against his better judgment is intentional, but the basketball player does not intentionally miss the shot. One may consequently seek to construct versions of the theses of logical and causal sufficiency that leave room for unintentional, but not (free) intentional, action against one's better judgment. Nevertheless, the Davidsonian and modified Davidsonian arguments considered here do not establish the impossibility of strict akratic action. And we have seen that one way of patching up Hare's version of the thesis of logical sufficiency is compatible with the occurrence of strict akratic action. The view that Hare uses the thesis of logical sufficiency to defend—namely, that "the typical case of moral weakness . . . is a case of 'ought but can't' " (1963, p. 80)—falls within the purview of the following section.

2. The Freedom Condition

On New Year's Eve Fred resolved not to eat an after-dinner snack for the entire month of January. It is now January 15 and he still has not succumbed to temptation. Tonight, however, Fred finally gives in. While watching the NBC Sunday night movie, he experiences a desire to eat the piece of chocolate pie that he has set aside for tomorrow's dessert. He is not at all surprised by the desire's nagging presence since he has had similar desires almost every night for the last two weeks. He has been able successfully to resist them by rehearsing the reasons for not acting on them and by making it evident to himself that these reasons far outweigh any competing reasons that he has. The reasons are now quite familiar to Fred, and the calculation is easy. Fred weighs his competing reasons on the basis of their respective merits, judges that it would be best, all things considered, not to eat the piece of pie, and decides to save the tempting tidbit for tomorrow's dessert. However, a short time later, during an advertisement for Michelob Light, Fred walks to his refrigerator for a beer (which neither Fred nor I count as a snack), spies the pie on the middle shelf, and, still thinking that it would be best not to eat it, removes it and a container of Dream Whip from the refrigerator. Fred carefully spreads the whipped cream over the pie, carries the dessert to his seat in front of the television, and, admitting to himself that, all things considered, he ought not to do what he is about to do, proceeds to eat the pie.

What we have here is ostensibly an example of strict incontinent action. The purpose of the present section is to ascertain whether intentional action against a consciously held better judgment about something to be done here and now can be free. Since I shall argue that it can, I shall make matters more difficult for myself by supposing that Fred wants not to have the desire, *D*, on which he acts and has no second-order desire to have *D*. (Again, I use 'want' and 'desire' interchangeably in a familiar, broad sense of these terms. See Ch. 1, n. 9.)

This pair of suppositions yields the result that Fred's desire to eat the pie was, in some sense, against his will: He desired not to have this desire and he had no desire whatsoever to have it. However, it does not follow from this that, in acting on his desire to eat the pie, Fred was acting against his will and therefore unfreely. If it was within Fred's power successfully to resist acting on this desire, then the desire did not *compel* him to eat the pie, in which case (other things being equal) his eating the pie was a free action.

Could Fred have resisted successfully? Wright Neely contends that "a desire is irresistible if and only if it is the case that if the agent had been presented with what *he took to be* good and sufficient reason for not acting on it, he would still have acted on it" (1974, p. 47). He claims, accordingly, that "a man is free with respect to some action which he performed only if it is true that, if he had been presented with what he took to be a good and sufficient reason for not doing what he did, he would not have done it" (p. 48).

If Neely is right, Fred's desire to eat the pie was irresistible and his eating the pie was unfree; for, Fred took there to be good and sufficient reason for not eating the pie (that evening) but ate it nonetheless. However, Neely's contentions depend upon the assumption that if an agent's belief that there is good and sufficient reason for not acting on a desire, *D*, fails to generate successful resistance of *D*, it was not within his power successfully to resist acting on *D*. This assumption, I shall argue, is false.

David Pugmire, in a recent paper (1982), employs a slightly more modest version of Neely's assumption in arguing that akratic action of the sort at issue here is unfree. It will prove useful in assessing this assumption to see it in operation. The core of Pugmire's argument is as follows. When a person "put himself through a deliberation that opened him, as much as anything in his power could, to what he was doing, and . . . reached a dissuasive all-things-considered value-judgment, resolved and set himself against what he then did anyway," he did all that he could have done to resist (p. 189). But "if the available resources for resistance failed, it would be arbitrary to insist that the desire was resistible on the occasion and his action clearly voluntary" (p. 189). "As everything stood the desire does seem to have been as good as irresistible by him then," for it defeated "his best efforts" (p. 188).

The crucial flaw in the argument is that it depends upon the false premise that there is nothing more that the agent could have done by way of resistance. If there are akratic actions, the akratic agent is evidently less motivated, at the time of action, to perform the action judged best than he is to perform some competing action. Successful resistance is resistance that prevents the agent's final motivational balance from falling on the side of incontinent action. And there is more that Pugmire's agent could have done to prevent this. An agent can, for example, refuse, at the time of action, to focus his attention on the attractive aspects of the envisioned akratic action and concentrate instead on what is to be accomplished by acting as he judges best. He can attempt to augment his motivation for performing the action judged best by promising himself a reward (e.g., a night on the town) for doing so. He can refuse to entertain second thoughts about the judgment that he has just very carefully reached. He can practice more sophisticated self-control techniques prescribed by his behavioral therapist.[5] This is not to say that every agent is at all times capable of making such efforts of resistance; and for my purposes there is no need to insist on such universality. It is sufficient to notice that Pugmire ignores nondeliberative modes of resistance of the sort just described and that measures such as these are plainly capable of having a salutary influence on the balance of one's motivations at the time of action.

There is a general lesson to be learned here. When we ask whether an akratic action was motivated by an irresistible desire, we should ask whether it was in the agent's power at the time to augment his motivation to perform the action judged best, or to decrease his contrary motivation— or, more precisely, whether it was in his power to bring it about that the bulk of his motivation lay on the side of his better judgment. If it was in his power to do the latter, he *could* successfully have resisted the recalcitrant desire(s), and therefore was not motivated by an *irresistible* desire or desires. In the case of Fred, for example, it may well be true both (1) that if, upon noticing the pie or upon returning to his seat with it, he had forced himself to avoid focusing his attention on its attractive aspects, to picture it as something decidedly unattractive to him (e.g., a plate of chocolate-coated chewing tobacco),[6] and to represent vividly to himself some of his stronger reasons for not eating the pie, he would not have succumbed to temptation, and (2) that he was capable at the time of taking these measures.

Neely and Pugmire ignore a whole range of modes of resistance and are thus led to unacceptably weak conceptions of 'irresistible desire.' An agent's acting on a desire that he takes there to be good and sufficient reason not to act on is not a sufficient condition of the desire's being irresistible, even if the action occurs in the deliberative setting that Pugmire describes. An agent in the cognitive condition imagined by Neely or Pugmire may well fail to employ modes of resistance that are open to him at the time and would lead to continent action. In such a case, the offending desire, though not successfully resisted, is resistible.

Of course, if an agent who is alleged to have incontinently A-ed was able successfully to resist his desire to A, one would like some explanation of his failing to do so. Why would someone who wants to resist his desire to do A, who wants not even to have this desire, who has no second-order desire whatsoever to desire to do A, and who *can* successfully resist the offending desire, nevertheless succumb to it? If no adequate answer is forthcoming, we may be forced to retract our supposition that he was able to resist successfully. Gary Watson notices these points (1977); and he argues that the failure in question cannot be explained by the agent's *choosing* not to resist, nor by his making a culpably insufficient *effort* to resist, and that we are therefore left with a single explanation—the agent was *unable* to resist (pp. 336–338).

I shall focus on a segment of Watson's argument, a segment designed to show that the explanation at issue cannot be that the agent "misjudged the amount of effort required" (p. 338). It is not clear, Watson says, how misjudgment of the sort in question is to be understood; and "even if misjudgment were involved, that would be a different fault from weakness of will." The point of the final claim, presumably, is that if an agent's acting contrary to his better judgment is to be attributed to his making a misjudgment of the sort in question, it cannot also be attributed to "weakness of will." Watson does not attempt to defend this claim.

One possibility that Watson overlooks is that in some cases of akratic action an agent may make no judgment whatsoever about "the amount of effort required" to resist his recalcitrant desire(s). Indeed, this appears to be more than just a possibility. Consider the following case.[7] Alex's friend, Bob, has proposed that they affirm their friendship by becoming blood brothers, since Alex is about to go away to prep school. The ceremony involves the boys' cutting their own right palms with a sharp new pocket knife and then shaking hands so that their blood will run together. Alex is averse to drawing blood from himself; but he carefully weighs his reasons for accepting the proposal against his competing reasons (including, of course, the aversion just mentioned) and judges that, all things considered, it would be best to accept the proposal and to perform the ceremony at once. He decides, accordingly, to cut his hand with the knife here and now, thus forming an intention to do so; and, without considering that he may find the task difficult to accomplish, he grasps the knife and moves it toward the right palm with the intention of drawing blood. However, as he sees the knife come very close to his skin he stops (intentionally),[8] defeated by the abovementioned aversion. (Upset at himself for having failed, Alex resolves to try again, this time without looking. The second attempt is successful.)

Perhaps Watson would want to assimilate this case of nonjudgment to a case of *mis*judgment about the effort required to resist. If so, he would take the position that if Alex's refraining from cutting his hand is to be attributed to his failing to appreciate "the amount of effort required," it is not to be attributed to *akrasia*. Is it clear, however, that *both* items cannot enter into the explanation of his action? It is true, we may suppose, that if Alex had correctly gauged "the amount of effort required," he would not have acted against his better judgment. But can we suppose, consistently with this, that if he had been 'stronger' or more self-controlled there would have been no need for him to make a special effort to resist?

It will prove useful, in attempting to answer this question, to distinguish between two quite different kinds of resistance—what we may call *skilled* and *brute* resistance. In a case of skilled resistance, the agent actively manipulates his motivational condition. He may adopt strategies that he hopes will increase his motivation for performing the action judged best, or attempt to decrease his motivation for doing the contrary action (e.g., by concentrating on the unattractive features of that action). He may even attempt to control his motivation by altering his environment: For example, a heavy smoker who has decided to try to cut back to three cigarettes a day may keep his cigarettes in an out-of-the-way place so that he will have plenty of time to make a special effort of self-control when he is tempted to smoke.

Brute resistance, on the other hand, is what we have in mind when we speak, in ordinary parlance, of someone's resisting temptation by sheer effort of will. Since this use of 'will' makes many philosophers (the author included) uneasy, I shall attempt to unpack the idea less provocatively. To say simply that the agent *intends* to do *X*, the action that he judges best, does not capture the notion of brute resistance; for, an agent may have such an intention when there is nothing to resist. *S*'s intending to do *X* with the awareness that he is faced with competing motivation comes closer to what we want. But this leaves unrepresented the element of *effort* involved in brute resistance. Moreover, whereas brute resistance is intentional, one may intend to do *X* without intentionally intending to do *X*. I suggest, therefore, that we understand brute resistance as follows: To make an effort of brute resistance in support of one's doing *X* is to form or retain an intention to do *X* in order to bring it about that, rather than succumbing to temptation, one *X*-s. That is, it is with a *further intention* that the agent exercising brute resistance forms or retains the intention to do *X*—with the intention, namely, of bringing it about that he *X*-s rather than *Y*-s. This account captures the intentional element, and therefore the element of effort, involved in brute resistance. The brute resister *intentionally* forms or retains the intention to *X*. And anything intentionally done plainly requires *some* effort. (Of course, some instances of brute resistance may involve more effort than others.)

An exceptionally resolute individual may not need to rely on resistance of any sort—even in cases of strong temptation—to act as he judges best. His better judgments may yield intentions that are sufficiently firm as not to require support. Others may find that brute resistance is sometimes called for, and typically sufficient, to prevent incontinent action, while yet others may need to resort more often to skilled resistance. In any case, now that we have a better sense of what resistance involves, it is easy to see how an action may be explained *both* by an agent's failing to make a judgment about "the amount" (or sort) of resistance required to avoid being defeated by recalcitrant desires *and* by his 'weakness.' For, it may be true both that an agent would not have done *A* if he had seen what he needed to do to mount a successful resistance against his desire to do *A* and that, if he had been stronger or more resolute, a special effort of resistance would have been unnecessary. (We may also note that an agent's failure to see what sort or "amount" of resistance is required may itself be due to *akrasia*.)

This point applies as well, of course, to the case of *misjudgment* about requisite effort. It may be true both that an agent would not have acted against his better judgment if he had not mistakenly deemed brute resistance sufficient and that, if he had been stronger, his unsuccessful brute effort would have been sufficient. Similarly, an unsuccessful effort of *skilled* resistance may be explained by pointing out that the agent made this insufficient effort because he was mistaken about the amount or kind of resistance required *and* by observing that, if he had been stronger, this effort, or even mere brute resistance, would have been successful.

I am unwilling to accept the inference from '*S* would successfully have resisted *D* (a desire that prompted him to act against his better judgment) if he had had a greater capacity for self-control' to '*D* was resistible by *S*.' (Compare: 'It is false that *S* was unable [at *t*] to lift the weight [at *t*], for if he had been stronger he would have lifted it.') However, we are still left with the eminently reasonable suggestion that, in some cases, *S* would successfully have resisted *D* if he had exercised his powers of self-control in a way or ways open to him at the time, and that in these cases *D was* resistible by *S*. Watson might object that in these cases the "fault" which explains *S*'s action is not *akrasia*. But this contention, as we have seen, is false. Nonjudgment and misjudgment of the amount or kind of effort required to resist (successfully) a pertinent desire quite properly enter into explantions of strict akratic actions. Furthermore, as I shall argue next, it is far from clear that strict akratic action *depends* upon nonjudgment or misjudgment of this sort.

The target of the preceding few paragraphs is Watson's contention that an action's being partially explained by the agent's misjudgment about "the amount of effort required" to resist his recalcitrant desire is incompatible with its being akratic. That is why I have focused on cases in which misjudgment (or nonjudgment) does enter into the explanation of the action. However, I see no compelling reason to deny that an agent who *does* see how to resist a desire may perform a strict akratic action in accordance with that desire.

Watson's claim that akratic action cannot be due to an agent's *choosing* not to resist a recalcitrant desire merits discussion in this connection. He offers two pieces of support for the assertion. First, to make a choice of the sort at issue "would be to change [one's] original judgment" (1977, p. 337): "The weak drinker's failure to resist her desire to drink is a failure to implement her choice not to drink. To choose not to implement this choice would be to change her original judgment, and the case would no longer be a case of failure to implement judgment" (pp. 336f.). Second, to attempt to explain what purports to be an akratic action by postulating a choice of this sort would be to assimilate "the weak case to the reckless case" (pp. 336f.) and, therefore, to treat the action as having been done in accordance with the agent's better judgment (see p. 324).

Neither of these claims is convincing. The argument about the weak drinker's failure depends upon a disputable identification of better judgment with choice.[9] Perhaps to choose not to implement a *choice* would be to abandon the choice; but it does not follow that one who chooses not to exercise self-control in support of one's better judgment no longer holds that *judgment*. We may, without obvious contradiction, describe a case in which an agent judges that all things considered it is better to do *A* than *B*, but due in part to his taking his reasons for doing *A* to be only slightly more weighty than his reasons for doing *B*, decides to indulge himself and to refrain from exercising self-control in support of *A*. In such a case, the agent may think his doing *B* to be *permissible*, even though he judges *A* to be better; and he may self-indulgently opt for the lesser alternative.

The following example illustrates the point. Mike, who is visiting New Orleans for the first time, is strolling down Bourbon Street when he notices a number of clubs featuring strip-tease acts. He has never before seen ecdysiasts perform, and he would like to take this opportunity to do so. However, he has moral qualms. He believes that watching ecdysiasts, though by no means seriously wrong, is somewhat exploitive of women. Though Mike does not believe that moral reasons are always the better reasons for action, he does judge that he has slightly better reason, all things considered, not to enter the clubs than to enter them. Now, Mike has a painless desire-eradicating device in his pocket. He realizes that he can bring it about that he acts on his better judgment simply by pressing a button: In the absence of a desire to see ecdysiasts he certainly would not enter a strip joint. But he decides to indulge himself—against his better judgment.

The central argument against Watson in this section does not, of course, depend upon my intuitions about this example. For Mike does see how to resist the desire that competes with his better judgment, and my primary concern has been with Watson's contention about cases in which the agent is mistaken about what is required by way of resistance. However, it is worth noting that Watson does not succeed in blocking the possibility of strict akratic action on this other front either. He fails to show that an agent's freely choosing not to exercise self-control in support of his decisive better judgment and his freely acting on the unresisted desire are incompatible with his retaining that judgment.

A possible source of confusion about the central argument should be removed. I have not suggested that 'D was resistible by S at t' follows from 'S would not have acted on D at t if he had done X at (prior to) t.' S must also have been able to do X at the time in question, or, more precisely, he must have been able to do it *in order to* prevent himself from acting on D. Although it may be true that an agent would not have succumbed to the temptation, say, to eat a piece of pie if he had convinced himself that his eating it would result in his immediate death, it does not follow from this that his desire to eat the pie was resistible by him. For it may well be the case that it was not within his power at the time to produce this conviction in himself. Similarly, from the fact that an agent's killing himself at t would prevent him from acting on D, it does not follow that D was resistible by the agent at t. Even if the agent could bring himself to commit suicide in some circumstances, it may not be within his power to kill himself to avoid eating a piece of pie.[10] The resistibility of a desire depends upon the agent's having at his disposal—that is, in his 'resistance-repertoire'—what we may call 'subjectively reasonable' modes of resistance. If he does have such modes of resistance at his disposal, and if one or more of them, if executed, would prevent the agent from acting on D, then D does not compel the agent to act as he does.

If and when we act akratically our problem is, in part, that, at the time of action, the balance of our motivations lies on the side of the akratic action performed. But, in at least some ostensible instances of strict incontinent action, it is open to the agent to prevent his being in this motivational condition by exercising his powers of self-control. *While* he is capable of preventing the condition in question from obtaining, an agent plainly is not under the sway of irresistible desires. And, in some cases at least, the desires in accordance with which an agent ostensibly acts incontinently are resistible at the very time at which the akratic action commences. In cases of this sort, since desires that are resistible at t do not *compel* at t, the ostensible akratic actions (other things being equal) are free.

3. A Loose End

Before bringing this chapter to an end, I shall comment briefly on an additional puzzle about the possibility of free action against one's better judgment. Cases are imaginable in which an agent who cannot at *t* resist his desire to do *A* at *t* could have made an earlier attempt to resist that desire such that, if he had made it, the desire would have been resistible by him at *t*. Can an agent properly be said to have done *A* freely in such a case? If not, can he have akratically done *A*?

Since a sustained attempt to defend an answer to the former question would take us too far afield, I shall directly address the latter only. First, if an action is not freely performed, it is not a *strict* akratic action. Second, actions not freely performed may nevertheless be akratic. Consider the following case. Andy, a semireformed heroin addict, now has a strong desire to drive to Harry's house and to purchase and use some heroin there, but he judges his not acting on this desire to be best, all things considered. Let us suppose that Andy is able *now* to resist his desire to drive to Harry's house for the purpose of 'shooting up,' but that once he were to see the drug there, his desire to use some (against his better judgment) would be irresistible. Andy's freely leaving his house for Harry's against his better judgment would be a *strict* akratic action. And Andy's using the drug at Harry's after having driven there for that purpose would be akratic even if its being motivated by an irresistible desire renders it unfree. For it would indirectly manifest the weakness or *akrasia* that is directly exhibited by Andy's strict incontinent action. This is not to say, of course, that every action having a strict akratic action as a causal antecedent is itself akratic. Andy may drive over a bicycle in the entrance to Harry's driveway—and even do this against his better judgment, due to an irresistible impulse—without that action's being akratic.

My primary purpose in this chapter has been to refute some challenging arguments for the claim that strict akratic action is impossible. In each case, fatal flaws were revealed. It does not follow from this, of course, that strict akratic action *is* possible. In particular, some interesting causal puzzles remain to be resolved. What has been established thus far is that the proponent of the commonsensical view that there are strict akratic actions may successfully avoid a number of pitfalls. Akratic action does not depend upon the agent's holding contradictory decisive better judgments, nor upon his simultaneously having competing intentions. Furthermore, an agent's engaging in intentional behavior that is contrary to a better judgment that he consciously holds at the time of action is compatible with his being moved only by *resistible* desires.

3

Akratic Action:
Causes, Reasons, Intentions

Causal theories of action have a long and distinguished history. Proponents include Aristotle, Aquinas, Hobbes, Spinoza, Locke, Kant, and William James. Due in significant part to the work of Ryle and Wittgenstein, causal accounts of action fell into general philosophical disfavor for a time; but the last two decades has witnessed a powerful revival of the older view. The causal approach to action-explanation is once again the orthodox approach.

The occurrence or apparent occurrence of a particular variety of strict akratic action—namely, akratic action against a 'here-and-now' intention—raises an interesting and instructive problem for causal theories of action. It is the purpose of this chapter to show that the problem can be surmounted and, more generally, that the occurrence of akratic action of this sort is compatible with the truth of a *causal theory of action* (*CTA*). In the course of establishing this compatibility, I shall begin to construct an explanatory framework for akratic (and continent) action on a modified belief-desire model.

The question to which this chapter is addressed is motivated by Donald Davidson's attempted resolution of "the logical difficulty" of *akrasia* in his justly celebrated article, "How Is Weakness of the Will Possible?" (1970a; henceforth *WWP*). In his introduction to a recent collection of his essays, Davidson observes that "causal theories of action are challenged by intentional actions that are contrary to the actor's best judgment. For if reasons are causes, it is natural to suppose that the strongest reasons are the strongest causes" (1980, p. xii) It is this challenge—though he does not make this explicit there—that *WWP* is designed to meet. He attempts to meet it by arguing that the occurrence of akratic actions is compatible with the truth of a pair of principles that "derive their force" from a "very persuasive," *causal* "view of the nature of intentional action and practical reasoning" (p. 102). But, as we shall see, these principles jointly entail that strict akratic action of the type just described never occurs. And if they entail something false, one who finds a *CTA* attractive, as I do, will surely want to ask whether a *CTA* depends upon these, or *any*, principles which have the result that there are no strict akratic actions against here-and-now intentions.

1. The Causal Theory

By a causal theory of action (*CTA*), I mean any theory of action that makes the following claim:

> C. For all actions A, A is an intentional action only if A's agent had a reason for A-ing and (his having) that reason was a cause of his A-ing.[1]

(A closely associated claim, endorsed by any *CTA*, is that to explain an action by citing the reason(s) for which it is done is to give a causal explanation of the action.) *C,* of course, provides us only with a necessary condition of an action's being intentional. A sufficient condition is not difficult to locate. That an action is done for a reason is, I suggest, a sufficient condition of its being an intentional action. But what it is for an action to be done for a reason is a notoriously difficult matter. A causal theorist will want to give a causal account. But the account cannot be this, that an action A was done for a reason just in case the agent had a reason for doing A and his having that reason was a cause of his A–ing; for the causal connection between an agent's reason for doing A and his A-ing might be inappropriate. For example, a chemist who is working with cyanide near his colleague's cup of tea may desire to kill his colleague and believe that he can do this by dropping some cyanide into the tea (which desire and belief constitute a *reason* for his dropping some cyanide into the tea), and this desire-belief pair may so upset him that his hands shake, with the *accidental* result that he drops some of the poisonous substance into the tea. This, of course, is an instance of the problem of 'wayward causal chains.'[2]

Fortunately, a detailed examination of sufficient conditions of an action's being intentional is unnecessary for my purposes in this chapter. For, as we shall see, what is distinctive about incontinent action is not the nature of the causal connection between the action and the reasons for which it is done, but rather that the agent acts for certain reasons rather than for others. Thus, for example, akratic action poses no special difficulty for the idea that a sufficient condition of A's being intentional is that its agent had a reason for A-ing and that his having this reason was, "in a certain characteristic way" (Goldman, 1970, pp. 57–63), a cause of his A-ing. I shall return to this point toward the end of Section 6.

2. Davidson on Incontinent Action

In his *WWP* Davidson formulates the following pair of principles in an attempt to give expression to a "doctrine that has an air of self-evidence" (pp. 94–95):

> *P1*. If an agent wants to do x more than he wants to do y and he believes himself free to do either x or y, then he will intentionally do x if he does either x or y intentionally.
>
> *P2*. If an agent judges that it would be better to do x than to do y, then he wants to do x more than he wants to do y.

These principles entail P^*, which connects judgment and action:

> P^*. If an agent judges that it would be better to do x than to do y, and he believes himself free to do either x or y, then he will intentionally do x if he does either x or y intentionally. (cf. Davidson's formulation, p. 95)

However, Davidson characterizes incontinent action as follows:

> *D*. In doing x an agent acts incontinently if and only if: (a) the agent does x intentionally; (b) the agent believes that there is an alternative action y open to him; and (c) the agent judges that, all things considered, it would be better to do y than to do x. (p. 94)

And since (by definition) the judgment against which the incontinent agent acts is an 'all-things-considered' judgment, and therefore (in Davidson's terminology) a "conditional" judgment, the occurrence of incontinent actions does not falsify P^*; for, the judgments with which P^* is concerned are *unconditional* judgments (p. 110).

Of course, Davidson's attempt to reconcile incontinent action with *P1–P2* depends upon the correctness of his characterization of the former. In particular, if his *D, minus* the crucial phrase "all things considered," adequately describes some cases of akratic action, then some cases of akratic action plainly falsify P^*; for, in instances described by the modified version of *D*, the agent judges (without qualification, i.e., unconditionally) that it would be better to do A than B, and believes that he may do either A or B (thereby satisfying the compound antecedent of P^*), and yet intentionally does B, falsifying P^*'s consequent. Thus, one wants to ask why we should believe that we never act against the *unconditional* judgment that it would be better to do y than to do x in the circumstances described in D.

Davidson has little to say on this score in WWP^3; but it is plain at least that his notion of an unconditional judgment must play an important part in any answer to the present question. In WWP he unfortunately fails to make it entirely clear what an unconditional (practical) judgment is. But in a later article (1978), Davidson contends, as we have seen, that a certain kind of unconditional or all-out judgment, "a judgment that something I think I can do . . . is desirable not only for one or another reason, but in the light of all my reasons, . . . is . . . an *intention*" (p. 58); and in WWP we are told that "every judgment is made in the light of all the reasons in this sense, that it is made in the presence of, and is conditioned by, that totality" (p. 111).

This clarifies matters considerably. Davidson claims in WWP that:

> Intentional action . . . is geared directly to unconditional judgments like 'It would be better to do a than to do b'. Reasoning that stops at conditional judgments . . . is practical in its subject, not in its issue. (p. 110)

What this reasoning stops short of is the formation of an intention. And what happens in cases of incontinent action, on Davidson's account, is that the agent does not intend to do what he judges to be best, all things considered. His weakness (*akrasia*) is exhibited, not in a failure to act on an unconditional judgment—that is, on an intention—but rather in his failure to intend (and, hence, to act) in accordance with an all-things-considered judgment, a judgment that is conditional in form.[4]

Davidson's tack is helpful in reconciling at least some cases of akratic action with $P1$–$P2$. This pair of principles is concerned with unconditional judgments or intentions; and it does seem that an agent's weakness may at least sometimes be manifested, not in action against an intention, but rather in a failure to intend in accordance with an all-things-considered better judgment.[5] However, one still wants to ask whether people ever act akratically when their practical reasoning does *not* stop at a conditional judgment, but issues in an intention to do an A here and now.

This last question is quite plausibly answered in the affirmative. Consider the following case. John's present Biology 100 lab assignment is to determine what his blood type is by pricking one of his fingers with a needle and examining a sample of his blood under a microscope. Although John does not mind the sight of his own blood, he is averse to drawing blood from himself. John weighs his reasons in favor of carrying out the assignment

against his contrary reasons and judges that, all things considered, he ought
here and now to prick his finger with sufficient force to release an appropriate amount of blood for the experiment. But his reasoning does not stop
here. He judges *unconditionally* that this is the best thing to do, that is, he
intends to prick his finger at once[6]; and he moves the needle toward his
finger with the intention of drawing blood. However, as he sees the needle
come very close to his skin, he stops. It is more difficult than he thought
to carry through. He decides that if he did not look at the needle, it would
be easier to complete the task. And he tries again, this time without looking.
But when he feels the needle touch his finger, he stops. Now, as Chapter
2.2 indicates, it is not necessary to suppose that John is psychologically
unable to perform the task. Rather, it looks as if John's failure is due to
weakness (*akrasia*): Because he is weak, he fails to do what he judges to
be best, all things considered, *and* what he intends to do.

Davidson's account of akratic action does not help us here. Indeed,
this case is inconsistent with *P1–P2*. For, given the agent's unconditional
judgment, *P2* implies that he wants to draw blood from his finger more
than he wants not to, and (assuming that John has the appropriate belief
about what he is free to) *P1* implies that he will intentionally draw blood
from his finger if he intentionally draws, or fails to draw, the blood; and
John's failing to draw blood from his finger certainly appears to be
intentional.

It is obvious that a person may intend to do an *A* here and now and yet
fail to do so: An agent might lack the ability to act as he intends, or we may
prevent him from doing so. Davidson is not denying this. What he is
denying is that this failure is ever an *akratic* failure. For Davidson,
weakness may explain why an agent fails to intend to do what he judges to
be best, all things considered; but it cannot explain an agent's failing to act
in accordance with a here-and-now intention, that is, with an 'unconditional judgment' about what it is best to do here and now.

3. Intentions and the Balance of Motivation

If *P** (the implicate of *P1–P2*) is falsified by akratic action of a certain
type, must we abandon hope of understanding ''what it is to act with an
intention'' and ''how we explain an action by giving the reasons the agent
had in acting'' (*WWP*, p. 102)? Must we reject, in particular, a causal
theory of action? I think not.

In our case of the biology student, the agent judged that it would be
better to do *A* than to do *B*, all things considered, and he intended to do *A*

straightaway. But he intentionally stopped short of doing A. This is perplexing indeed. For, the reasons for which he refrained from doing A were taken into account in the process of reasoning whereby his intention to do A was formed. He had, as it were, already given the reasons for doing A the upper hand. His subsequent action is not inexplicable, however, unless it is supposed that the balance of an agent's motivations must always be in line with his here-and-now intentions. And this, as we shall soon see, is not a supposition that a proponent of a causal theory of action is committed to making.

There are several possible explanations of our student's being more motivated to refrain from pricking his finger than to prick it. For present purposes, they may be divided into two sorts, depending upon whether John is more motivated to prick his finger than to refrain from pricking it when he forms the intention to prick it. I start with the less interesting possibility—that the balance of John's motivation is in line with his intention when he forms the intention.

Even if John is in this motivational condition when he forms the intention to prick his finger, the balance of his motivation may shift as he attempts to execute his intention. For example, as he sees or feels the needle approach his skin, his desire not to harm himself may grow stronger[7]. Indeed, it may grow so strong that he now wants to refrain from pricking his finger more than he wants to prick it. I think, for reasons which will become clear later, that this can be at most a partial explanation of John's having the balance of motivation in question. But it should be observed that the imagined (partial) explanation does not, at least in any direct way, contradict the central thesis of a *CTA* articulated above. The claim again is that A is an intentional action only if A's agent had a reason for A-ing and (his having) that reason was a cause of his A-ing. Our agent *intentionally* refrained from pricking his finger ('intentionally R-ed,' for short). But it is not difficult to supply a reason for which he R-ed. On a Davidsonian account of practical reasons, his reason consisted, presumably, in a desire to avoid harming himself and a belief that he would harm himself if he pricked his finger. Nor is the explanation at issue, at least on the surface, inconsistent with the idea that John's wanting not to harm himself and his believing that he would harm himself if he were to prick his finger (i.e., his having the reason in question) causally contributed to his refraining from pricking his finger. And, as we shall see later, there are no conclusive grounds for thinking that the causal connection between his having this reason at t and his refraining at t from pricking his finger is different from 'the characteristic' causal connection between the reason(s) for which one A-s and one's A-ing.

On another possible account of our student's being more motivated to refrain from pricking his finger than to prick it, he was *not* more motivated to do the latter when he formed the intention to do it. It will be helpful in this connection to distinguish between two senses or uses of 'wants more.' Gary Watson (1977, pp. 320–321) has suggested that 'wants more' has both an evaluative and a motivational use.[8] In the evaluative use, to say that '*S* wants *x* more than he wants *y*' is to say that *S* '*prefers x* to *y* or ranks *x* higher than *y* on some scale of values or "desirability matrix",' whereas in the motivational use, it is to say simply that '*S* is more strongly motivated by considerations of *x* than by considerations of *y*.' Now, it is sometimes said that one function of the practical reasoning of people who have conflicting wants is to determine what the person wants more or most; and the point that I want to make is that, if this is true, the sense of 'wants more' or 'wants most' which makes it true is not, at least typically, the motivational sense. We do not characteristically attempt to decide which of our competing wants has the most motivational force; if anything, we try to determine, from the point of view of our own system of values (again, conceived broadly so as to include desires, fears, principles, etc.), which want it would be best to satisfy. Thus, our biology student, for example, may attempt to determine whether it would be better to satisfy his want to complete his assignment or his want not to harm himself; but it is unlikely that he would try to determine which of these wants has more motivational force. Indeed, unless he is also a student of philosophy or psychology, it is unlikely that the latter question would even occur to him.

That the motivational force of a want may be out of line with the agent's evaluation of the object of that want seems to me obvious. Someone who has decided, for reasons of health, to quit smoking after having smoked a pack of cigarettes daily for fifteen years may occasionally desire more strongly to buy a pack of cigarettes than to refrain from buying one, even though he judges at the time that not buying a pack is better, all things considered, than buying one—that is, even though he gives his not buying cigarettes a higher evaluation than his buying them. Or someone with a severe fear of flying may judge that his flying would be better than his not flying on a particular occasion (say, because it is the only way to get to an important job interview), and yet be so anxious about flying that, in the motivational sense, he wants less to board the plane than to refrain from boarding it. Perhaps in these cases the agents are faced with compulsive desires. But this is beside the present point, namely, that evaluation and motivation can be out of line with one another.

There is no need to rely solely on 'real world' examples, of course. Imagine that an evil genius is able to implant and directly maintain very strong desires in people, and that he does this to Susan. However, because she knows both that her desire to *A* was produced by the evil genius and that he does this sort of thing solely with a view to getting those in whom the desires are implanted to destroy themselves, Susan gives her *A*-ing a very low evaluative ranking. She believes that her not *A*-ing would be much better, all things considered. Nevertheless, the genius's control over the strength of Susan's desire to do *A* is such that the balance of her motivation falls on the side of her *A*-ing.

Let us return now to our biology student. Suppose that, when faced with his competing desires, he attempts to decide (from the perspective of his own system of values) which desire it would be better to act on. He observes that the harm that he would inflict upon himself in executing the assignment is minor and that he has good reason to complete the assignment, since he wants to earn a high grade in the course and to make a good impression on his teacher; and he judges that, all things considered, it would be best to complete the assignment even though this entails harming himself by pricking his finger. Now if, in the evaluative sense of the term, John wants to execute the assignment more than he wants to avoid harming himself by pricking himself with a needle, it does not follow that this is also true in the motivational sense of 'wants more.' And even if he *intends* to complete the assignment, he may be more motivated not to harm himself; for his intention is based (at least primarily), *not* on the relative motivational force of his competing wants, but rather on his evaluation of the objects of these wants. This is not to say that his evaluation *must* result in an appropriate intention. An agent might, for example, judge that it would be better, all things considered, to act on want *W1* than on want *W2*, and yet he might fail to intend to act on *W1* because, say, he believes that he cannot avoid acting on *W2*, or, if Davidson is right, because of weakness. But it is true (given the details of the example) that, in this case, his evaluations led to an appropriate intention.

The preceding two paragraphs provide us with a partial explanation of the possibility of an agent's forming a here-and-now intention to do *A* without being more motivated at the time to do *A* than to refrain from doing *A*. When an agent forms a here-and-now intention on the basis of practical reasoning in a situation in which he has conflicting wants, any ratiocinative weighing of wants typically is not a weighing in respect of motivational force, but rather a ranking in respect of *value;* and what an agent wants more in the evaluative sense need not be what he is most motivated to do.[9] This is only a partial explanation, for we need, among other things, an explanation of the possibility of disparity between wanting more in the evaluative sense and wanting more in the motivational sense.[10] But I think that the answer must be, at least in significant part, that the motivational force of wants typically is not under our control to the extent to which the evaluative ranking of wants is. Evaluative ranking is a matter of 'making up one's mind,' or deciding, about the relative value of the objects of competing wants; but if the idea of deciding to be more motivated by one of one's wants than by another even makes sense, the decided-upon balance of motivation surely is something distinct from the decision and something that depends upon factors other than the decision.

I suggested earlier that one explanation for the balance of our biology student's motivation, at the time of action, is that he was most motivated to prick his finger when he formed the intention to prick it and that his balance of motivation shifted when he began to execute the intention. A second explanation of his final motivational balance might run as follows. His intention was formed on the basis of practical reasoning about the relative merits of the objects of his competing wants; and the motivational force of his competing wants at the time was not in alignment with his ranking of them, since, as a result, say, of an unpleasant childhood experience in which he injected a staple into his finger, the strength of his desire not to prick himself exceeded what was warranted by his evaluation of the object of the desire. Consequently, he was less motivated to prick his finger than to refrain from pricking it at the very time at which he formed the intention to prick it. Here again the explanation of the balance of the student's motivation is, at least on the surface, consistent with the central thesis of a *CTA* articulated earlier. It is for a reason that John refrained from pricking his finger; and the preceding explanation does not contradict in any direct way the claim that his having the reason for which he refrained from doing this is a cause of his refraining. Moreover, as we shall see in Section 6, there are no compelling grounds for thinking that the causal connection between his having at *t* the reason for which he refrained at *t* from pricking his finger and his refraining is not a connection of the sort that obtains in ordinary cases of continent action.

One point that emerges clearly from the preceding discussion is that if a *CTA* is to leave room for the occurrence of akratic actions against here-and-now intentions, it cannot pretend that every intentional action is adequately explained by the reason(s) for which it is done. Our biology student intentionally refrains from pricking himself; but we would not be satisfied if, in response to the question why he refrained from doing this, we were told that he wanted not to harm himself and believed that the finger-pricking would hurt. After all, the agent also wanted to execute the assignment and believed that in order to do this he must prick his finger. We want to know why he acted on the former want or reason *rather than* the latter; and to cite the (specified) reason for which he refrained from pricking his finger is not to answer *this* question.

Brief attention to the idea of an 'adequate reasons-explanation' of an action will prove useful. Consider the following case. Sam tells us that he desires states of affairs *S1* and *S2*, that he believes that actions *A1* and *A2* are conducive to the achievement of *S1* and *S2* respectively, and that he believes that he can do either *A1* or *A2* but that he cannot simultaneously do both. He then does *A1*. Now if Sam were to respond to our question "Why did you *A1*?" with the answer "Because I wanted *S1* and I believed that *A1* was conducive to *S1*," we would not be satisfied. We want to know why Sam did *A1 instead of A2*. The following answer would (in light of what Sam has already said) satisfy us: "Because (evaluatively speaking) I wanted *S1* more than I wanted *S2*." And this answer can easily be filled out as an explicit 'reasons-explanation' as follows: "My reason for doing *A1* instead of *A2* was that I wanted that for the sake of which I did *A1* more than I wanted that which I believed I would achieve by doing *A2*." This, I take it, is an adequate 'reasons-explanation' of what Sam did. It provides us not only with the agent's reason for doing *A1*, but with his reason for doing it *instead of* the envisaged alternative.

Let us now imagine, if we can, a case of akratic action in which the agent weighed up all the relevant facts known to him at the time and all of his pertinent occurrent desires and attitudes and judged, on the basis of these facts, desires, and attitudes, that *A* was the best thing for him to do. Let us imagine further that, upon making this judgment, he intentionally did something else, *B*. If we were to ask why the agent did *B*, someone might answer: "Because he had a desire for *C* and believed that *B* was conducive to the achievement of *C*." But, as in the preceding case, we would not be satisfied. We want to know why the agent did *B instead of A*. Now even if there is some 'reasons-explanation' for this—for example, he thought that doing *B* would generate more short-term pleasure than doing *A*, and he had some desire to maximize his short-term pleasure—we would still rightly want to know why the agent acted on this reason instead of on his reason for doing *A*. And at this point the 'reasons-explanations' would seem typically to come to an end.[11] Of course, one might want to say that his reasons for doing *B* are motivationally stronger than his reasons for doing *A*; but if the agent had no reason for having this unhappy balance of strength, then factors other than reasons must be brought into an adequate explanation of his action.

The fact that, in such a case, an adequate explanation of the agent's action must go beyond his reason for acting provides no solid evidence, however, against the idea that any action done for a reason has that reason as a cause. If a proponent of a *CTA* maintains the view that, in a certain range of cases of conflicting wants, the reason (or set of reasons) which the agent takes to be, say, 'of greatest import' is a cause of the agent's *A*-ing, then he will have to hold that, in all *relevantly similar* circumstances, reasons which agents take to be of greatest import are causes of what they intentionally do. But as we shall see in more detail later, he is *not* committed to the claim that such reasons are causes of the agent's intentional actions in *all* cases of conflicting desire. In some cases, conditions may be such that the agent's intentional action is not caused by the reason which he takes to be of greatest import. We would, of course, like to know what the conditions are that are responsible for the inefficacy of a reason of this sort; and I shall have more to say about this shortly. But this is beside the present point, namely, that a proponent of a *CTA* is not committed to holding that there is an adequate reasons-explanation for every intentional action.

If agents can act akratically even against an unconditional practical judgment, then practical reasoning does not have the power that some philosophers have claimed for it. It does not follow from this, of course, that practical reasoning, reasons, and judgments have no motivational force, but only that other forces must be taken into account in explaining (some) actions. These "other forces" are commented upon briefly in Section 5 below and at greater length in Chapters 6 and 7.

4. Intentions, Unconditional Judgments, and Incontinent Actions

Near the end of *WWP* Davidson writes:

> There is no paradox in supposing a person sometimes holds that all that he believes and values supports a certain course of action, when at the same time those same beliefs and values cause him to reject that course of action. If *r* is someone's reason for holding that *p*, then his holding that *r* must be, I think, a cause of his holding that *p*. But, and this is what is crucial here, his holding that *r* may cause his holding that *p* without *r* being his reason; indeed, the agent may even think that *r* is a reason to reject *p*. (p. 111)

Part of what Davidson is claiming here, as I understand him, is that when an agent judges, in the light of "the sum of his relevant principles, opinions, attitudes, and desires" (p. 110), that, all things considered, *A* is better than *B*, this same sum of principles, opinions, and so on—that is, the sum of reasons (which I should add, is itself treated as a reason by

Davidson)[12]—may cause him to judge unconditionally that B is better than A. Thus, an agent may act, and act *intentionally,* contrary to his all-things-considered judgment; for his unconditional judgment *is* an intention. An agent may judge that, all things considered, A is better than B and yet, due to weakness, both fail to intend to do A *and* intend to do B. The above-mentioned sum of reasons (r) does not constitute the *akrates' reason* for judging unconditionally that B is better than A. Indeed, the agent thinks that r warrants denying that B is better than A. Nevertheless, r causes the agent to make this judgment; and, presumably, some member of r is the agent's reason for doing B. (Cf. *WWP,* p. 104: "The incontinent man believes it would be better on the whole to do something else, but he has a reason for what he does, for his action is intentional.")

One may think this (or something similar) an attractive initial move to make in explaining how someone who judges that, all things considered, A is better than $B,$ may nevertheless akratically intend to do B. But I have suggested that a person who makes the 'conditional' judgment in question may form an *intention* to do A here and now and yet, due to weakness, intentionally do B. And, one wants to ask, what happens to the intention to do A in that case?

Akratic actions, as I intimated in the preceding chapter, are (at least at first glance) divisible into those that involve a change of mind and those that do not. A person who has judged unconditionally that it is better to do A than B here and now may be prompted to reverse his judgment (i.e., to judge unconditionally that it is better to do B than A) by the fear or anxiety elicited by his attempt to execute the judgment. For example, the novice swimmer who experiences a pang of anxiety upon making an effort to execute his unconditional judgment that it is better to jump now into the pool of water before him than to refrain from jumping in, may suddenly judge unconditionally that it is better not to jump in. Of course, not every action in accordance with a change of mind exhibits *akrasia.* If circumstances are such that we think a change of mind reasonable—if, say, the anxiety which a person experiences upon attempting to execute an unconditional judgment is so great that we believe it outweighs (evaluatively speaking) those "principles, opinions, attitudes, and desires" that the agent takes to support his judgment—we are disinclined to count his acting in accordance with his change of mind as akratic.[13] But if, given the agent's own values and beliefs (i.e., principles, opinions, attitudes, and desires), his change of mind seems to us unreasonable, we are inclined to say that the change of mind itself exhibits weakness; for, we want to say, if he had got a grip on himself, if he had exercised self-control, he would have retained his initial judgment.

It is worth noting, before we turn to akratic action which does not involve a change of mind, that Davidson's *P1–P2* may be made compatible with akratic action of the type just discussed by means of the addition of appropriate temporal references. The formation of an unconditional judgment—even a judgment about something to be done here and now—is not, in general, simultaneous with the performance of a corresponding intentional action. It takes time to act. Davidson is committed to the idea that one who judges unconditionally at t that it is better to do A at t^* than to do B at t^*, and who has the appropriate beliefs about what he is free to do, will intentionally do A at t^* if he does either A or B intentionally at t^* and retains at t* the unconditional judgment in question. But, of course, this leaves room for the rejection or reversal of an unconditional judgment—even if that judgment is about something to be done 'here and now.'

What Davidson's principles, appropriately sharpened, rule out are cases of the other sort at issue here—cases in which the agent does not change his mind, but rather retains at t his unconditional judgment that it would be better to do A than to do B and yet intentionally does B (at t) even though he believes himself free to do A. That there are such cases is, I think, obvious. Consider again our biology student's first failure to prick his finger. There is no need to suppose that at some time prior to his intentionally refraining from pricking his finger he changed his mind and judged unconditionally that it would be better not to prick it than to prick it. Indeed, it would appear that he retained his judgment, for he proceeds to make a second attempt. And if we were to ask *him,* we would not be terribly puzzled if he told us that even though he intentionally refrained from pricking his finger he did not change his mind, *even for a moment,* about the best course of action. It is true, I think, that when he intentionally refrained from pricking his finger he no longer had the here-and-now intention to prick it. Failing to prick his finger was something that he intended to do; that is, when he refrained, he intended to refrain. And I do not think it possible for one both to intend at a moment m to do A (under that description) at t and to intend at m not to do A (under that description) at t. (The logic of 'intends' differs in this way from that of 'wants'.) But this issue is distinct from that of failing to retain judgments.

If what I say in the preceding paragraph is correct, unconditional judgments are *not* (Davidson's contention notwithstanding) identical with intentions; for, one may retain an unconditional judgment without retaining an intention. (As I noted in Chapter 2, if one insists on identifying a sort of judgment with an intention, my reply is that strict akratic action is not properly defined in terms of that sort of judgment.) It is also worth noting that our biology student's intention to refrain from pricking his finger is quite implausibly regarded as an unconditional judgment that refraining from doing this is best or better than doing it. *He* does not take himself to have made this judgment; nor, in general, do those of us who are subject to *akrasia* find it plausible to say that we always do what we judge unconditionally to be best. Sometimes what we do, at the very time at which we are doing it, seems to us to be, without qualification, rather distant from the best available option.

We now have the ingredients for two rough and incomplete answers to our present question about the here-and-now intention against which an agent may akratically act. One makes reference to changes of mind. The other does not. But both assert that intentions—even here-and-now intentions—may be defeated by opposing wants and fears, and that these wants and fears may lead to new intentions. More needs to be said, of course. Thus far, our answer is on a par with Davidson's remark that a person may hold "that all that he believes and values supports a certain course of action, when at the same time those same beliefs and values cause him to reject that course of action" (*WWP*, p. 111). We want to know *how* this can happen, and how here-and-now intentions can be defeated by opposing wants and fears. Thus, we come again to the issue raised at the end of the preceding section.

5. Akrasia, Self-Control, and the Balance of Motivation

In Section 3, I suggested that we have more control over how we rank the objects of our wants in respect of value than over the relative motivational force of our wants. This is not to say that we have no control at all over the latter. As Richard Brandt has observed (1979, Ch. 6), wants may be extinguished by a kind of "cognitive psychotherapy." Aristotle has pointed out (*NE* 1150b21-25) that a person who has alerted himself to the probability of an upcoming "danger," for example, is less likely, other things being equal, to be overcome by fear and the attendant wants when the danger arrives than is a person who is taken by surprise. And the psychological literature on self-control is filled with discussions of useful techniques designed to attenuate or enhance the strength of a desire.[14] I suppose that the ideal condition with respect to the balance of one's motivations is to be so disposed that this balance will always, under any conditions, be in accordance with one's unconditional practical judgments and the corresponding intentions. The suggestion is extreme that anything less than this is *akrasia* (i.e., the *trait*); but it is natural, as we have seen, to define 'lack of self-control' in relation to *some* standard of 'self-control' (or *enkrateia*).[15]

Wants do not bear a fixed motivational force or weight. Although when *S* sets out to decide what to do here and now he may want *x* (in the motivational sense) more than he wants *y*, the balance may be reversed when he evaluates *x* and *y* in the light of other of his wants and relevant beliefs of his. If he is a perfectly self-controlled person and he judges decisively (in the sense defined in Ch. 1) that *y* is better than *x*, the balance of his motivations *will* be reversed. And this reversal will occur *because*— I do not say "just because"—he has so judged. If he is less than perfectly self-controlled, however, the decisive judgment that *y* is better than *x*, and even the intention to do *y* in preference to *x*, may not elicit (or be accompanied by) a reversal of motivational balance. As I shall explain in more detail in Chapter 6.3, what the agent is most motivated to do, and hence what he *does,* depends upon his capacity for self-control; and a *CTA* that ignores this point cannot account for akratic action against a here-and-now intention. The causal theorist rightly holds that the reasons on the basis of which decisive better judgments and intentions are formed have a motivational element; but (barring wayward causal chains) whether those reasons result in action depends not only on the agent's being able to act accordingly and the absence of external prevention, but also on the extent to which he is self-controlled.

Davidson has suggested that the following "principle of continence" is one which "the rational man will accept in applying practical reasoning": "Perform the action judged best on the basis of all available relevant reasons" (*WWP*, p. 112). "What is hard," he continues "is to acquire the virtue of continence, to make the principle of continence our own. But there is no reason in principle why it is any more difficult to become continent than to become chaste or brave." He is, I think, correct in this. What he fails to see is that the extent to which we have acquired the trait of continence does not, at the point at which a here-and-now intention is formed, cease to be causally relevant to what we do. The person who is not fully self-controlled may be "defeated," to use Aristotle's term, even though he has formed an intention to do *A* here and now. And his being defeated, rather than showing that a *CTA* is untenable or that the reasons for which we act sometimes do not contribute causally to what we do, ought to suggest to us that reasons, decisive better judgments, and intentions, even in the presence of ability and the absence of external interference, do not tell the whole story. The story is to be filled in, I have suggested, partly by attending to what *akrasia* and self-control are. This is taken up in greater detail in subsequent chapters.

6. Causal Theories of Action (CTAs) and Akratic Actions

What does a *CTA* amount to when it is admitted that the story is to be filled in in this way? I shall start with two obvious points. First, no *CTA* holds that an agent's having a reason at *t* to do *A* at *t* is a causally *sufficient* condition of his doing *A* at *t;* for the agent may lack the ability (at *t*) to do *A* at *t,* or he may be prevented by some external force from doing so. Second, no reasonable *CTA* holds that the three elements just mentioned— that is, having a reason, ability, and absence of external prevention—are jointly causally sufficient for an agent's doing *A* at *t;* for the agent may also have a reason at *t* for doing *B* at *t,* and he may know that he cannot do both, have the ability to do *B,* and not be prevented by an external force from doing *B.*

Here the proponent of a *CTA* is faced with an interesting and important question. When an agent has competing reasons at *t,* which reason(s) will lead to action at *t?* Davidson's answer seems to be this: (1) whatever an agent is most motivated to do by the sum of his reasons, he will unconditionally judge best, that is, intend to do (provided that he believes that he is free to perform the action in question); (2) his unconditionally judging *A* best—that is, his intending to do *A*—is caused by his reason(s) for *A*-ing; and (3) the agent's unconditional judgment or intention will lead to (cause) his *A*-ing (provided that he is able to *A* and is not prevented by an external force from doing so).

This answer, I have argued, is false; but notice what its three parts jointly imply. First, an agent will do whatever he is most motivated to do, provided that he is able to act accordingly, believes himself free to do so, and is not prevented by an external force from doing so. Second, an agent's reason(s) for doing what he does will be (a) cause(s) of what he does. This pair of propositions, with the inclusion or appropriate temporal references, is, I think, quite plausible, provided that we are speaking only of *basic* actions. (Recall the example of the basketball player in Ch. 2. Sometimes, even under the conditions specified, we do not succeed in performing the nonbasic actions that we attempt.) I am not suggesting that the pair of propositions at issue expresses a strict psychological law. Rather, the pair is comparable to the claim that soluble things dissolve when placed in water. As Davidson observes, "Explaining why something is dissolved by reference to its solubility is not high science, but it isn't empty either, for solubility implies not only a generalization, but also the existence of a causal factor which accounts for the disposition: there is something about a soluble cube of sugar that causes it to dissolve under certain conditions" (1976, p. 274). Nor is it high science to explain someone's doing *A* rather than B by saying that he was more motivated at the time by his reasons for doing A than by his reasons for doing B. But it may be that, as in the case of solubility, there is something about being more motivated by one's reasons for doing A than by one's reasons for doing B that causes one's A-ing 'under certain conditions.'

The important point here is that the phenomenon of incontinent action is compatible with (havings of) reasons being causes of actions. From the fact that agents, due to weakness, sometimes fail (1) to intend (and, hence, act) in accordance with the reasons which they take to be best, and even (2) to act in accordance with decisive judgments of the best and corresponding here-and-now intentions, it does not follow that there is no causal law connecting havings of reasons with intentional actions. Perhaps all cases of doing what one is most strongly motivated to do by one's reasons fall under neurophysiological laws linking the relevant psychological antecedents, under physical descriptions, with the actions, under physical descriptions.[16] But in all cases of *incontinent* action, one does what one is most motivated to do by one's reasons (broadly conceived). Akratic actions do not falsify the claim that havings of reasons are causes of action. The agent who akratically does A, does A for a reason. That he took his reason to do a competing action, B, to be a better reason—even if he formed an intention to do a B—does not show that his having the reason for which he acted is not a cause of his action.

Something should be said in this connection about the 'characteristic way(s)' in which (havings of) reasons cause intentional actions. The notion of a 'characteristic' causal connection between reasons and actions is introduced into a causal analysis of intentional action in order to deal with the problem of wayward causal chains (see Goldman, 1970, pp. 57–63). Even if S's having a reason R for doing an A is a cause of his A-ing, A might not be an intentional action; for, the causal connection between (S's having) R and S's A-ing may be a deviant one. However, the precise nature of the causal connection between reasons and actions in virtue of which actions done for reasons are intentional has no significant bearing on the question whether the occurrence of akratic actions against here-and-now intentions is compatible with its being the case that some *CTA* or other is correct; for what is distinctive about akratic actions is not the nature of the causal connection between the actions and the reasons for which they are done, but rather the fact that the agent acts for certain reasons rather than for others, that is, rather than for the reasons that yield his decisive better judgment. Of course, if a reason's causing an action 'in a certain characteristic way' is not only a sufficient condition of that action's being intentional but a necessary condition as well, then what we have seen about akratic action is inconsistent with *some* ways of spelling out this connection. It would be wrong, for example, to suppose that the characteristic way involves making a decisive judgment that A is best; for, sometimes what we do intentionally we do not decisively judge best. But this does not show that there can be *no* successful causal analysis of an action's being an intentional action.

The central point of the preceding paragraph may be illustrated as follows. Suppose that Myles Brand is correct in claiming that although "there are diverse chains leading to the peculiar kind of mental event that causes [intentional] action . . . there is one kind of mental event that proximately causes the action" (1979, p. 183; cf. 1984, p. 35). Let us call mental events of this type *m*-volitions. An *m*-volition is a volition that one has just prior to *m* (where *m* is a moment) to do an A beginning at *m*. If all A-ings proximately caused by an *m*-volition to A are intentional A-ings, then we have located the 'certain characteristic way' in which havings of reasons cause intentional actions. We may suppose that an agent's having a reason R for doing an A beginning at *m* causes 'in the characteristic way' his A-ing beginning at *m* just in case his having R is a cause of (or identical with) his having an *m*-volition to do an A and that *m*-volition is the proximate cause of his A-ing. *How* R led to the *m*-volition to do an A, and *why* R led to this volition rather than some competing reason leading to another *m*-volition, are irrelevant to the matter at hand. There are diverse chains, as Brand says, leading to what we are supposing to be the proximate cause of intentional action. What makes an A intentional, on our present supposition, is simply that it was proximately caused by an *m*-volition to do an A. My claim is not, of course, that a certain event-type is in fact the proximate cause of intentional action, but only that the occurrence of akratic actions—even akratic actions against here-and-now intentions—does not preclude there being some successful causal account of an action's being an intentional action.

The final point to be made here is that the conclusions at which I have arrived in this section are consistent with its being the case, as I suggested earlier, that reasons "do not tell the whole story"—that, in the case of akratic action, the (psychological) explanation is to be filled in by attending to other points about the agent, such as his capacity for self-control. When S intentionally does A, believing that he has, on the whole, better reasons to do some competing action, B, we want to know why he was more motivated to do A than B. For this he has no reason. And if he had been perfectly self-controlled, the balance of his motivations would not have been what it was.

7. Conclusion

We may, and should, reject Davidson's *P2*—the claim that any agent who judges (unconditionally) that it is better to do *x* than to do *y* is more strongly motivated to do *x* than to do *y*—without having to abandon a causal theory of action. *P2* is false. The connection between better judgments and the balance of an agent's motivation is more complex than Davidson thinks; and this holds as well for the connection between intentions and motivation. The extent to which an agent is self-controlled is also an important factor. This is not to say, however, that there is no connection, nor that to explain an intentional action by citing the reason(s) for which it was intended and performed is not to give a causal explanation of the action.

The primary purpose of this chapter has been to show that the occurrence of the most challenging variety of strict akratic action—akratic action against and intention to do an *A* here and now—is compatible with the truth of a causal theory of action. Thus, my central concern here, as in Chapter 2, has been with the *possibility* of strict akratic action. In the course of the discussion, I made some suggestions about the explanation of akratic action. This issue is addressed much more fully in Chapter 6 below; and in Chapter 7 I examine the implications of strict akratic action for a traditional causal model of action-explanation. The model, I shall argue, is in need of extensive revision. Among the elements that must be added are some that revolve around the notion of self-control. It is to this notion that I turn now.

4

Self-Control and The Self-Controlled Person

Although *akrasia* has received a great deal of attention for a great many years, its opposite, *enkrateia* or self-control, has largely been ignored by philosophers. The reason for this, I think, is that whereas akratic behavior poses interesting difficulties for influential theories in ethics and the philosophy of mind, self-control and the behavior in which it manifests itself seem unproblematic. However, we cannot hope to understand *akrasia* in isolation from self-control. Indeed, the former is properly defined in terms of the latter.

In this chapter I characterize the traits of self-control and *akrasia* and begin to construct a case for their influence upon behavior. I argue that this influence extends beyond action to practical thinking and to the formation and retention of beliefs, and I develop accounts of self-control and *akrasia* which apply to both actional and doxastic phenomena.

Since the notion of *akrasia* is derivative from that of self-control, I focus on the latter and comment in passing on the former. In the first two sections I develop an account of self-control as an ability of a certain sort. This is self-control to a first approximation, or *SC1*. In Section 3, I argue that to have *SC1* is not yet to have the *trait* of self-control and I contend that a certain motivational component must be added. A derivative account of *akrasia* appears at the end of that section.

The ultimate purpose of this chapter is to set the stage for an attempt to integrate self-control and its opposite into a conceptual framework for explaining continent and incontinent action. The explanatory model that I shall develop in chapters 6 and 7 is a modified belief-desire model. On a simple belief-desire model, actions are explained solely in terms of reasons constituted by beliefs and desires and of standing conditions such as ability (see, e.g., Davidson, 1963; Goldman, 1970). A more complex belief-desire model adds intending to the explanatory apparatus, intending being treated as irreducible to belief and desire (see, e.g., Brand, 1984, Part III; Davidson, 1978, 1985a, p. 196). However, Chapter 3 makes it evident that this addition is not enough. Even here-and-now intentions can be defeated in cases of strict akratic action. Among the items that I shall add is an executive element, to be spelled out in terms of self-control.

My interest in self-control in this chapter is not, however, purely instrumental. Self-control is deserving of philosophical attention in its own right. This chapter and the next constitute what I hope is a persuasive, if indirect, argument for this claim.

1. Self-Control, Action, and Evaluation

Akrasia is exhibited in behavior that is contrary to one's better judgment; *enkrateia,* in behavior in accordance with one's better judgment. This does not get us very far, however, in understanding self-control. Is self-control exhibited *only* in behavior that is in accordance with the agent's better judgment? Do we exhibit self-control *whenever* we act as we judge best? Is self-control the sort of thing that can be *exercised?* These are among the questions that must be addressed here.

Two of our preliminary questions are answered—incorrectly, I shall argue—by David Pugmire (1982). According to Pugmire, "'strength of will'," or, as I prefer to say, self-control, "consists in doing what seems best simply on the ground that it seems best" (p. 196). He envisages a case in which an agent "put himself through a deliberation that opened him, as much as anything in his power could, to what he was doing, and . . . received a dissuasive all-things-considered value-judgment, resolved and set himself against what he then did anyway" (p. 189). Pugmire goes on to ask rhetorically: "If we decline to take literally the energy metaphors of *willpower, strength of will, struggle, exertion, resistance, overcoming,* etc., how else than in the abovementioned way could he have tried to resist? What more could he have done?"

Pugmire is mistaken on two counts. First, as we saw in Chapter 2, there is much more to self-control than what he suggests, and there is more that his agent could have done even after careful deliberation. An agent can, for example, keep clearly in mind, at the time of action, the reasons for doing the action that he judged best; he can refuse to focus his attention on the attractiveness of what might be achieved by performing a competing action, and concentrate instead on what is to be accomplished by acting as he judges best; he can refuse to entertain second thoughts concerning matters about which he has just very carefully made up his mind; he can seek to add to his motivation for performing the action judged best by promising himself a reward (e.g., an expensive dinner) for successfully resisting temptation. Such exercises of self-control can have a desirable effect upon the balance of his motivation at the time of action.

Second, self-control as commonly conceived is, like *akrasia,* exhibited only where there is competing motivation. Motivation which competes with one's better judgment need not actually be present at the time at which self-control is exhibited; for one may exercise self-control as a precautionary measure against motivation that one expects to arise later (e.g., upon finishing dinner, when his desire for food has been satisfied, a weight-conscious person may steel himself against the foreseeable onslaught of a desire to have a late snack). And we may wish to say as well that a person who, through an effort or efforts of self-control, succeeds in purging himself of a 'standing' desire that is contrary to a better judgment of his, displays his self-control simply in his no longer having the desire in question. But where there is no (actual or foreseeable) motivation contrary to one's better judgment, there is no occasion for a manifestation of self-control in support of one's better judgment. Consequently, since not every case of doing what seems best simply because it seems best is a case involving competing motivation, not every case of the former sort is a case of self-control.

It is worth noting that there are many ways of exercising self-control other than those mentioned above. A person may, in the course of his deliberation about an important matter, remind himself to look carefully for practical implications of the data being considered, and take pains not to be led by his wants into careless thinking, biased interpretation of his situation, one-sided evidence-gathering, inattention to significant features of his present circumstances, or ignorance of pertinent data. One might try to ascertain how one's highest goals would be affected by courses of action that one is considering. One might resist acting impulsively in anger by, for example, counting to ten or by calling to mind a previous resolution not to be a slave to anger. A deliberator may remind himself of resolutions that he has made about proper modes of deliberation, or ask himself whether he is reasoning in a way that is likely to generate a sound decision. An agent who has already made a decision may attempt to anticipate, and steel himself against, recalcitrant motivation that is likely to arise or increase in strength as the time to execute the decision draws near, and he may work out a detailed plan of resistance.[1] Such an agent may even have time to practice Brandtian "cognitive psychotherapy."[2]

It will be useful to have at least some crude conceptual machinery for the classification of methods of self-control. One classificatory principle is temporal. Some modes of self-control have as their target the agent's behavior in the nonimmediate future[3] whereas others are intended only to influence what one will do here and now. Another classificatory dimension is the method's locus of operation. Some modes of self-control involve the agent's altering his physical or social environment (e.g., by destroying his cigarettes or by anouncing his continent intentions to people who will think less of him if he fails to act accordingly).[4] The operation of others is wholly internal to the agent. Furthermore, while some modes of self-control are primarily cognitive (e.g., the attentional strategies described above), others are essentially conative (e.g., brute resistance, as defined in Ch. 2).

More important for present purposes is a point about the scope of self-control. Self-control, as should by now be clear, is exhibited on two practical fronts, the motivational and the evaluative. It may be exercised in order to generate or preserve a condition in which the balance of one's *motivations* is in alignment with one's better judgment; and it may be used as well to promote rational *evaluation*. Evaluations or values may be motivational. Perhaps placing a positive value upon X entails being motivated to some degree to pursue or promote X, provided that the agent believes himself capable of doing so. But, as we have seen, the degree to which we are motivated by a want is not always in strict alignment with our evaluation of the object of that want. For example, the motivational force of my want not to experience the discomfort of having a tooth pulled may be wholly out of line with the low evaluative ranking that I give the object of that want in deciding to make a dental appointment. A self-controlled person is disposed to bring his motivations into line with his evaluations and to maintain that alignment. But there is more to being self-controlled than this, for one's evaluations themselves can be warped in various ways by one's wants or motivations. Hence, a self-controlled person must also be disposed to promote and maintain a collection of evaluations that is not unduly influenced by his motivations.

Self-control exercised on the evaluative front merits further attention. Not every case of faulty evaluative thinking exhibits a failure (or absence) of self-control. Some such thinking is due simply to unmotivated careless- ness, to lack of skill in drawing inferences, to innocent mistakes about sound procedures for arriving at evaluative conclusions, and the like. Akratic evaluative thinking can, I think, be characterized on the model of akratic action—thinking, after all, is a kind of action. And *self-controlled* evaluative thinking, or evaluative thinking that exhibits self-control, may be characterized accordingly. We say (speaking now of 'external' actions, or actions upon the world) that a person acts akratically when he performs an intentional, uncompelled action that is contrary to his (decisive) better judgment. Since akratic action is, by definition, intentional action, there is no need to specify that it is motivated (for all intentional action is motivated action). But the 'motivatedness' of akratic evaluative thinking may be overlooked, and therefore requires emphasis. Akratic evaluative thinking, I suggest, is (uncompelled) motivated evaluative thinking that is contrary to a decisive better judgment of the thinker—a judgment, that is, about proper modes of evaluation, evaluative principles, and the like. Thus, for example, an agent is guilty of akratic evaluative thinking if he is moved by a desire or desires in such a way that, in deliberating about a change of careers, he violates a decisive judgment that it is best to take the interests of his family into account in making decisions which will affect their welfare. And if, though he is tempted to ignore his family's interests in reaching his decision, our agent gives them due consideration, he exhibits self-control (at least to some degree and in *this* connection) in his evaluative thinking.

Self-control, I propose, is roughly the ability to master motivation that is contrary to one's better judgment—the ability to prevent such motivation from resulting in behavior that is contrary to one's decisive better judgment.[5] This is self-control to a first approximation, or *SC1*. The better judgments in question include judgments about proper evaluative conduct as well as judgments about 'external' action, so that a single account of self-control applies to judgments of either sort. And, in both cases, exercises of self-control are responses to (actual or foreseeable) motivation that is contrary to a better judgment of the agent, whether the judgment in question be explicitly held or only implicitly endorsed.[6]

The proposal just made about self-control is compatible with there being particular exercises of self-control that are not in the service of a better judgment. Suppose that young Freddy, against his better judgment, has accepted a dare to break into the Smiths' house this evening while they are out. If Freddy decides for the 'right' reasons not to go through with the break-in, we would not attribute his decision to weakness of will. But if, due simply to a failure of nerve, he refrains from breaking into the house, a charge of weakness may be appropriate. Similarly, if Freddy masters his fear and breaks into the house (against his better judgment), it seems that this mastery should be counted as an instance of self-control. However, from the fact—if it is a fact—that one can exhibit self-control that is not in the service of a better judgment, it does not follow that self-control is not *at least* an ability to master motivation that is contrary to one's better judgment. Nor does it follow that self-control is simply an ability to master motivation that is contrary to one's decisions or intentions (i.e., whether or not the decisions or intentions are in accordance with one's better judgment). Freddy can exhibit self-control in *refraining from* acting in accordance with his decision to break into the house. He can exercise his powers of self-control in such a way as to resist the temptation of which his decision to break into the house is reflective—that is, in such a way as to master the motivation that *supports* his akratic decision. And this exercise of self-control need not serve some *other* decision or intention, but may rather be in the service of his *judgment* that it is best not to break into the house.

My suggestion, which will derive further support from subsequent discussion in this chapter, is that self-control to a first approximation is the ability specified above and that the 'powers' of mastery and resistance which the possession of this ability involves may sometimes be exercised in the service of decisions and intentions that are not reflective of one's better judgment.

2. Self-Control and Belief

Although my discussion thus far has been conducted in a practical or 'actional' context, doxastic matters being given only derivative attention, self-control and its opposite seem to have a broad and significant bearing on the formation and retention of (nonevaluative) beliefs. What we want to be the case plainly has a significant influence on what we believe to be the case.[7] And although our beliefs, unlike many of our actions, are not (at least in general) under our direct voluntary control, what we come, or continue, to believe is often subject to our *indirect* control. For example, in executing my decisions about how to gather evidence in a certain situation, or in acting on my judgments about which data merit consideration and which do not, I clearly influence what I come, or continue, to believe.

In the present section, I shall ask whether the account of self-control articulated above is successfully applied to the doxastic realm. The account, again, is this: Self-control to a first approximation (*SC1*) is the ability to master motivation that is contrary to one's decisive better judgment. The element of this account which, for present purposes, is most in need of discussion is the notion of a better judgment. What sort of 'better judgment' is it that is served by *doxastic* self-control?

The phenomenon of self-deception, which has been compared to akratic action in some recent literature,[8] may profitably be considered in this connection. Beliefs that agents are self-deceived in holding are, like akratic actions, motivated (or so I shall argue in Ch. 9). Moreover, just as the person who incontinently does *A*, acts against his better judgment due to contrary motivation, the self-deceived person, again due to some motivational element, typically *believes* against his 'better evidence,' or against better evidence which he would have had, or could easily have acquired, if it were not for the motivational element in question.[9] Not every case of self-deception need be a case of incontinence, however. Suppose, for example, that Sarah (nonakratically) decided long ago that it is best, all things considered, not to attend to unpleasant matters about which she can do nothing. Suppose further that she is now in possession of excellent evidence that there will soon be a Third World War, and that, due in part to a want-influenced failure to focus her attention on this evidence, she acquires, or retains, a belief that there is no significant danger of another world war. On these suppositions, Sarah is conducting herself in accordance with her better judgment and, therefore (on the assumption that she is not violating some other, incompatible better judgment of hers), she is not guilty of incontinence—even though she *is* self-deceived.

What sorts of better judgment are violated by self-deceived persons? Many general judgments fit the bill. For example, the judgment that it is best (1) to conduct oneself in such a way that one will believe what is true and will not believe what is false; (2) to assess evidence objectively; or (3) not to allow what one wants to be the case to determine what one believes *is* the case. Some specific judgments are also candidates; for example, the judgment (4) that the evidence for *p* is very strong and much stronger than the evidence for not-*p*. How the general judgments may be violated is not difficult to see; and we may even imagine a violation of the specific judgment which does not involve us in an investigation of the various paradoxes associated with self-deception. To judge that there is very strong evidence for *p* is not necessarily to believe that *p*. We may, without contradiction, imagine that *S* believes, say, that the evidence that his wife is having an affair is quite strong and yet sincerely and accurately reports that he does not believe that she is having an affair, since his faith in his wife is such that he believes that there must be some other explanation, however implausible it may be, of the data in question.

To believe that not-*p* while one holds (4) is not, however, to believe akratically, unless some appropriate (explicit or implicit) higher level judgment is involved. A person who holds (4) but does not judge it best always to bring it about that his beliefs conform to the evidence, may continently believe that not-*p*; for example, he may think (nonakratically) that in some cases it is best to believe 'against' the weightiest evidence and that his present situation is just such a case. There may be a sense in which a person who holds (4) is committed to believing that *p* (and to not believing that not-*p*): He may be so committed by some epistemic principle of rationality. But not every commitment is, as it were, a *self*-commitment, a commitment of the self *by the self* (rather than by some principle that is not the self's). Although we may say that, morally speaking, or from a moral point of view, an agent who thinks he ought morally to do *A* is committed to doing, or to trying to do *A*, this commitment is not a *self*-commitment unless the agent takes this moral judgment (or moral judgments of this *type*, or moral judgments in general) to override any competing judgment that he may hold. And in the absence of such a self-commitment, his failing to try to do *A* might exhibit moral imperfection, but not *akrasia*. Similarly, a person who holds (4) and believes not-*p* rather than *p*, but does not violate a self-commitment in so doing, may exhibit doxastic irresponsibility (having violated some epistemic principle of rationality), but he does not believe akratically.

We have just located a disanalogy of sorts between akratic action and akratic belief. The judgment that it is better (without qualification) to do *A* than to do *B* constitutes a self-commitment; but the (in some ways) comparable judgment that the evidence for *p* is strong and stronger than the evidence for not-*p* does not. The explanation is instructive. The former judgment is grounded in the agent's own system of values, while the latter is grounded only in the subject's beliefs about evidence; and whereas a person may take considerations of evidence to be evaluatively overridden by other considerations (e.g., by his faith in, or commitment to, a person or institution), the actional judgment in question has 'built-in' evaluative overridingness.

I asked, near the beginning of this section, whether the account of self-control in Section 1 is successfully applied to the doxastic realm and how the notion of 'better judgment' that it involves is to be construed in a doxastic context. The answer to the second question is that better judgments in the requisite sense are judgments that constitute doxastic self-commitments or that, when conjoined with such judgments, yield further doxastic self-commitments (e.g., the self-commitment to believe that *p*). When the notion of better judgment is understood in this way, the account at issue seems well suited to the doxastic arena. Where there is no doxastic self-commitment there can be no doxastic self-control, since there is nothing for the latter to defend against recalcitrant motivation. Doxastic self-control to a first approximation is the ability to master motivation that is contrary to a doxastic self-commitment (and to the judgments that generate such a commitment), whether the commitment be to a way of assessing, gathering, or attending to evidence, or to holding (or not holding) a certain belief.[10]

3. Self-Controlled Agents

Since self-control and its opposite obviously have a marked influence on what we do and believe, they ought, it seems, to be taken into account in philosophical theories of human behavior. For example, if, as I argued in Chapter 3, we can act akratically even against an intention to do an *A* here and now, then causally sufficient conditions of intentionally *A*-ing cannot be articulated wholly in terms of intending, physical and psychological ability, the absence of external prevention, and 'the cooperation of the world.' An executive element must also be brought into the causal picture—something that explains an agent's executing his intention rather than abandoning it in the face of competing motivation. In the case of continent action, self-control is a promising candidate.

In the present section, I shall lay more of the groundwork for the integration of self-control and *akrasia* into explanations of continent and incontinent behavior by characterizing the self-controlled agent. My account of self-control to a first approximation (*SC1*), as we shall see, does not fully capture what it is to be a self-controlled agent, that is, to have self-control as a trait of character. Though, as I suggest in Chapter 7.4, characterological explanations of actions are at best promissory notes of a sort, an examination of self-control as a trait of character will prove helpful later in explaining how the notes may be redeemed.

To understand the *trait* of self-control we must look more closely at self-control *qua* ability (i.e., at *SC1*). In what does *SC1* consist? The discussion in Chapter 2 of skilled versus brute resistance suggests an answer: A person's capacity for self-control is a function of the modes of skilled resistance that he has at his disposal and his powers of brute resistance. *SC1* is analogous in some respects to the ability to wrestle well. The latter ability involves not only strength, but skill.

The wrestling analogy can be pushed further. One can conceive of a wrestler who is familiar with a number of holds and other maneuvers and can execute them well but who is a very bad tactician. He lacks a talent for selecting appropriate holds or moves for particular situations. Such a person lacks the ability to wrestle well. Similarly, someone who has learned, and can successfully execute, a number of self-control techniques, but who generally is unable to identify an appropriate technique when he needs to employ one, would be possessed at most of a rather distant approximation of *SC1*.

This indicates that an individual's *SC1* is more than the collection of resistance-techniques and powers of brute resistance that he has at his disposal. *SC1* also involves an ability to see when self-control is called for and to identify expedient measures of self-control in particular situations.

There is, however, a sort of self-controlled person—perhaps a purely fictitious sort—whom this account does not fit. Consider the exceptionally resolute person (commented upon in Ch. 2.2), one who has no need to make an effort of self-control even when faced with strong competing desires. His commitment to his decisive better judgments is such that his corresponding intentions carry the day without the assistance of skilled, or even brute, resistance. It is precisely because his will is so strong, we might say, that he is not in need of self-control techniques—including the brute technique (see Ch. 2.2) of forming or retaining the intention to do *A* in order to bring it about that he acts, not as he is tempted to do, but rather as he judges best. This agent's ability (or better, power) to counteract motivation that is contrary to his better judgment—that is, his *SC1*—is not the sort of thing that can be actively exercised. Rather, it lies simply in the firmness of his intentions. Such a person has no need to see when self-control is called for.

Does self-control involve a motivational component—perhaps motivation to exhibit self-control? Some analogies suggest that it does not. For example, someone with the ability to wrestle well may retain that ability (for a while) even if he loses all motivation to wrestle well, or to wrestle at all. Similarly, a physically strong person may retain his strength (for a time) even if he loses his motivation to utilize it. Certain traits of *character,* on the other hand, plainly have a motivational component. Generosity, for example, involves motivation to behave generously. Is self-control more like physical stength or generosity in the relevant respect?

On the face of it, the assertion that someone has remarkable powers of self-control but is no longer motivated to exercise them does not seem self-contradictory. Such a loss of motivation might be generated by a personal tragedy. Someone who has just lost his entire family in an automobile accident may not now care what he does and may make no attempt to pull himself together even though he is able to do so. We may suppose that, out of habit, he continues to make judgments about what it would be best to do, but that he makes no effort to bring the balance of his motivation into line with his decisive better judgments, and that, as a result, he often acts incontinently.

Clearly, such a person would not be a *self-controlled person* at the time; but it does not follow from this, at least in any obvious way, that he has lost his remarkable powers of self-control. We must distinguish in this connection between having powers, skills, and so on of the sort that constitute self-control *qua ability* (i.e., *SC1*) and having self-control as a *trait of character*. To have self-control as a character trait is to be a self-controlled person. And part of what it is to be a self-controlled person is to be appropriately motivated to act as one judges best. A self-controlled person is disposed to exhibit self-control in appropriate circumstances; and he does this, most characteristically, by successfully resisting motivation that competes with his decisive better judgments (with a view, of course, to acting on those judgments).

In short, a self-controlled person is someone who is appropriately motivated to conduct himself as he judges best and has the ability to master motivation to the contrary. This is not to say, of course, that he will always behave continently. Nor should we suppose, as I have mentioned, that a person who exhibits self-control in some areas (e.g., eating) will also be self-controlled in others (e.g., smoking). And, of course, self-control comes in degrees.

One consequence of the accounts just advanced of self-control and the self-controlled person is that even someone who *always* acts in accordance with his better judgment need not have the trait of self-control. This consequence, though it may initially strike one as odd, is a desirable one. Suppose that Sonny, through no effort of his own, has at most exceedingly weak desires for any course of action that is contrary to his better judgment.[11] Suppose also, however, that he is possessed of none of the skills and powers of the sorts discussed above, and that if he were to be faced with a moderately strong competing desire whose strength is such that most people could, with a little effort, resist it, he would act against his better judgment. Such a person lacks the trait of self-control. He acts as a self-controlled individual would typically act (i.e., in accordance with his better judgment); but his actions do not exhibit self-control.

A word is in order, finally, about *akrasia* and the akratic individual. *Akrasia* is literally a lack of self-control. However, as the classical Greek term is employed by the philosophers who used it, it does not denote a total absence of self-control. Aristotle tells us, for example, that the akratic individual is *less* self-controlled than most people (*NE* 1152a25–27). Similarly, he asserts that the enkratic individual is better than most people at resisting temptation.

Akrasia and *enkrateia* lie on a continuum whose endpoints are, on the one hand, the agent who is totally lacking in self-control (*qua* ability) and wholly without motivation to act as he judges best and, on the other, the perfectly or ideally self-controlled person. Both sorts of agent, if not philosophers' fictions, are very rare indeed. Just what the respective conditions are of 'normal' akratic and self-controlled agents is, of course, an empirical matter. The cases of akratic action examined in the philosophical literature often depict an agent who is motivated to exercise self-control but fails to do so successfully. Living examples include people who would like to lose weight, save money, quit drinking, and the like, but fail to do so on their own and consequently join a support group composed of individuals with similar aspirations and problems. Another sort of akratic action is performed by agents who suffer from acedia—they are apathetic, and consequently lack motivation to exercise self-control. The earlier example of the man who lost his family falls under this heading. We might identify as akratic *agents* people who are subnormal either in their possession of *SC1* or in their motivation to exercise self-control, or both. But we must not forget Amelie Rorty's observation (1980a, p. 205) that "*akrasia* is characteristically regional."

4. Conclusion

In this chapter, I have been concerned to develop a notion of self-control which is properly contrasted specifically with *akrasia*. There is also a broader notion of self-control. To have self-control, one might say, is to be in control of oneself; and, one might add, there is more to being in control of oneself than having and exhibiting the power to master motivation that is contrary to one's better judgment.[12] A person whose better judgments rest on values generated and maintained by brainwashing, for example, may be self-controlled in my sense; but he seems not to be in control of himself in the broader sense. He is ruled, ultimately, not by his 'self' but rather by his brainwasher. This broader notion is certainly worth examining; but this is not the place. I shall be satisfied if I have clarified the narrower notion and contributed to our appreciation of the practical and doxastic significance of self-control in this sense.

5

Self-Control: A Paradox

A certain paradox about self-control has gone largely unnoticed by philosophers.[1] It revolves around a very plausible assumption about the relationship of motivation to intentional action—roughly, that whenever an agent acts intentionally he does what he is most motivated (occurrently) to do at the time.[2] Of course, this formulation of the assumption cries out for qualification. Among other things, physical and psychological ability must be taken into account. Fortunately, refinements along these lines require little attention for present purposes.

The paradox lies just beneath the surface of the following schematic story. S is now most motivated to do A here and now (i.e., at t), but he judges it best, all things considered, not to do A at t. He attempts to control himself by uttering a self-command: "Don't do it," he firmly says. The attempt is successful. Now, it looks as though S's intentionally not doing A entitles us to infer that he is more motivated at t not to do A at t than to do A at t. However, this contradicts a central element in the story. S *is* most motivated at t to do A at t: That is why he makes an attempt at self-control.

One attempt to resolve the contradiction involves dividing t into smaller units, t_1 and t_2. We might suppose that at t_1 S is most motivated to do A at t_2, and that at t_2, as a result of his self-command, he is most motivated not to do A at t_2. But we are still saddled with a problem. If, at t_1, S is most motivated to do A at t_2, how can we explain his uttering a self-command at t_1 with a view to bringing it about that he does *not* do A at t_2? If, at t_1, he is most motivated to do A at t_2, it looks as though he must be more motivated at t_1 not to utter the self-command than to utter it; for, it seems, his motivation at t_1 to utter the self-command at t_1 is identical with his motivation at t_1 not to do A at t_2, and that motivation is weaker, by hypothesis, than his motivation at t_1 to do A at t_2.

One might attempt to employ the time-slicing strategy again: Perhaps at t_{1a} S is most motivated to do A at t_2, whereas at t_{1b} he is most motivated not to do *A* at t_2 and, consequently, most motivated to exercise self-control; and perhaps the motivation shifts spontaneously, without any intervention on *S*'s part. One could object that, in that case, there is no need for self-control, since *S* will do what he is most motivated to do anyway. But, of course, *S* may fear that another sudden shift in his motivation is about to occur, and take measures to ensure that this does not happen. There is, however, a problem with the second application of the time-slicing strategy. Suppose that *S* is *already* doing *A*; for example, he is watching Monday Night Football, and he judges it best to stop doing this here and now (cf. Alston, 1977, p. 81). If he *is* watching it, this is what he is now most motivated to do (now). Indeed, we may suppose that it is precisely because he realizes that he is most motivated to *continue* watching the game against his better judgment that he thinks an attempt at self-control to be in order. But if he is now most motivated to continue watching the game, how can he intentionally utter a self-command now for the purpose of bringing it about that he now *stops* watching it?

The puzzle here directly concerns not the *successful* use of self-control but the use of self-control at all in a certain type of case. If (roughly) we always act in accordance with the balance of our occurrent motivations, and we are most motivated at *t* to *A* at *t** (which may or may not be identical with *t*), how can we exercise self-control at *t* for the purpose of bringing it about that we do not *A* at *t**? What gives the paradox its bite (for one who holds the common-sense view that we can exercise self-control in such cases) is the supposition that the agent's motivation to exercise self-control is precisely his motivation not to do *A*—that is, the *weaker* motivation. If it is the weaker motivation, how can it result in intentional action?

There is another side to our paradox. If, at *t*, an agent is more motivated to exercise self-control in support of his *A*-ing at *t* than he is to refrain from exercising self-control, and if his motivation for exercising self-control and his motivation for refraining from doing so are identical, respectively, with his motivation for *A*-ing at *t* and his motivation for not *A*-ing at *t*, then, at *t*, he is more motivated to *A* at *t* than he is not to *A* at *t*. But in that case his exercising self-control seems pointless.

The immediate purpose of this chapter is to resolve both sides of the paradox. In so doing, I shall lay more of the groundwork for an explanation of incontinent and continent action.

1. Identifying the Scope of the Paradox

Some exercises of self-control are quite unproblematic. Consider, for example, the cigarette smoker who, at the end of another day of coughing, wheezing, and offending militant nonsmokers with his disgusting exhaust, decides to try to kick the habit. Given that he is not now under the sway of an occurrent desire to smoke, it may well be the case that he is now less motivated to smoke tomorrow than he is to refrain from smoking tomorrow. Furthermore, because he knows that he will be sorely tempted tomorrow to smoke over his morning coffee, he may now be strongly motivated to take measures designed to decrease the chances that he will give in to the anticipated desire, and this motivation may be greater than any motivation that he may have for not making an attempt at self-control. For example, he may now be most motivated to destroy his supply of cigarettes.

There is nothing paradoxical about this; for the agent's current balance of motivation concerning the exericse of self-control is in line with his current balance of motivation concerning his smoking tomorrow. Paradox arises only when (1) it looks as though one's balance of motivation concerning the exercise or nonexercise of self-control in support of one's A-ing (at t) is at odds with one's contemporaneous balance of motivation concerning one's A-ing or not A-ing (at t) or (2) one is most motivated to exercise self-control now in support of one's A-ing here and now. In the first instance, the lack of alignment itself is puzzling. Moreover, as we have seen, it is difficult to understand how someone who is more motivated at t to do A at t^* than not to do A at t^* can be sufficiently motivated at t to exercise self-control in defense of his not A-ing at t^*. Let us call this the paradox of *uphill self-control*. What renders (2) problematic, on the other hand, is the supposition that the two motivational sets that compete over one's exercising or not exercising self-control in support of one's A-ing are also the competitors over one's A-ing or not A-ing. If this is right and S is most motivated to exercise self-control at t in support of his A-ing at t, his motivation to A would seem to be such that an attempt at self-control is pointless. This is the paradox of *downhill self-control*. The paradox of uphill self-control poses a problem about the *possibility* of exercising self-control in a certain range of cases, while its counterpart raises a question about the *point* of exercising self-control in another range.

2. Uphill Self-Control: The Weak Paradox

The former paradox—the more challenging of the two—will receive the bulk of the attention in the present chapter. In some cases, it is not difficult to see how this paradox should be resolved. There are instances in which the agent's motivation for exercising self-control in the way he does is not limited to his motivation for performing the continent action supported by his exercise of self-control. Such cases pose what I shall call the *weak paradox of uphill self-control.*[3]

Consider the following science-fiction case. Harry, a heroin addict, is now under the influence of a craving for the drug so strong that he cannot resist it by ordinary means. Although he wants not to be an addict and has some motivation to refrain from using the drug now, the strength of his craving is such that, other things being equal, he will now use the loaded syringe resting on the table before him. Fortunately, however, there is a motivation-eradicating device on the wristwatch that Harry just acquired. He sets the dial to his craving for heroin and presses a button, with the result that he is no longer motivated to use the drug now. Harry wonders whether the watch can be used to eradicate his addiction in one fell swoop. If not, he decides, he will gradually rid himself of his addiction by using the watch whenever he craves the drug; for he judges it best, all things considered, to put an end to his addiction and, consequently, to refrain from using the drug.

Why did Harry act on his desire to eradicate the craving rather than on the craving? If (again roughly) we always do what we are most motivated to do, Harry must have been more motivated to eradicate the craving by using the watch than to use the drug, even though, at the time at which he decided to press the button, his craving for heroin was stronger than his desire not to use the drug. How can this be?

Part of the answer is that Harry's desire to eradicate the craving by pressing the button does not rest wholly on his motivation to refrain from using the heroin at *t*. Eradicating the craving in this way is not simply a means of bringing it about that he refrains from using the heroin. It is also a means of putting an end to the pain of an unsatisfied craving; and, we may suppose, Harry desires it (in part) as such. It is the pain that gives the craving so much motivational power. And Harry has at his disposal two different means of eliminating the pain. He can satisfy the craving, or he can eradicate it. These means are equally quick and effective, but Harry prefers the second to the first for the very reasons that support his desire not to use the drug.

Why, if this is so, do these reasons not render his motivation not to use the drug stronger than his craving, so that no effort of self-control is required? The answer is implicit in what I have just said. In this example, we can identify three alternative courses of action, broadly conceived: (1) refraining from using the drug at *t* even if one craves it at *t* (this is not a genuine option for Harry); (2) using the drug at *t* should one crave it at *t*; (3) pressing the button, thereby bringing it about that one refrains from using the drug while *not* craving it. Courses of action (2) and (3) have an important consequence that (1) does not: They eliminate the pain of an unsatisfied craving. This is why they are desired more strongly than (1). Courses (2) and (3) are supported equally, we may suppose, by Harry's desire to eliminate the pain of an unsatisfied craving for heroin. The relative strength of his desires for (2) and (3) (or, more precisely, of his desires to press the button and to use the drug) is a function of other motivators—Harry's desire not to be a heroin addict, his desire for the euphoric feeling that a shot of heroin will bring, and so on. Thus, Harry's reasons for pressing the button *rather than* using the drug fight only a limited battle. And this is why they can have the result that he is more motivated to press the button than to use the drug without also (directly) rendering his motivation not to use the drug stronger than his craving. Although these reasons motivationally outweigh their competitors, Harry's motivational condition prior to pressing the button is such that, unless it changes, he will use the drug at once.

In pressing the button to eradicate his craving, Harry is not acting simply to eliminate the pain of an unsatisfied craving. Nor is he acting simply to bring it about that he does not use the drug. What he wants most is to bring it about that he refrains from using the drug without suffering the pain of an unsatisfied craving. This is what his desire-eradicating device enables him to do. Since he has motivation to push the button which is not also motivation to refrain from using the drug (viz., his desire to eliminate the pain of an unsatisfied craving), his being more motivated to press the button than to use the drug is quite compatible with the latter motivation's being stronger than his motivation to refrain from using the drug.

The point of the preceding discussion is not limited to science-fiction cases. Many dieters take appetite suppressants for roughly the reason that Harry uses his watch—namely, not only to increase their chances of acting as they judge best but also to eliminate the pain of an unsatisifed appetitive desire. Of course, in both instances, the self-control technique promotes continent behavior *by* eliminating the pain; but the fact remains that use of the technique in cases of the sort imagined is not motivated solely by the desire to resist temptation. (Of course, *some* dieters who take appetite suppressants may do so from the desire to lose weight alone.)

Substitution strategies of self-control work in a similar fashion. For example, people who chew a great deal of gum while attempting to quit smoking often do this not only to improve their chances of kicking the habit but also to make the process less unpleasant. Again, in these cases, the self-control technique may contribute to continent behavior *by* making it more tolerable; but this is quite compatible with an independent desire's partially motivating the substitution of gum for tobacco.

Once we notice that an agent's motivation to exercise self-control in defense of his *A*-ing need not be limited to his motivation to *A*, certain apparently problematic cases of self-control become intelligible. These cases raise what I have called the weak paradox of uphill self-control—the paradox that has just been resolved.

3. Uphill Self-Control: The Strong Paradox

The philosophically most challenging instances of uphill self-control are those in which one's motivation to exercise self-control in the way that one does is limited to one's motivation to perform the action that the exercise of self-control is intended to support. If *S*'s motivation to exercise self-control in a particular way—his motivation to *X*—*is* his motivation to *A*, and his motivation to *A* is *weaker* than his motivation not to *A*, how can he do *X*? If to *X* is to act on the weaker motivation, *S*'s *X*-ing seems impossible. This is the *strong paradox of uphill self-control*.

The introduction of some technical terminology will facilitate the ensuing discussion. Let us say that the *positive motivational base* of a desire is the collection of all occurrent motivations of the agent that make a positive contribution to the motivational strength of that desire. Not every occurrent motivation that figures in the causation of a particular desire is in the positive motivational base of that desire. For example, in the course of deliberation undertaken with a view to the achievement of a desired end, *E*, *S* may discover that his doing *A* is a necessary condition of his achieving *E*, and he may consequently desire to do *A*. This latter desire may prompt a bit of deliberation about how best to put himself in a position to do *A*, resulting in a desire to perform some basic action, *B*. In such a case, *S*'s desire to do *A* may be a causal antecedent of his desire to do *B* without making a positive contribution to the *strength* of *S*'s desire to do *B*; for the strength of the latter desire may be wholly derivative from the strength of *S*'s desire for *E*. Conversely, an occurrent motivation may be in the positive motivational base of a desire without contributing causally to the formation or retention of that desire. Suppose that, having already acquired the desire to do *B*, *S* discovers that *B*-ing will contribute to the satisfaction of his desire for *C*. If this strengthens his desire to do *B*, his desire for *C* will be in the positive motivational base of the former desire. And not only is the latter desire not a cause of the formation of the former, it need not even causally *sustain* *S*'s desire to do *B*. *S*'s continuing to desire to do *B* may be causally independent of his desire for *C*.

Now, among our desires are both *intrinsic* and *extrinsic* desires.[4] An intrinsic desire is a desire of something for its own sake. An extrinsic desire, on the other hand, is a desire of something for its conduciveness to something else that is wanted. Thus, for example, I may desire my happiness intrinsically and financial security extrinsically, as a means to happiness. Many desires are mixed, in the sense that their objects are wanted both for themselves and for their conduciveness to something else. I may desire to relax now both for its own sake and in order to refresh myself for the next order of business. I shall say that a desire is *strictly intrinsic* if and only if its object is wanted for itself alone and, similarly, that a desire is *strictly extrinsic* if and only if its object is wanted only for its (believed) conduciveness to something else. A mixed desire is partly intrinsic and partly extrinsic.

The positive motivational base of any intrinsic desire is at least partly internal to the desire itself. Thus, if I desire to jog now partly for the sake of the activity itself, this desire is the source of part of its own motivational strength. Of course, the same desire may also derive strength from other occurrent desires of mine. I may also want to jog now in order to amuse my children.

Many desires have not only a positive motivational base but also what I shall call a *negative motivational base*. The negative motivational base of a desire is the collection of all occurrent motivations of the agent that make a negative contribution to the motivational strength of that desire. Consider, for example, the case of a semireformed smoker who now has a desire to buy a pack of cigarettes. In addition to the motivation that contributes to the strength of that desire, he may also have motivation that makes the desire less strong than it would otherwise have been. The attenuating motivation can prevent the strength of the desire in question from reaching a level that it would otherwise have reached, decrease the strength that the desire actually has at a given moment, or both.

One might attempt to account for the motivational influence of subjective probabilities in terms of motivational bases. For example, if S's desire to do A is stronger than his desire to do B because he believes that A has a better chance than B of producing E, one might suppose that he has a desire to take the most effective means to E and that this desire is in the positive motivational base of his desire to do A but not of his desire to do B (or that it is in the negative motivational base of the latter but not the former desire).

The positive and negative motivational bases of a desire constitute its *total motivational base*. The total motivational base of a desire need not *determine* its motivational strength even if the motivational influence of subjective probabilities can be captured in terms of positive or negative motivational bases. The strength of a desire can also be influenced, as we have seen, by such cognitive matters as vividness of representation. Someone who sees a delectable hot fudge sundae being prepared may be more motivated now to order one than he was only a few moments earlier, even if the earlier and later desires for a hot fudge sundae have the same total motivational base.

Consider now a case of uphill self-control. Ian turned on the television about a half-hour ago when he started eating lunch. He decided to have a quick meal so that he would have time to finish painting his shed before his wife came home from work. (He wanted to surprise her.) Ian has just finished eating and he is thinking that he ought (all things considered) to get back to work now. However, he is enjoying the golf tournament on TV and he remains seated. He tells himself that he will watch the match until the next commercial break; but the commercial comes and goes and Ian is still in front of the set. Thinking that he had better drag himself away from the television now, Ian utters a self-command: "Get off your butt, Ian, and paint that shed!" Ian turns off the set, picks up his painter's cap, and walks into his backyard.

If we suppose that Ian is more motivated to continue watching the golf game than to stop watching it when he utters the self-command and that his motivation for uttering the command *is* his motivation for getting back to work, we have a problematic case of the sort at issue in this section.

Thus far, we have identified three determinants of the motivational force of a desire: its positive motivational base, its negative motivational base, and cognitive elements. I am supposing that Ian's desire to utter the self-command (Dc) has the same positive motivational base as his desire to get back to work (Dw) and that Dw (prior to Ian's uttering the self-command) is weaker than his desire to continue watching television (Dtv). But precisely because a desire's positive motivational base is not the sole determinant of its motivational force, it does not follow that Dc has the same strength as Dw, nor, consequently, that Dc is weaker than Dtv.

Of course, one would still like some explanation of the relative strengths of these desires; but before that issue is broached, let us briefly consider some attempts to block the supposition that Dc and Dw have the same positive motivational base. One might suggest that Ian has motivation to utter the self-command that is not also motivation to get back to work. As support for the suggestion, one might offer the following. (1) Ian may have a generic desire to act in accordance with his better judgments and to exercise self-control when necessary; but this plainly is not a desire to get back to work, and it is not in the positive motivational base of Dw.

(2) Ian *desires* to utter the self-command; but since this is not itself a desire to get back to work, Ian has motivation to utter the self-command that is not also motivation to get back to work.

Contentions (1) and (2) are both unconvincing. First, if Ian has a generic desire to act as he judges best, we may suppose that this is also motivation that he has to get back to work. Normally, if an agent who occurrently has this generic desire sees that he can satisfy it only if he does *A* (in this case, gets back to work), his prospective *A*-ing will receive the generic desire's full motivational support. We may reasonably suppose not only that Ian's generic desire is in the positive motivational base of *Dw*, but also that it provides no greater motivation to utter the self-command than to get back to work. Second, although *Dc* is not a desire to get back to work, we may reasonably suppose that it is a strictly extrinsic desire, whose strength is wholly derivative from Ian's motivation to get back to work. We may suppose, in short, that the positive motivational base of *Dc* is identical with, or a segment of, the positive motivational base of *Dw*.

Once we grant that *Dc* has the same positive motivational base as *Dw*, what we are inclined to say is that it is easier for Ian to utter the self-command than to get back to work now and that this helps to explain (in a loose sense of the term) why he was sufficiently motivated to utter the self-command but not to get back to work (prior to uttering the command). The relative ease of uttering the self-command is a psychological matter, of course. Though a brief uttering may burn fewer calories than does rising from a chair, this is not the sort of ease in question. What, then, is the sense of 'easier' at issue, and in virtue of what is the utterance psychologically easier for Ian than getting back to work?

Let us suppose, for the sake of argument, that *Dc* has the same negative motivational base as *Dw*. That is, all occurrent motivations which have a negative effect upon the strength of *Dw* also have a negative effect upon the strength of *Dc*, and vice versa. Let us suppose further that the negative motivational base of these desires is precisely the positive motivational base of Ian's desire to continue watching television (Dtv) and that the latter is an intrinsic desire. Given these suppositions, Dtv will be in the negative motivational base of both *Dc* and *Dw*. It is at this point that the issue of ease enters. *Dw* competes *directly* with Dtv: To satisfy either is to frustrate the other. However, there is only indirect competition between *Dc* and Dtv: Ian can utter the self-command *while* watching the tournament. Thus, one may expect Dtv's resistance to be stronger in the first instance. And this would make it *easier* for Ian to utter the self-command (at *t*) than to get back to work (at *t*).

One may try to unpack the point about relative ease further in at least two ways. One approach employs what I shall call the *negative* strategy. It might be argued that because Dtv is directly opposed to Dw, but not to Dc, it (i.e., Dtv) exerts a stronger negative influence upon the motivational force of Dw, with the result that Dw is weaker than Dc. Another approach utilizes what I shall call the *fine-grained* strategy. The emphasis here is upon the relative strength of the motivation with which Dc *directly* competes. The idea (in part) is that, other things being equal, Dc need only be stronger than its *direct* motivational competition to result in action (i.e., the self-command) and that the direct competition may be weaker than Dtv. Since Ian can act on Dtv and Dc simultaneously, he can act on the latter even if it is weaker than the former. What is crucial, as far as Dc is concerned, is its direct competition (e.g., Ian's desire, if he has one, not to command himself to return to work).

How might Dc's direct competitor be weaker than Dtv? Notice that watching the golf tournament is attractive to Ian in a way that his not making an attempt at self-control is not. He is *enjoying* the former, but not (we may suppose) the latter. Even if Ian feels certain that his not making an attempt at self-control is a necessary condition of his continuing to watch the tournament, the effect of his enjoyment upon the strength of Dtv need not be matched in the case of Dc's direct competitor. Ian may have a relatively weak desire to refrain from making an attempt at self-control; and if Dc is stronger than its direct competitor, we should expect Ian to act on it even though Dtv is stronger than Dw. Notice also that an agent's attentional condition (as we have seen) can have a marked influence on his motivational condition.[5] Ian's attention, we may suppose, is focused much more on the TV than on the prospect of not making an attempt at self-control. Thus, we should not find it surprising that he is more motivated to continue watching TV than he is to refrain from making an attempt at self-control. Moreover, when the thought of uttering the self-command occurs to him, he may be much more attentive to the prospect of surprising his wife with a freshly painted shed than to his reasons for refraining from making the attempt at self-control. This would give Dc the advantage of vividness of representation over any desire that Ian may have not to utter the self-command. (In contrast, the thought of getting back to work may make the prospect of continuing to watch *TV* even more attractive.) Thus, it is possible that Ian is more motivated to utter the self-command than to refrain from uttering it even though, at the same time, he is more motivated to continue watching TV than to get back to work.

The question remains, of course, how Ian's uttering the self-command can have the result that he gets back to work. This takes us beyond the scope of the present investigation; but a brief comment is in order. First, Ian may be in the *habit* of obeying his self-commands. Consequently, his uttering the command may tap an additional source of motivation. Second, his utterance may focus his attention in such a way as to enhance his motivation to get back to work (while, perhaps, diminishing his motivation to remain in front of the set).

In any case, the key to resolving the strong paradox of uphill self-control is the observation that the motivational strength of a desire is not always a function simply of its positive motivational base, nor even of its total motivational base. Two desires having the same total motivational base may differ in strength. For example, one's desire to exercise self-control in support of one's A-ing can be stronger than one's desire to A even when both desires have the same total motivational base. This is true as well of one's desire to B and one's desire not to exercise self-control in support of an action that is incompatible with one's B-ing. Moreover, the desire to exercise self-control in support of one's A-ing and the desire to A can be, respectively, stronger and weaker than their direct competitors.

4. Downhill Self-Control

In an apparently problematic instance of downhill self-control, the agent is more motivated at *t* to exercise self-control in defense of his A-ing at *t* than he is not to exercise self-control. In such a case, one might wonder what point an attempt at self-control can have; for, it may seem that if one's motivational balance vis-à-vis self-control is as just described, one would already be most motivated to do A, in which case an attempt at self-control seems pointless.

The solution to this paradox should by now be obvious. First, as we saw in Section 2, an agent may have motivation to exercise self-control in support of his A-ing that is not also motivation to A. When this happens, the agent may be more motivated to exercise self-control than not to do so while also being more motivated to do B than to do A (where A and B are competing actions). In such a case an attempt at self-control is in order. Such an attempt can reverse the balance of one's motivation with respect to A and B. Second, as I argued in the preceding section, one may be more motivated to exercise self-control in support of one's A-ing than not to do so even when the motivations that compete on this front have the same total motivational bases as their respective counterparts on the pertinent actional front *and* one is more strongly motivated to do B than A. Here again, an attempt at self-control is far from pointless; for unless the agent's balance of motivation concerning A and B is reversed, he will do B rather than A.

5. An Unsuccessful Attempt: Higher-Order Motivation

At one point in my thinking about the paradoxes of self-control, I was strongly inclined to make central use of Frankfurt's notion of a second-order desire in attempting to resolve them. Since this approach has probably occurred to a number of readers, I would like to explain why I have not taken it.

On Frankfurt's account, an agent "has a desire of the second order either when he wants simply to have a certain desire or when he wants a certain desire to be his will" (1971, p. 10).[6] We can say, more generally, that a higher-order desire is a desire whose propositional content makes essential reference to another actual or possible desire of the agent. Thus, the desire that my desire to smoke not be so strong as it is and the desire that my desire to diet be stronger are also properly counted as higher-order desires.

Now, it is tempting to try to resolve the paradox of self-control, as initially formulated, by postulating two orders or levels of motivation, one concerned with altering one's motivational condition and the other with more mundane action (cf. Alston, 1977). Thus, one might suppose, although a smoker is more strongly motivated at the first level to smoke than not to smoke at *t*, the balance of his higher-order motivation may favor his making an attempt to bring it about that he is more motivated not to smoke than to smoke at *t*.

In some instances, this may well be the case; but the appeal to different levels of motivation will not generate a perfectly general resolution of any of the paradoxes of self-control. Although there are second-order motivations, they do not enter into even some quite ordinary examples of self-control. The case of Ian illustrates the point nicely. Although we could suppose that he has a second-order desire to bring it about that the motivational balance of his first-order desires is reversed, there is no need to suppose that he does, nor that he has any other pertinent second-order desire. (As evidence for this claim, I offer the fact that I made sense of the case without supposing that Ian had any relevant second-order desires.) Ian might not think at all in terms of motivation. Rather than having the second-order desire at issue, he may simply desire to get back to work and utter the self-command as a means of getting himself to do so. Ian has a desire to get back to work, and he has a desire to get himself to get back to work. But neither of these desires is a second-order desire. One might try to redescribe the latter desire as a desire to bring it about that he is sufficiently *motivated* to get back to work. But this misrepresents Ian's actual psychological condition, or so at least I am entitled to suppose.

(After all, this is *my* example!) Ian has no thought whatsoever of operating on his motivational condition.

William Alston (1977) carves up the motivational terrain a bit differently than Frankfurt does, and specifically for the purpose of addressing the phenomenon of intervention into one's own motivational condition. Alston attempts to make conceptual room for what he calls "self-intervention" by distinguishing between two "levels" (e.g., p. 79) or "systems" (e.g., p. 83) of motivation, one concerned with action "designed to influence the current motivation of the agent" (p. 79) and the other with action not so designed. In some cases, both sorts of motivation may indeed be importantly involved. But the example of Ian is not such a case. His act of uttering the self-command is not done with the *design* or intention of influencing his current motivation. Rather, he utters the self-command simply with a view to bringing it about that he gets back to work. He has no thought of altering his motivational condition, much less an intention to do so.

Alston claims that in instances of successful self-intervention there is some point at which "one of the systems must contain a *W* [i.e., a want] that is lacking in the other, or a given *W* must differ in strength in the two systems" (pp. 85f.). In the case of Ian, however, only one motivational system is at work, a "system" that involves his desires to get back to work, to get himself to get back to work, to continue watching television, and so on. And although Ian does intervene "into [his] own motivational processes" (p. 76), he does not intend to do *that*. What he intends to do is to utter the self-command, with a view to getting himself back to work.[7]

6. Conclusion

In Chapter 4, I suggested that self-control is deserving of philosophical attention in its own right. That this is so should by now be obvious. However, my examination of self-control in this and the preceding chapter was conducted with an ulterior motive. In the following chapter, I bring the notion of self-control to bear upon the explanation of akratic action. And in Chapter 7, I sketch and defend a modified belief-desire model of action-explanation in which self-control and the concept developed here of the total motivational base of a desire play significant roles.

6

Strict Akratic Action: A Paradox of Irrationality

An adequate explanation of akratic action will preserve the elements of rationality involved in akratic actions without rendering the actions themselves rational. Akratic action is subjectively irrational; that is, it is irrational from the *agent's* point of view. For, it is contrary to his own better judgment. Nevertheless, elements of rational explanation apply to akratic behavior. Agents of akratic actions act for *reasons*. What is potentially puzzling is that the reasons for which they act are not the reasons on which they judge it best to act.

A more general version of the problem that I shall address in this chapter is framed as follows by Donald Davidson:

> The underlying paradox of irrationality, from which no theory can entirely escape, is this: if we explain it too well, we turn it into a concealed form of rationality; while if we assign incoherence too glibly, we merely compromise our ability to diagnose irrationality by withdrawing the background of rationality needed to justify any diagnosis at all. (1982, p. 303)

The purpose of this chapter is to show how this paradox (*PI*) can be resolved in a representative instance of strict akratic action. In Sections 1 and 2 I criticize Davidson's attempted resolution and a modified Davidsonian counterpart. I develop, in the process, a partial basis for a resolution of *PI* as it applies to strict akratic action. Section 3 more systematically lays the foundation for the resolution advanced in Section 4.

1. Davidson's Resolution: The Partitioning Hypothesis

Davidson claims that we can resolve *PI* and explain irrationality only by partitioning the mind (1982, p. 300; cf. p. 303). The strategy of dividing the mind to explain irrational behavior is, of course, as old as Plato. But Davidson employs a new principle of partitioning. It is "the breakdown of reason-relations,'' he tells us, that "defines the boundary of a subdivision'' (p. 304). More perspicuously, two mental items are located in different mental subdivisions if one is a cause of, but not a reason for, the other (cf. p. 303).[1]

The central argument of Davidson's paper may be set out as follows:

1. An adequate explanation of subjectively irrational behavior depends upon there being mental causes that are not reasons for mental items that they cause. (pp. 297–304, passim)

2. The supposition that the mind has "two or more semi-autonomous structures'' is "necessary to account for mental causes that are not reasons for the mental states they cause.'' (p. 303)

3. Therefore, an adequate explanation of subjectively irrational behavior depends upon mental partitioning: "Only by partitioning the mind does it seem possible to explain how a thought or impulse can cause another to which it bears no rational relation.'' (p. 303)

In the present section, I shall show that this argument is unsuccessful. We shall see later, in Section 4, that an adequate explanation of strict akratic action does not depend upon Davidsonian mental partitioning.

The first premise may be accepted for the sake of argument. My concern is with incontinent action, and I am willing to grant that an agent's acting against his better judgment involves mental causes that are not reasons for mental items that they cause. I shall refer to such causes hereafter as *MCNR-s*.[2]

The second premise merits close inspection. It is noteworthy that from Davidson's principle of partitioning alone it follows that there is mental partitioning wherever there are *MCNR*-s. The principle, again, is that "the breakdown of reason-relations defines the boundary of a subdivision'' (1982, p. 304). And the existence of an *MCNR* constitutes precisely such a breakdown.

Davidson's case for premise (2) rests entirely upon his case for this principle. His reasons for accepting the principle are difficult to ascertain; but I suspect that the attractiveness that it has for him is due to his not having cast his net widely enough. In his concern to explain irrational action, Davidson overlooks a variety of roles that *MCNR*-s may have in rational behavior, and he opts too hastily, as we shall see, for an interpersonal model of the mind in attempting to make sense of *MCNR*-s.

Davidson makes a move toward explaining how it is possible for one mental event to cause, in the same agent, another mental item for which it is not a reason by observing that this sort of thing is not at all puzzling in an interpersonal case (1982, p. 300). For example, even if my wanting you to *A* is not a reason for *you* to want to *A*, the former want may lead me to engage in behavior—for example, inviting you to *A*—which results in your wanting to *A*. He then suggests that "the idea can be applied to a single mind and person. Indeed, if we are going to explain irrationality at all, it seems we must assume that the mind can be partitioned into quasi-independent structures" (1982, p. 300). If the structures are identified in accordance with the interpersonal model that Davidson envisages, the mental cause will be found in one mental partition and the effect for which it is not a reason in another.[3]

But why appeal to an interpersonal model at all? Suppose that Bart wants to memorize the names of the seven hills of Rome so that he can pass a test. He uses an acronym in preparing for the test; and when his teacher asks him for the names, he first thinks the acronym, which leads him to think 'Caelian', 'Capitoline', and so on. Bart's thinking the acronym is a cause of his thinking the names of the various hills, but it is not a reason for his thinking these names.[4] Here the relationship between an *MCNR* in an agent and its intended effect in the *same* agent is not at all paradoxical.

The following cases bring us closer to home:

CASE 6.1

Veronica is afraid of flying. Wishing to get over her fear, she adopts a program of desensitization. Each night, after making herself as comfortable as possible, she imagines that she is flying to visit a friend. After several weeks, her association of images of flying with feelings of comfort has met with considerable success. Veronica is now much less fearful about flying than she had been.

CASE 6.2

Jim has decided that, all things considered, it is best to quit smoking. He has now gone thirty-six hours without a cigarette. When he sees a friend light up after lunch, he is sorely tempted to ask him for a cigarette. However, he remembers a self-control technique that his wife described to him. Hoping that it will work, but intending to ask the friend for a cigarette if it doesn't, Jim decides to give the technique a try. He says the word 'stop' to himself, takes a deep breath, relaxes while exhaling, and then imagines that he is floating pleasantly in a small boat in the Carribean.[5] Much to his surprise, it works. Jim now has only a mild desire for a cigarette and he proceeds to form a firm intention to refrain from having an after-lunch smoke.

In both cases, mental events contribute causally to mental items for which they are not reasons. Veronica's acts of imagination result in an attenuation of her fear of flying and Jim's employment of the self-control technique contributes to the weakening of his occurrent desire for a cigarette and to his forming an intention not to smoke at this time. If we want to speak about mental partitioning at all in these cases, we may well be inclined to place the mental causes in the same partition as the mental effects identified. After all, in both cases the effects are the intended products of a project that centrally involves the mental causes at issue, and the causes operate in an intelligible way to generate a predictable result. In both cases, as in the acronym example, talk of a goal-directed functional system seems quite appropriate. Indeed, it is difficult to see how matters could be made clearer by supposing that, because the imaging and self-control activities are not reasons for their intended mental effects, they must be placed in different partitions from their effects. When one mental item causes another for which it is a reason, there is, to be sure, a certain coherence or intelligibility in what happens.[6] But we have just seen that some instances of causation involving *MCNR*-s have a coherence or intelligibility of their own. If, in the case of 'reason-causes,' it is coherence that inclines us to place cause and effect in the same mental system, we should be equally so inclined in the cases of Bart, Veronica, and Jim. In short, it looks as though we *can* "account for" some *MCNR*-s without adopting Davidson's principle of partitioning.

What about incontinence? Is there good reason to think that in order to make sense of incontinent action we must suppose that certain mental effects of mental causes that are not reasons for these effects are located in different partitions than their causes? If we are going to answer this question, we shall need to know more about the identity of the effects in question. Davidson claims that in any instance of akratic action "the agent goes against his own second-order principle that he ought to act on what he holds to be best, everything considered" (1982, p. 297). And he maintains that irrationality enters when the agent's desire to do A (i.e., the incontinent action) causes him to "ignore or override his principle"; for although his desire to do A is "a reason for ignoring the principle, it [is] not a reason against the principle itself." This is puzzling. For while a major theme of the paper is that the existence of *MCNR*-s is essential for an adequate explanation of incontinent action, there seems to be no mention here of a mental effect whose cause is not a reason for the effect. The mental effect that we are after cannot be the ignoring or overriding of the principle, since Davidson says that the desire to do A *is* a reason for these things. (This is not to say, of course, that it is a *good* reason.) Nor can it be, say, the agent's believing that it would be rational to reject the second-order principle; for he does not believe that. Nor is the effect at issue the agent's *A*-ing: Even though actions are mental events for Davidson (1980, p. 211), the desire to do *A* is a "consideration in favor of"—that is, a reason for—*A*-ing (1982, p. 297). And to the extent that this desire is a reason for *A*-ing, it would also seem to support, as a (possibly very poor) reason, an intention or decision to *A*. We might suppose that the desire is a cause of, but not a reason for, the agent's not intending to act as he judges best. But do negative states of this sort have a particular mental location?[7]

I do not wish to deny that *MCNR*-s play a significant role in the generation of incontinent actions. We have already seen, in the cases of Veronica and Jim, that *MCNR*-s can have a pronounced influence on a person's motivational condition. This is true as well in instances of incontinent action. For example, a person's focusing on and vividly representing the prospective pleasant results of an action, *A*, that is contrary to his better judgment may increase his motivation to do *A* even though these mental events are not *reasons* for him to be more motivated to do *A*. At the same time, such mental events may block various routes of resistance. For example, such focusing and representing may prevent Jim from recalling his wife's advice or from successfully executing the suggested technique even if the advice is recalled. However, in these examples, as in the examples of desensitization and resistance described above, it is far from clear what is to be gained by placing the mental causes and their effects (e.g., the agent's focusing on *A* and the increased motivation to do *A* that this generates) in different partitions. Moreover, these causes and effects appear to be elements in a coherent action-generating causal nexus. If this is right, we have another telling objection against Davidson's argument for his partitioning principle: Even in some instances of incontinent action we can account for the existence and the efficacy of *MCNR*-s without placing them in different partitions from their mental effects (e.g., the intentions that they generate).

To say that Davidson's argument is unsuccessful is not, of course, to deny that an adequate explanation of irrational behavior depends upon mental partitioning. What we are entitled to conclude at this point is that Davidson has failed to show that his brand of mental partitioning must be postulated to explain the effects of *MCNR*-s. If we had good reason to think, with Davidson (1982, p. 300), that the workings of *MCNR*-s can only be accounted for on an interpersonal model, we would have grounds for accepting his partitioning principle. But we have seen, in a variety of cases, that an interpersonal model is not required for this purpose. Moreover, it is unclear what the explanatory force of the partitioning principle is. *How* does placing *MCNR*-s and their pertinent mental effects in different mental partitions help to explain the generation of those effects?

2. Partitioning and Explanation:
Pears's Modified Partitioning Hypothesis

The central idea of Davidson's paper (1982) is that "if parts of the mind are to some degree independent, we can understand how they are able to harbour inconsistencies, and to interact on a causal level" (p. 300). Davidson admits that his partitioning hypothesis "leaves much unexplained, for we want to know why this double structure developed, how it accounts for the action taken," and so on. What he wants to emphasize is that "the partitioned mind leaves the field open to such further explanations, and helps to resolve the conceptual tension between" the Socratic idea that no intentional action can be subjectively irrational "and the problem of accounting for irrationality" (p. 301). However, attention to one way in which the partitioning hypothesis may be held to account for particular incontinent actions suggests, as I shall argue in the present section, that we can explain such action without invoking the hypothesis.

David Pears has developed a modified version of Davidson's principle of partitioning (1984, Ch. 5).[8] Although Pears applies this principle to the explanation of a certain sort of motivated irrational belief, he does not use it in his treatment of incontinent action. Nevertheless, brief consideration of Pears's work on partitioning will prove instructive since he gives substance to Davidson's notion of a mental subsystem.

Pears maintains that a mental element is assigned "exclusively to a sub-system if and only if it failed to interact in a rational way with an element in the main system with which it ought to interact in a rational way" (1984, p. 105; cf. pp. 97f.). In the case of motivated irrational belief, only one element, "the cautionary belief," is assigned *exclusively* to a subsystem (p. 95). The cautionary belief is a belief about the proposition that one wishes to believe; it is the belief that it would be irrational to believe this proposition. The analogue in an instance of a strict incontinent action, *A*, would be the belief that it would be irrational to do *A*, or a decisive better judgment against doing *A*. But, of course, to assign such a belief or judgment to a subsystem is not to explain the agent's incontinently *A*-ing. We need at least to be told why the belief or judgment failed to prevent the incontinent action. If the answer is that it failed precisely because it was in a subsystem and not in 'the main system,' we must ask how it came to be restricted to this particular location.

In the case of motivated irrational belief, Pears has an answer. The subsystem contains a wish (which is present in the "main system" as well) that the agent (or his main system) hold a certain belief; and this wish prevents the agent's cautionary belief from interacting with items in the main system:

> The sub-system is built around the nucleus of the wish for the irrational belief and it is organized like a person. Although it is a separate centre of agency within the whole person, it is, from its own point of view, entirely rational. It wants the main system to form the irrational belief and it is aware that it will not form it, if the cautionary belief is allowed to intervene. So with perfect rationality it stops its intervention. (1984, p. 87)

Consider the following representative instance of strict akratic action. For the last hour Susan has been preparing for tomorrow's history midterm. Boredom and restlessness are beginning to set in, and she is now entertaining the prospect of a solitary stroll through the quad on this quiet Spring evening. She decides that it would be best, all things considered, to remain in her dormitory room and study. The recent rash of muggings on campus really is quite frightening; and, in any case, she has a lot of work to do tonight if she is to pass the test. Susan judges that each of these considerations provides her with a good and sufficient reason to forego the stroll; but a short time later, against her better judgment, she leaves her room for a solitary walk through the quad. (On her way down to the main floor, Susan encounters a friend who expresses surprise when Susan announces her intention to go out alone tonight. Susan sincerely, if light-heartedly, replies: "This is what my philosophy professor calls *akrasia*.")

Pears's model may be applied to this case as follows:

1. The sub-system (*Ss*) is built around the wish for a solitary stroll through the quad. It wants Susan to take this stroll and it is aware that she will not do so if her better judgment (or her belief that strolling alone would be irrational) is allowed to intervene. So it stops the judgment's (or belief's) intervention.

Although it is not clear exactly what the intervention of the above-mentioned better judgment (*BJ*) or belief (*B*) would consist of, the upshot of its successful intervention would be that Susan does not take a solitary stroll. One way for *BJ* or *B* to generate this result is by bringing it about that the balance of Susan's motivation at the time falls on the side of continent action. *Ss* can employ a variety of strategies in preventing Susan's *BJ* or *B* from having the latter effect. Promising measures include getting "the main system" (*Sm*) to focus on the attractive features of a solitary stroll at the expense of attention to reasons for Susan's not strolling, getting *Sm* to engage in vivid representation of previous pleasant strolls through the quad, and the like. Measures such as these can increase Susan's overall motivation for strolling while blocking potential routes to increased motivation for staying indoors—for example, routes such as *Sm*'s focusing on reasons for Susan's not strolling or vividly representing a particularly frightening stroll-scenario.

One problem with this account, as I shall argue, is that it is unnecessarily anthropomorphic. *Ss*, rather than simply being constituted of wants, beliefs, and the like, *has* wants, *is aware* of certain things, and so on. It is noteworthy that, given its wish that Susan take a solitary stroll and its awareness or belief that Susan will not stroll if her *BJ* or *B* is allowed to intervene, *Ss has a reason* to prevent *BJ* and *B* from intervening and that it acts *for* this reason: "with perfect rationality"—"from its own point of view," of course—"it stops [their] intervention" (Pears, 1984, p. 87).

Ss can be made less anthropomorphic by turning the psychological items that it is supposed to *have* into constituents of the system. We can, for example, characterize the system as follows:

2. *Ss* is built around a constituent desire that Susan take a solitary stroll through the quad. The function of the system is to bring it about that Susan takes the stroll, and one of *Ss*'s elements is the belief that Susan will not do so if her *BJ* (or her *B*) intervenes. So *Ss* stops the intervention of Susan's *BJ* (or her *B*).

However, this still leaves *Ss* with agency: It acts for a reason (though now a reason which *Ss* in part *is* as opposed to one that it *has*). Indeed, "the essential point" of the functional theory of systems, according to Pears, "is that the sub-system is an internally rational system of agency" (1984, p. 104).

Now, we shall see that the story can be told without this element of subsystemic agency. But this is not a way of saving the Pearsian subsystemic explanation of Susan's behavior. It is a way of *undermining* it. Without the element of agency that Pears plays up, his functional theory of systems lacks explanatory power. On Pears's account of partitioning, to say that a particular mental item is located exclusively in a subsystem is precisely to say that it does not rationally interact (as it ought) with any elements in the main system (1984, p. 105). The explanatory power of the theory lies, as Pears says, not in the idea that one mental item is partitioned off from others, but rather in "its account of the internal structure and organization of the sub-system" (p. 104)—that is, in its account of what maintains the partitioning. And at the heart of the structure is internally rational agency.

On the Pearsian account of Susan's behavior that I constructed, the use of certain cognitive measures is part of a strategy adopted by a subsystem with a view to an end. However, one need not appeal to subsystemic agency to bring processes such as these—that is, focusing, representing, and the like—into the explanatory picture. The more we want to do something, the more we tend to think about doing it, to entertain pleasurable images (including memorial images) of our doing it, and so on. These cognitive processes do not require an inner agent to set them in motion; nor need they be set in motion for reasons. They often occur quite 'automatically.' Susan's incontinently walking across the quad does not depend on a subagent's successful employment of a strategy designed to make her better judgment ineffective. Her desire to stroll can speak up for itself. If it speaks loudly enough, processes such as those just described may be activated, with the potential result that Susan's desire to stroll will carry the day.

When we drop subsystemic agency from the explanatory apparatus applied to Susan's irrational behavior, we may still find it useful to talk of subsystems. Presumably, some aspects of Susan's mental condition contribute to her strolling, whereas others do not; and we may wish to treat the contributors as constituting an action-causing subsystem. However, this subsystem is composed simply of such things as her desire for a solitary stroll, supporting desires of hers (e.g., her desire for fresh air), and the psychological events (e.g., selective focusing) as a result of which she is more motivated to take the stroll than to refrain from doing so. To say that these elements constitute a system is (roughly) to say that *together* they generate (or are capable of generating) a certain result. The explanatory work is done by the elements and their interrelationships, not by the supposition that they are somehow partitioned off from other mental items. Nor is the subsystem just mentioned defined, as Davidson would have it, by the breakdown of reasons-relations.

I do not wish to claim that Pears's notion of subsystemic agency lacks application entirely in the sphere of action. It may apply, for example, to genuine instances of split personality.[9] My contention thus far is that we do not need to postulate the existence of a Pearsian subsystem to explain Susan's irrational behavior, a representative example of incontinent action. Moreover, a more modest explanation of the sort just sketched seems decidedly preferable, if only because it is so much more modest. Postulation of subsystemic agency to explain Susan's behavior looks like a clear case of overkill.

Davidson's own partitioning hypothesis fares no better. Not only is his argument for it unsuccessful, but it is unclear how his nonagential subsystems are supposed to function and, therefore, how they are to help us to understand irrational actions (1982, p. 304). Furthermore, as we shall see in more detail later, there is no need to suppose that subsystems defined by the breakdown of reasons-relations are at work in the case of Susan.

3. Explaining Akratic Action: Proximity and Attention

The rough materials for a resolution of the paradox of irrationality identified by Davidson *(PI)* are present in the preceding sections. The purpose of this section is to develop them more systematically. The results will be used in Section 4, in an attempt to meet the challenge posed by *PI* in the case of Susan.

When an agent akratically does A, while consciously holding a decisive better judgment in favor of his performing a competing action, B, he is evidently more motivated to do A than B. If we can explain how he came to have this balance of motivation, we can explain his akratic action. Now, we have already seen that the balance of an agent's motivation can be out of line with his decisive better judgment even about something to be done here and now. Better judgments are often formed on the basis of the agent's evaluation of the objects of his wants, and one's evaluation need not match the motivational force of the want. But what might *explain* this disparity, and the associated disparity between better judgment and overall motivation, in an instance of akratic action?

In this section, I shall consider two answers to this question. The first is derived from the work of George Ainslie on what he calls ''impulsiveness''—roughly, the free ''choice of less rewarding over more rewarding alternatives'' (1975, p. 463; cf. Ainslie, 1982). The second has been advanced by Amelie Rorty. I shall argue that they jointly provide a basis for a very plausible explanatory hypothesis.

Ainslie's guiding concern is strikingly similar to Aristotle's in Chapter 7 of *De Motu Animalium*. There Aristotle asks (701a7–8): ''How does it happen that thinking is sometimes followed by action and sometimes not, sometimes by motion, sometimes not?''[10] Similarly, Ainslie wants to know not only why we sometimes freely pursue ''the poorer, smaller, or more disastrous of two alternative rewards even when [we] seem to be entirely familiar with the alternatives'' (1975, p. 463), but also why we seek the better or larger reward when we do. His position, which rests on research with animals (Ainslie, 1974; Ainslie & Herrnstein,

1981; Navarick & Fantino, 1976; Rachlin & Green, 1972) and with human subjects (Ainslie & Haendel, 1983; Solnick et al., 1980), may be summarized as follows:

1. "The curve describing the effectiveness of reward as a function of delay is markedly concave upwards" (1982, p. 740). That is, a desire for a "reward" of a prospective action, other things being equal, acquires greater motivational force as the time for the reward's achievement approaches, and after a certain point motivation increases sharply.

2. Human beings are not at the mercy of the effects of the proximity of rewards. They can bring it about that they act for a larger, later reward in preference to a smaller, earlier one by using "pre-committing devices," a form of self-control (1975, 1982). "Rewards that are due at different times will be chosen in proportion to their actual amounts, as long as the choice is made far enough in advance" (1975, p. 472). And if someone who chooses early believes that his "preference for the better alternative is apt to change," he will be motivated to exercise self-control (1982, p. 743). (He can bind himself, for example, as did Odysseus, or employ techniques that increase the motivational force of the preferred alternative.) In some cases, exercises of self-control are both required and successful.

Ainslie does not make it clear whether he is supposing that when an agent "chooses" or changes his "choice" he forms or changes a *better judgment*. Thus, one cannot be sure what he would say about strict akratic action, as defined above. However, an explanatory hypothesis for strict akratic action can certainly be derived from Ainslie's work. Again, we can explain a strict akratic action by explaining how it happened that the agent was more motivated at the time of action to do A than the competing action that he judged best. Ainslie's points about "pre-commitment" and the motivational strength of proximate rewards generate a straightforward explanation: The agent judged it best to do C, but the level of his motivation to do C was such that, due to the (perceived) proximity of the rewards of A, to his earlier level of motivation to seek those rewards, and to his failure to make effective use of self-control techniques that he had at his disposal, he was more motivated to do A.

Although I shall call this the *proximity explanation,* it is important to note that four elements enter into it: (1) the agent's level of motivation to do C (the prospective continent action); (2) his earlier level of motivation to do A (the akratic action); (3) the agent's failure to make effective use of self-control; and (4) proximity. The last item is not sufficient to explain strict akratic action. Sometimes (even in the absence of an exercise of self-control) one's motivation to wait for a larger reward, relative to one's motivation to seek a competing earlier reward, is sufficiently great that proximity-enhanced motivation for the earlier reward does not surpass it. (Consider a moderately hungry person who can pull in to a McDonald's drive-in window now or eat at his favorite restaurant in thirty minutes.) On other occasions, as Ainslie emphasizes (1975; 1982), the effects of proximity are overcome by means of self-control. Thus, a complete proximity explanation of strict akratic action involves all four of the items in question.

A fuller account of strict akratic action would explain why proximity has such a pronounced influence on motivational strength. An attractive hypothesis may be gleaned from some experimental work on delay of gratification. This issue will be addressed shortly.

A comment on the generality of Ainslie's position is in order. Consider the following case. On May 15, Mary bought an expensive new dress to wear to her five-year college reunion at the end of June. She purposely bought an undersized dress as incentive to lose the fifteen pounds that she has gained since her college days. During the first week Mary sticks to her demanding diet and loses nine pounds. Although she is very pleased with her progress, Mary comes to believe that her diet is much stricter than necessary and that it is taking a toll on her health. She judges that it would be best to increase her caloric intake by twenty percent and decides accordingly to order a chef's salad, one of her favorite dishes, for lunch. She gives the waiter her order, but when he returns with her salad she apologetically makes the incontinent request that he bring her a serving of low-fat cottage cheese instead—thinking all the while that eating the salad would be quite pleasant.

In this case, proximity of reward is not a deciding feature. To be sure, Mary may now be *intrinsically* motivated to remain on the strict diet; and her refraining from eating the chef's salad may consequently be immediately rewarding. But this immediate reward competes with another—the pleasure of eating the salad. Whether human beings as they actually are can behave as I have had Mary do is an empirical matter on which I shall not take a stand. However, in the absence of a convincing argument that behavior of this sort is open only to fictional characters, I shall not advance Ainslie's hypothesis as a completely general one. (Another reason for limiting the scope of the hypothesis will be discussed shortly.)

The second view to be considered in this section is developed by Amelie Rorty in a pair of papers published in 1980. In these papers, Rorty identifies three "attractive strategies of akrasia," strategies that "often augment and supplement each other'' (1980a, pp. 209f.; 1980b, pp. 913f.). I shall refer to them respectively as the *attentional, habitual,* and *social* strategies.

1. *The Attentional Strategy:* An agent's balance of motivation at the time of action is sometimes importantly influenced by the focus of his attention. In a case of strict akratic action, an agent's desires may be such that the "akratic alternative . . . has more salience for him" than the course of action judged better. His attention may be drawn, for example, to the features of the pie which would make eating it so pleasant—and at the expense of attention to his reasons for eschewing the dessert. This may have the consequence not only that his motivation to pursue the akratic alternative increases but that his motivation to perform the action judged better is weaker than it would otherwise have been. Rorty observes that an alternative can "dominate attention" in a variety of ways: It can fill the visual field; it can have "imagined intensity or excitement"; it can "promise absorbing pleasure"; and so on.

2. *The Habitual Strategy:* Habit makes akratic action easier in two ways. First, action of a sort that one habitually performs has an attractiveness that goes beyond "its surface attractions." Consider someone who is in the habit of smoking while writing. He is motivated to smoke while he writes not only by the felt attraction that smoking has for him at the time, but also by the habit itself. Second, "perceptual habits of attending and focusing, cognitive habits of structuring or interpreting situations, habits of inference and narrative expectations . . . often support the akratic alternative." A person's habits may contribute to an akratic balance of motivation as a result not only of their built-in motivation for the habitual action but also of their capacity to influence an agent's cognitive behavior in such a way as to increase the attractiveness of the akratic alternative while shifting attention away from the action judged best, one's reasons for performing it, useful measures of self-control, and the like.

3. *The Social Strategy:* This strategy, like the preceding one, may be termed an *impetus* strategy. An agent's habits incline him in a certain direction; and when the direction is an akratic one, the impetus makes akratic action easier. Similarly, impetus makes it easier for one who is following a charismatic religious leader or working for a political party to follow the leader or party officials into incontinent courses of action.

I do not know whether Rorty would agree with everything that I have said about these three strategies. But this is not important for my purposes.

My immediate aim is to ascertain what an explanatory framework that does not explicitly give a central place to proximity of reward can add to a proximity account of strict akratic action.

Given this aim, the attentional strategy is the most important of the three. The impetus strategies may be subject to a deeper explanation in terms of proximity of reward (or the agent's attentional condition); but the attentional strategy may help to explain the motivational influence of (perceived) proximity. Why does an agent's motivation to do A tend to increase as he approaches the time at which the rewards of his doing A are available? Perhaps partly because the thought or representation of those rewards in some way dominates his attentional field. Surely, it is not *mere* proximity of reward that shapes motivation. The agent must at some level be aware of the reward's proximity. And it is a plausible hypothesis that this awareness has significant attentional ramifications. (This is not to suggest, of course, that one will always perform an action of the sort that is dominating one's attention.)

Though the influence of attention upon motivation and action is largely ignored in the philosophy of action, it has generated considerable discussion in experimental psychology. Unfortunately, the most extensive body of research that is directly applicable to the phenomenon of akratic action has been conducted with preschool children. It would be rash to generalize the results to adults. But a brief review of the literature will prove instructive.

In 1970, Walter Mischel and Ebbe Ebbesen reported the results of a study designed to test the hypothesis that "conditions in which [a] delayed reward was present and visually available would enhance attention to it and hence increase voluntary delay time for it" (Mischel & Ebbesen, 1970, p. 331). However, the results of the enhanced attention were quite the reverse. Preschool subjects were informed that they would receive a particular preferred reward if they waited for the experimenter to return and that, if they signaled him to return, they would receive instead a particular lesser reward. When both rewards were present during the delay period, the mean delay time was 1.03 minutes. When both rewards were absent, on the other hand, there was a mean delay of 11.29 minutes before the experimenter was signaled to return. Two further conditions were tested as well. When only the preferred reward was present, mean delay time was 4.87 minutes. When the lesser reward alone was available for attention, the mean delay time was 5.72 minutes. Mischel and Ebbesen suggested, plausibly, that "the presence of the rewards serves to increase the magnitude of the frustration effect and hence decreases delay of gratification by making the waiting period more difficult" (p. 337).

Inattention to the rewards, in this experiment, was much more effective in generating delay of gratification.

Another study, reported two years later, produced the same results and a predictable new datum (Mischel, Ebbesen, & Zeiss, 1972). When the rewards were absent and the children were instructed to "think fun" during the delay period, the mean waiting time was 14.48 minutes, compared with .78 minute for children instructed to think about the reward objects. (The mean delay time for children given no instructions was 12.86 minutes.) Mischel and his colleagues were careful to note that one cannot properly generalize from these results "to the role of cognition in forms of self-control other than the delay-of-gratification paradigm" (p. 216). However, a tempting generalization *within* the paradigm must also be resisted—namely, that preschool children who attend in no way to the rewards will tend to delay longer than those who do attend to them, independently of the *manner* of attention.

This generalization is undermined in Mischel and Moore (1973). The experimental design is similar to that of the two earlier studies. The most salient difference is in the presentational conditions. During the delay period subjects were presented with: (1) slide-presented images of the reward objects; (2) slide-presented images of irrelevant reward objects; (3) an illuminated, blank screen; or (4) an unilluminated screen. Also, the four different presentational conditions were studied under two different activity-conditions, waiting and working; and the presentations were periodic for some subjects and continuous for others. The results were as described in Table 6.1.

Table 6.1. Mean Delay Time (in Minutes) for All Groups

Task and imagery schedule	Imagery (slide content)			
	Relevant rewards	Irrelevant rewards	Blank	No slide
Wait				
Periodic	9.53	5.91	5.06	8.28
Continuous	9.40	3.98	3.30	7.07
Work				
Periodic	8.83	6.58	5.94	3.33
Continuous	8.65	6.12	4.17	4.14

Adapted from Mischel and Moore, 1973, Table 1, p. 176. Subjects are not permitted to delay more than ten minutes.

In each of the four conditions specified at the left of the table, subjects presented with slides of relevant rewards delayed the longest. How can this be squared with the results of the earlier studies? Mischel and Moore offer a plausible answer. Following Berlyne (1960),[11] they distinguish between the "motivational (arousal) function" and the "cue (informative) function" of a stimulus (p. 178). Their proposal is twofold. First, in the earlier experiments, the subjects viewing the reward objects or thinking about them in their absence were focusing on their motivational or arousing qualities, with the frustrative result mentioned above. Second, subjects attending to the slides were attending primarily to their informational qualities.

Subsequent studies designed to test this proposal (e.g., Mischel & Baker, 1975; Moore, Mischel, & Zeiss, 1976; Mischel & Moore, 1980) provide substantial support. In investigating the influence of "cognitive transformations" on delay of gratification, Mischel and his colleagues discovered that children instructed to focus on the "consummatory" qualities of relevant reward objects delayed for a much shorter period than did children instructed to "transform" the desired pretzels and marshmallows into brown logs and fluffy, white clouds. Moreover, and importantly, subjects who transformed the rewards available to them into nonconsummatory objects delayed much longer than subjects instructed to do this with "irrelevant rewards." Mischel and his colleagues attribute the latter result to the tendency of subjects' transformational (nonconsummatory) ideation about relevant rewards to remind them of what is to be gained by waiting, without frustrating them by focusing attention on consummatory qualities (Mischel & Baker, 1975, p. 259; cf. Moore et al., 1976, p. 423).

The story continues, but I shall not recount any more of it here.[12] Enough has been said to suggest a reasonable hypothesis about the role of attention in generating the motivational effects of the increased proximity of a reward. It is this: (1) attention to the 'consummatory' or 'arousing' features of a desired item tends to increase as a function of the increasing proximity of the reward; (2) the curve, in Ainslie's words, is "markedly concave upwards"; (3) increased motivation tends to be a partial function of this increased attention. The hypothesis is testable and suggests a number of strategies of self-control (e.g., the strategy of distracting one's attention from the consummatory qualities of relevant rewards). Ainslie's preferred self-control strategy is that of the "private side bet"—roughly, piling up rewards contingent upon one's waiting for the preferred reward. But even this may benefit from consequent decreased attention to consummatory qualities of the competing earlier and later rewards.

Tests of the hypothesis in question cannot be constructed within

Mischel's typical delay-of-gratification paradigm. His standard experimental design is such that the earlier, lesser reward is always (roughly) immediately consummable. The child can have the less-preferred reward whenever he wishes. *That* reward does not become increasingly proximate. In light of this observation, Mischel's results raise a telling point against Ainslie's proximity hypothesis, construed now as having a perfectly general application to strict akratic action. An agent's opting for a lesser, earlier reward over a greater, later one is not always a function of the increased (absolute) proximity of the former; for, in some cases of the phenomenon, the proximity of the former does not increase.

In the remainder of this section I shall develop an approach to modifying Ainslie's proximity hypothesis in such a way as to incorporate the agent's attentional condition. On the proximity hypothesis, an agent S's performing a strict akratic action, A, is explained as follows: The level of the agent's motivation to perform the continent alternative (C) was such that, due to the (perceived) proximity of the rewards of A-ing, to his earlier level of motivation to do A, and to his failure to make effective use of self-control techniques that he had at his disposal, he was more motivated to A than to C. This tells us nothing, of course, about the etiologies of S's level of motivation to perform C and his failure to make an effective attempt at self-control. I shall consider each in turn.

The motivational question is subject to a variety of explanatory hypotheses. I shall mention only two. First, S's level of motivation to perform C (the continent alternative) is fixed by, and consonant with, his evaluation of his reasons for performing C. (On this account, his motivation to do C was appropriately strong, and his contrary motivation inappropriately stronger at the time of action.) Second, (some of) the factors that influence S's motivation to A also have an effect upon his motivation to C. This is suggested by the discussion above of the attentional strategy of *akrasia*: The perceived proximity of a reward may affect one's attention in such a way that not only is one's motivation to pursue the nearer rewards enhanced, but one's motivation to pursue the more distant rewards attentuated. The second hypothesis seems preferable in, for example, the case of incontinent pie-eating in Chapter 2, but there is conceptual space for instances in which appropriate motivation for the continent course of action is defeated by inappropriate motivation for a competing action.

Now, why might an agent fail to make an effective attempt at self-control? We can hark back to Chapter 2 for some possibilities: It did not occur to him to exercise self-control; he exercised self-control, but selected an inappropriate technique; against his better judgment, he decided to indulge himself and to refrain from exercising self-control. It is worth noting that the occurrence of any of these possibilities may itself be due, in significant part, to attentional factors. For example, an agent's failure to focus on his reasons for doing C may make it easier for him to decide to indulge himself. Or his preoccupation with the attractions of A may have the result that he makes a feeble, inappropriate attempt at self-control. However, attentional factors need not always play a crucial role at this juncture. Sometimes, for example, it just does not occur to an agent that an effort of self-control is required, as in the blood-brother example in Chapter 2.

The incorporation of an attentional element into the proximity hypothesis gives us what I shall call the *modified proximity hypothesis*. On this hypothesis, many strict akratic actions are adequately explained in terms of: (1) the perceived proximity of the rewards of the incontinent alternative; (2) the agent's level of motivation to perform the continent alternative and his earlier level of motivation to perform the akratic alternative; (3) the agent's failure to make an effective attempt at self-control; and (4) the agent's attentional condition. An explanation of the sort at issue will account for the occurrence of a strict akratic action by explaining the agent's balance of motivation at the time of action.

As I have already indicated, the items involved in a modified proximity explanation are themselves subject to explanation in particular cases (as are beliefs, desires, intentions, etc., in cases of rational explanation). And the elements in each of the four items just mentioned (1 through 4) are capable of influencing one or more of the others. We have seen that perceived proximity can affect one's attentional condition, and that the latter can contribute to a failure of self-control and to an attenuation of one's motivation to perform the continent alternative. Conversely, the conditions identified in (2) and in (3) can have attentional consequences. For example, a student whose attention is drifting from his work to a lively game of frisbee on the lawn beneath his window may, owing in part to a failure to exercise self-control, find that he has become wholly engrossed in the spectacle; or the low level of his motivation to complete his assignment may make it easier for him to slip into a pleasant daydream. Furthermore, (2), (3), and (4) can each have the result that the rewards of a possible incontinent action become more readily achievable. For example, an agent may find himself face to face with the prospect of incontinently entering his favorite pub on his way home from the office, owing to his level of motivation to take the longer route home that he had decided upon earlier as a method of self-control, or to a failure to exercise self-control in defense of this decision, or to his preoccupation with a philosophical puzzle. Thus, we are working with an interrelated system of causal elements.

As I mentioned earlier, the proximity hypothesis is incapable of explaining cases of *akrasia* falling within Mischel's typical delay of gratification paradigm.[13] If the effects of the increased proximity of a reward upon motivation are mediated by attentional events, one might seek a more general hypothesis about the etiology of akratic action that treats increased proximity only as an attention-modifier. On such a hypothesis, an agent's level of motivation at the time of continent or incontinent action is a function of earlier relevant motivation, his attentional condition, and his self-control behaviors (including failures to make an attempt at self-control).

4. Explaining Susan's Stroll

Davidson's paradox of irrationality (*PI*) challenges us to explain irrationality in such a way that we neither "turn it into a concealed form of rationality" nor withdraw the "background of rationality" needed to justify the contention that the behavior in question is irrational. In the present section I return to the example of Susan's stroll and argue that enough can be said about her irrational behavior to show how the challenge posed by *PI* may be met in her case.

Why did Susan stroll across the quad? The answer cannot be as simple as this: She strolled in order to get some exercise, fresh air, and solitude. For, she also had reasons to stay indoors, and she took the latter reasons to be the better reasons. One might suggest that Susan strolled because her reasons for doing so were motivationally stronger than the reasons that supported her all-things-considered better judgment. But many will take this for granted. A more informative answer along these lines would explain why the bulk of the motivation fell where it did.

How might this be explained on the modified proximity hypothesis (or on a more directly attentional hypothesis)? First, some obvious points. (1) The rewards of a solitary stroll were at hand. (2) Susan did not make a successful attempt at self-control; if she had, she would not have taken the stroll. (3) Susan's level of motivation to refrain from strolling was not, when she formed her decisive better judgment (nor later), sufficiently high to render unnecessary an effort of self-control in support of her judgment.

The first point requires no explanation. The explanation of the second depends upon further details of the case. Let us suppose that Susan made no attempt at self-control. We have already seen (Ch. 2.2) that this sort of thing is possible. And in the present case we may seek an explanation in Susan's attentional condition. Perhaps the focus of Susan's attention at a crucial juncture was on the pleasure of a solitary stroll and the dreariness of her present surroundings rather than on her reasons for staying in; and this may have made it easier for her to decide that strolling comes in a close second and that she will simply indulge herself (against her better judgment).

Some of the items just mentioned also figure in a plausible explanation of the third point. In light of Susan's attentional condition, the proximity of the pleasures of a solitary stroll, the unattractive features of her present surroundings and activities, and possible other factors, it is not difficult to understand her level of motivation to refrain from strolling. And, as we have seen, one's motivation to perform the continent alternative may be sufficiently weak as to require the support of an exercise of self-control if it is to be effective.

Now, to explain (2) and (3) *is* to explain why the final balance of Susan's motivation fell on the side of the incontinent solitary stroll. Susan's motivation to refrain from strolling was sufficiently weak that to generate a continent balance of motivation she had to make a successful attempt at self-control; but she made no attempt whatever. The important point, for immediate purposes, is that the disparity between her decisive better judgment and what she was most motivated to do is not inexplicable. We *can* understand how someone might judge it best, all things considered, to do *A*, and yet be more motivated to do *B*.

Does the explanation just sketched render Susan's behavior rational? She is still acting incontinently—that is, intentionally, freely, and contrary to her better judgment. And this is where the irrationality of her behavior lies. If an agent's assessment of his reasons does not *determine* their motivational impact, he may end up acting on what he takes to be the "lesser" reasons (evaluatively speaking, of course). To be sure, he will still be acting for reasons. But this is not sufficient to render his behavior rational. Rather, given his assessment of the reasons for which he acts, his (free, intentional) behavior is irrational.

Perhaps, then, I have foundered on the other side of the paradox. Have I withdrawn the background of rationality needed to justify my diagnosis of Susan's behavior as irrational? No. Susan is still possessed of a coherent collection of evaluations, and her practical thinking yields a judgment that is rational in light of her evaluations of her reasons for and against strolling. Moreover, she takes her solitary stroll *for* a reason or reasons: *That* aspect of rationality too is still among the 'background conditions.' What justifies the diagnosis of her behavior as irrational is the supposed fact that the behavior is intentional, free, and contrary to the decisive better judgment that the coherent collection of evaluations supports.[14]

A note of caution is in order. I have profited from a distinction between a coherent collection of an agent's evaluations and a related motivational condition of the agent. The idea is not that we have here two competing mental subsystems. The point, rather, is that reasons (broadly conceived) for action have two importantly different dimensions: the agent's evaluation of them (when he does evaluate them) and their motivational force or valence. These features are not wholly independent of each other; evaluations of reasons seem often to influence their motivational impact and vice versa. But, at least in some cases, the influence is just *that*—influence. An agent's evaluation of his reasons and the motivational force of those reasons need not always be in mutual alignment. (Thus, there is conceptual room for incontinent action.)

PI challenges us to explain a certain kind of subjective irrationality without rendering the behavior rational—namely, an agent's doing something that is irrational from his own point of view. To meet the challenge, we must explain how an agent can exhibit such irrationality while performing the action in question *for reasons*, and this involves explaining why his acting for reasons does not render his behavior rational. In the case of Susan, at least, we have seen how to construct an explanation of the requisite sort. And the explanation involves neither Davidsonian nor Pearsian mental partitioning.

7

Explaining Intentional Actions: Reasons, Intentions, and Other Psychological Items

My primary concern thus far has been with irrational action. It is time now to examine the implications of the preceding chapters for the project of explaining *rational* action and intentional action in general. An attempt to develop a full-blown theory of action-explanation is beyond the scope of this book. I shall be content to identify explanatory items that must be added to traditional causal belief-desire models of action-explanation if they are to be adequate to the full range of intentional action, and to elucidate their interaction with the traditional items. Beliefs, desires, reasons, intentions, and the like do have an important role to play in intentionalistic psychological explanations of intentional actions. But, as I shall explain, other psychological items must be integrated into the explanatory framework if it is to generate adequate accounts of intentional actions performed in instances of motivational conflict.

I began in earnest to set the stage for the project of the present chapter in Chapter 3. I argued there (in Sect. 5) that "reasons, decisive better judgments, and intentions . . . do not tell the whole story" about akratic (and, I might add, continent) action; and I suggested that attention to the nature of self-control and its opposite would prove useful in augmenting the story. The task of clarifying the notions of self-control and *akrasia* was taken up in Chapter 4. Chapter 5 resolved some puzzles about the exercise of self-control. And in Chapter 6, in the course of resolving a paradox about the explanation of akratic action, I developed an explanatory hypothesis about a central range of cases of strict akratic action and sketched an explanation of a representative example. The explanation was not a simple reasons-explanation: Central explanatory items included such things as the agent's attentional condition and her failure to make an attempt at self-control.

The first order of business below is to display the inadequacy of traditional belief-desire models of action-explanation in cases of motivational conflict. In Section 2, I distinguish among three grades of continent action and argue that actions of all three types are explicable with reference to a collection of psychological items that includes both the standard elements of belief-desire explanations and additional elements identified in previous chapters. More specifically, I argue that when there is conflicting motivation, the generating of an adequate (intentionalistic) psychological explanation of action is a two-stage process. This process involves both the identification of the reason(s) for which the agent *A*-ed and an explanation of his acting for the reason(s) he did rather than for his competing reason(s). In Section 3, I turn to the role of intentions in action-explanation. I argue that intentions do not have as decisive a role as many have thought, but that they are nonetheless plausibly regarded as making a significant causal contribution to action. Section 4 addresses the role of character in the generation of intentional behavior.

1. The Inadequacy of Reasons-Explanations

Traditional belief-desire models of action-explanation (*TBDM-s*) are designed to yield *reasons-explanations* of intentional actions.[1] A reasons-explanation of an intentional action, *A*, explains the agent's *A*-ing by specifying the reason(s) for which he *A*-ed. In Chapter 3 I argued that, typically, there is no adequate reasons-explanation of a strict akratic action. We do not explain the akratic agent's *A*-ing by identifying the reasons for which he *A*-ed. In cases of strict akratic action, the agent also had a reason or reasons for performing some competing action. What must be explained is the akratic agent's acting for the reason(s) that he did rather than for the competing reasons; and, typically, there is no adequate reasons-explanation of this.

To explain strict akratic action, we need not reject wholesale the traditional belief-desire approach to action-explanation. What must be rejected is the assumption that all intentional behavior admits of adequate reasons-explanations. However, a weaker version of this assumption is quite plausible, namely, that intentional actions are actions done for reasons[2] and that the reasons for which we act figure significantly in the etiology of our intentional actions. We shall see that one may incorporate, accordingly, the elements of *TBDM*-s into a conceptual framework for the explanation of strict akratic action. What I am after is a conceptual framework that will enable one both to give reasons-explanations when they are appropriate and to supplement attempted reasons-explanations when citing the reasons for which the agent acted leaves important parts of the explanatory story untold. (Of course, an agent's having the reasons that he had for doing A is never a *sufficient* condition of his A-ing. If he is to A, he must, for example, be *able*—in some sense of the word—to A. This part of the untold story may be bracketed for present purposes.)

When agents are not faced with competing motivations, reasons-explanations of their intentional actions seem adequate, at least for some purposes. If, in the absence of competing motivation, I shaved this morning in order to look presentable, I may (in certain normal contexts) successfully explain my shaving simply by citing the reason for which I shaved. But what explains an agent's acting as he does when he has competing reasons for action? One might try to find the answer in the notion of a better judgment: Though the agent had reasons to do A, and reasons to perform a competing action, B, he judged it better to do A, and consequently did A rather than B. This is Davidson's strategy in "How Is Weakness of the Will Possible?"; but we have seen (Ch. 3) that it is unsuccessful. In cases of strict akratic action, the agent (decisively) judges it best to do A and yet freely and intentionally does B.

One might attempt to resolve the problem by retreating to the position that, whatever an agent's better judgment may be, he acts as he is most motivated to act. The problem with this strategy is that it does not yield an *explanation* of the agent's behavior. That the akratic agent was most motivated to act as he did can be taken for granted. We have not explained his action until we explain his balance of motivation at the time of action.

The same problem must be faced in explaining continent action. Suppose that, though he is tempted to do B, S judges it best to do A and acts accordingly. Here again we cannot explain the agent's acting as he does simply by observing that he judged it best to do A; for if judging A best (in conjunction with such standing conditions as having the ability to A) were sufficient for A-ing, there would be no strict akratic action. Nor can we explain S's behavior by observing that he was most motivated to A. Again, we must explain *why* he was most motivated to A.

There is, then, a *general* problem about the application of *TBDM*-s to actions performed in instances of motivational conflict. The difficulty with reasons-explanations is evident not only in akratic action but in continent action as well (when competing motivations are present).

2. Three Grades of Continent Action

In the present section, I shall distinguish among three grades of continent action and comment generally on the explanation of continent behavior. Continent action is, at least roughly, action in accordance with one's better judgment. Now, an agent may act in accordance with a better judgment of his without that judgment's contributing to his action. In such a case, the better judgment does not enter into an adequate explanation of the action. A distinction between acting *in accordance with,* and acting *on,* a better judgment will prove useful in this connection. The distinction that I shall draw is similar to the familiar distinction between acting in accordance with a rule and following a rule. When a young boy, without any understanding of the rules of the game, strikes the cue ball on his mother's pool table with a cue stick, he is acting in accordance with a rule of pocket billiards, but he is not *following* the rule. One follows a rule only if one is cognizant of the rule and one's behavior is guided by the rule. Similarly, an agent acts on a consciously held better judgment only if that judgment guides his behavior.

With this distinction in hand, we may differentiate among three grades of continent behavior. The first grade is intentional behavior that is *merely* in accordance with one's better judgment. Consider, for example, the case of Gordon. Though he has decided to play in the big game tonight, he wonders whether this is the best thing to do in light of his recent injury. He decides that, all things considered, it is; but he would have played (intentionally) even if he had come to the opposite conclusion. Moreover, the better judgment in no way enters into the etiology of Gordon's behavior. This is not (we may suppose) a case of causal overdetermination, and Gordon's better judgment does not replace his earlier decision to play as a cause of his behavior.

The second grade of continent behavior occurs in, and only in, cases in which the agent acts *on* his better judgment, but independently of any supporting exercise of self-control. Second-grade continent action, unlike its first-grade counterpart, is guided by the agent's better judgment. Self-control may or may not be exercised in instances of second-grade continence; but if it is exercised, it does not enter into the etiology of the actions in question. (Sometimes we make unnecessary exercise of self-control; and an unnecessary exercise may fail to contribute to the action at issue.)

The third grade of continent behavior is intentional action on one's better judgment that is due (in part) to the agent's exercising self-control. One may wish to separate out cases in which the causal connection between the agent's exercise of self-control and his subsequent action is a deviant one; but for present purposes it is not necessary to do so.

Some might wish to define continent action more narrowly than I have done. As continent action is sometimes conceived, an agent acts continently in doing A only if he does A while having motivation to perform some competing action. The reader who accepts this stricter conception may easily modify my characterizations of the grades of continent action accordingly. Furthermore, readers who regard continent action as being necessarily *guided by* the agent's better judgment, are free to interpret the first grade as a type of quasi-continent action. However, quasi-continent or not, action of this sort is explicable; and explanation, not classification, is the primary topic of this chapter.

The preceding chapters have identified a number of items that can enter importantly into psychological explanations of intentional actions. There are, of course, the familiar elements of reasons-explanations: reasons, the beliefs and desires that constitute them, the abilities and skills presupposed by reasons-explanations, better judgments, intentions, practical reasoning. However, there are also the positive, negative, and total motivational bases of desires; the agent's attentional condition; the perceived proximity of a reward; self-control and *akrasia*; exercises and nonexercises of self-control; motivation to exercise, or to refrain from exercising, self-control. In the preceding chapter, we saw how these additional items can be used to fill the explanatory gap in the case of Susan's strict akratic action. In Chapter 5, several of these items were used to resolve puzzles about the possibility of an agent's exercising self-control in certain types of situation.

Instances of the three grades of continent action obviously require rather different explanations. Whereas a better judgment of the agent figures in the etiology of instances of the second and third grades, this is not true of the first grade. And an exercise of self-control is significantly involved in the generation of third-grade continent action, but not in its second-grade counterpart.

It would be tedious to work out (and to read!) detailed explanations of representative examples of each of the three grades of continent action. Indeed, this is rather more involved than one might think, since we may distinguish among various subtypes within some of the grades, each of which requires a different sort of explanation. For example, in some cases of second-grade continent action a better judgment may contribute to action by *altering* one's motivational condition, whereas in others it may do so by helping to maintain the balance of motivation that one has when the judgment is formed.

Some general comments are, however, in order. First, the explanation of first-grade continent action presumably lies primarily in the total motivational bases of the agent's competing desires, and perhaps as well in his attentional condition. Such things as practical reasoning and the perceived proximity of a desired reward may contribute—in a variety of ways—to the agent's final motivational balance. For example, both may influence the agent's attentional condition, and practical reasoning may augment the total motivational base of a desire by identifying a goal or countergoal to which action in accordance with the desire may be expected (to some degree) to lead.

Second, though better judgments may influence an agent's motivational condition by prompting an exercise of self-control, other avenues of influence are open to these judgments. If the agent has a generic want to act as he judges best, a decisive better judgment in favor of his *A*-ing may increase his motivation to do *A* by injecting the generic want into the positive motivational base of his desire to do *A*, or decrease his motivation to do a prospective competing action by introducing the generic want into the negative motivational base of his desire to do that action (or both). A decisive better judgment may also have a salutary influence upon one's attentional condition. For example, it may help to focus one's attention on the action judged best at the expense of attention to the desired consequences of competing actions.

Now, the agents of continent actions *do* act for reasons. The problem with *TBDM*-s is that they wrongly assume that to identify these reasons is, in all cases, to provide an adequate explanation of the action. It is at this juncture that explanatory items other that reasons enter the picture. They help us to see why the agent acted for the reason(s) that he did rather than for his competing reason(s) (i.e., when he had one or more competing reasons).

Explaining intentional actions performed in cases of motivational conflict may be regarded as a two-stage process. In the first stage, one identifies the reason(s) for which the agent *A*-ed. In the second, one explains why he acted for that reason (or those reasons) rather than for his competing reason(s). Again, we can arrive at the second-stage explanation by explaining why the agent was more motivated at the time of action to do *A* than its competitors. This approach to explanation is evident in the discussion in Chapter 6.4 of Susan's akratic stroll, and it is implicit in my treatment of Ian's effective exercise of self-control in Chapter 5.3.

3. The Role of Intentions in Reasons-Explanations

Intentions are often thought to mediate between the reasons for which we act and our intentional actions. As Davidson puts the point in a recent essay:

> Reasons cause the intention 'in the right way'. . . . If the intention exists first, and is followed by the action, the intention, along with further events (like noticing that the time has come), causes the action 'in the right way'. If the action is initiated at the moment the intention comes into existence, then the initiation of the action and the coming into existence of the intention are both caused by the reasons, but the intention remains a causal factor in the development of the action.[3] (1985a, p. 221)

An influential ancestor of this idea is found in Aristotle's work on human action. For Aristotle, action expressive of an agent's moral character is caused by a "choice" (*prohairesis*), which is in turn caused by a process of deliberation (*bouleusis*) that incorporates reasons for action (see, e.g., NE III.3, VI.2; cf. my 1984c). I have elsewhere argued that, in Aristotle's view, nondeliberative intentional action is caused by a similar process—a process in which practical inference generates a mental event akin to here-and-now intending, which in turn is the proximate cause of an intentional action.[4]

Although I am attracted to the view that intentions mediate between the reasons for which we act and our intentional actions, I shall not defend it here. Instead, I want to examine the implications of akratic action against here-and-now intentions for this view of the role of intentions in intentional action. My goal is to find a plausible role for intentions in a modified belief-desire explanatory framework that is adequate to the full range of intentional action, including strict akratic and continent action.

Some philosophers maintain what I have elsewhere called the *Intention/ Motivation Alignment Thesis* (*IMAT*)[5]—roughly, the view that we are always most motivated to do what we intend to do.[6] When conjoined with (a suitably qualified version of) the thesis that we always do what we are most motivated to do, the *IMAT* yields a thesis connecting intention and action.[7] If intention could be linked at the other end to reasons for action, the result would be an account linking reasons, via intentions, to intentional actions.

What typically motivates acceptance of the *IMAT*, I think, is the idea that a psychological[8] model for the explanation of intentional action must include an explanatory item that captures the notion ˙ of preponderant occurrent motivation and can serve as the proximate psychological cause of action. That is, what proponents of the *IMAT* are generally after is a psychological item that (1) initiates action without generating another psychological item that more proximately initiates action and that (2) is *sufficient* to initiate action provided that the pertinent bodily mechanisms are in proper working order. Intending is a prime candidate. (We might say that the proximate psychological cause of action initiates an *attempt* which, if successful, is part of the successfully attempted action. Notice that the proximate *psychological* cause of action is not necessarily the proximate cause *simpliciter* of action. Perhaps nonpsychological causes mediate between the former and intentional action. In the case of 'external' actions, or actions 'upon the world,' the success of an attempt depends, of course, upon the friendliness of the agent's environment.)

The central point of the preceding paragraph comes out quite clearly in the following passage from Alston's (1974):

> If we are looking for an internal 'psychological field' variable that is highly enough correlated with (attempted) intentional action to stand as a surrogate for actual overt behaviour in a nonphysiological theory, we need something like the concept of the strongest contemporary desire for a state of affairs deemed attainable (or possibly attainable) by present action. In our common-sense psychological scheme we have such a concept; the concept of a (present) intention to do so-and-so. My intention to do *A* right now can . . . be construed as a want for *S*, with the added stipulation that the agent takes *S* to be realisable by his behaviour (or at least having some chance of being so realisable) and that it is at that moment stronger than any want the realization of which would require incompatible movements. Thus a present intention to do *S* can be construed as what we might call an 'executive' desire for *S*, a desire that has come out victorious over any immediate competitors and that will therefore trigger off mechanisms leading to overt movement provided that the relevant mechanisms are working normally. (p. 95)

Unfortunately, certain instances of strict akratic action show that the *IMAT* is false (see Ch. 3.3). The problem with the *IMAT* is closely related to the problem with the idea that we are always most motivated to do what we (decisively) judge it best to do. Some intentions are based on the agent's better judgments; and when one's better judgment is not aligned with the bulk of one's motivation, a corresponding intention may be similarly misaligned (see Ch. 3.3). In the blood brother case of Chapter 2.2., for example, Alex decides to cut his hand—thereby forming an intention to do so—on the basis of a decisive better judgment arrived at via deliberation; yet the balance of his motivation at the time is in line neither with his better judgment nor with the intention to which it led.[9]

The ordinary, 'common-sense' notion of intending does double duty. Intentions are regarded both as initiators of intentional action and as items that often issue from one's evaluation of one's reasons for action, as in deliberation. These two aspects of intention often coincide.[10] We frequently form an intention to A on the basis of an evaluation of our pertinent reasons and then act on that intention. But occasionally the motivational force of evaluated items is out of line with our evaluations, and with the better judgments and intentions formed on the basis of our evaluations. In cases of this sort, intentions—even here-and-now intentions—may be overridden by competing motivation. Preponderant motivation is *not* built into the 'common-sense' notion of intention. Or, if it is, that notion is incoherent, given the role that it accords to evaluation in the formation of many intentions. For evaluation and preponderant motivation sometimes part company.

One may attempt to revise the *IMAT* by introducing a technical use of 'intention' ('intention*') that is stipulated to entail preponderant motivation, or by opting for a term whose ties to evaluation are weaker (e.g., 'volition'). Now, to be sure, we are often most motivated to do what we intend to do. What must be asked is whether, whenever this happens, preponderant motivation is *built into* the agent's intention—is a part of the structure of that intention. Or, taking a broader perspective, one should ask whether a successful intentionalistic psychological model for the explanation of intentional action must build preponderant motivation into some single, determinate item that is the proximate psychological cause of action (e.g., intention* or volition).

The last question is properly answered in the negative. Rather than build preponderant motivation into intention*, volition, or their ilk, we may treat the presence of supporting preponderant motivation as a causally necessary condition of an intention's initiating (in 'the right way') a corresponding intentional action. The concept of preponderant motivation can perform its theoretical function without our treating preponderant motivation as an essential property of intending (or some close relative). To be sure, one is free to understand the proximate psychological cause of action as intention *backed by* preponderant motivation; but this is not to specify a kind of intention that differs *intrinsically* from intentions not backed by preponderant motivation.

I suspect that the *IMAT* lies behind David Pears's recent attempt—which merits mention in any case—to account for strict akratic action by means of a distinction between *intending oneself to A* and *intending to A*

(1984, pp. 243ff.). To intend oneself to A, on Pears's account, is to intend to do something, X, with the intention that, as a result of doing X, one will intend to do A. For example, an agent who intends himself to refrain from drinking a third scotch may command himself to stop at two scotches, with the intention that the self-command will result in his intending *to* stop at two scotches (see Pears, pp. 243f.). Pears's idea is reminiscent of Davidson's view, in "How Is Weakness of the Will Possible?," that the akratic agent fails to intend in accordance with an all-things-considered better judgment (see above, Ch. 3.2). For Davidson, the akratic agent judges it better to do A than B, but does not intend to do A in preference to B. For Pears, the agent of a "last ditch" akratic action judges it best to do A and *intends himself* to do A, but he does not *intend to* do A. Though Pears allows the akratic agent to go a bit further than Davidson does, both stop short of the *last ditch*—akratic action against a here-and-now intention to A.

The falsity of the *IMAT* does not prevent intentions from playing a mediating causal role in intentional action. Perhaps, as Davidson claims, intentional actions are caused (in part) by intentions that are in turn caused (in part) by reasons. Some intentions—including some here-and-now intentions—are defeated in cases of akratic action. But, as we have seen, the agent of an akratic action acts for a reason (or reasons); and the reason(s) for which he acts may result in action by contributing to the generation of an (effective) intention.

The idea that intentions have the mediating role in question is compatible as well with my suggestion in the preceding section that explaining intentional actions performed in cases of motivational conflict is a two-stage process, involving both a specification of the reason(s) for which the agent A-ed and an explanation of his acting for the reason(s) that he did rather than for his competing reason(s). In focusing in this way on reasons, I do not mean to exclude intentions from the causal story.

What I do want to contend is that intentions do not have as decisive a role in action as proponents of the *IMAT* would give them. It is admitted on all sides that we do not always do what we intend to do. This should be uncontroversial even in the case of here-and-now intentions. Sometimes we are physically or psychologically unable to execute them successfully. Sometimes the world is not friendly enough. What I have shown (Ch. 3) is that there is another, generally overlooked defeater of here-and-now intentions: A here-and-now intention can be defeated by opposing motivation (even when the agent is physically and psychologically able to act on the intention).

Why are here-and-now intentions defeated by opposing motivation in some cases and not in others? The ingredients of an answer should by now be familiar. Here-and-now intentions are defeated or undefeated by opposing motivation depending upon the agent's balance of motivation at the time of action. And we have seen how to construct explanations of an agent's motivational balance in particular cases.

In Chapter 4, I suggested that to explain intentional action we must bring into the causal picture something that explains an agent's executing the intention that he does rather than abandoning it. Now, executing an intention to A entails A-ing. Thus, in the case of an 'external' action, an action upon the world, the execution of an intention depends both upon the agent and his environment. Like the suitors in Homer's *Odyssey,* an agent may do all that he can to string a bow, and yet fail to do so because of the rigidity of the wood. What I had in mind in Chapter 4 was the *agential* aspect of execution.

I am not suggesting that we incorporate into the causal picture an executive *faculty*—for example, the will—which performs executive actions, such as volitions to execute intentions. My contention is much more modest. First, when an agent behaves continently or incontinently in the presence of competing motivation, we do not adequately explain his action by explaining his intention to perform that action; for, intentions can be defeated by opposing motivation. Second, to explain why an agent acted on his intention to A in a case of motivational conflict, we must explain why he was most motivated to A at the time. In some cases, the explanation does involve executive actions—the successful exercise of self-control at work in third-grade continent action. In other cases, it does not.

Why should intentions be brought into the causal picture at all if—putting aside ability, the friendliness of the world, and the like—we can explain intentional action by explaining why the agent was most motivated at the time of action to act as he did? A straightforward answer, a defense of which is beyond the scope of the present work, is that intention mediates between overall motivation and intentional action. This is compatible, of course, with the attractive idea that intending itself has a motivational component.[11] An intending may mediate between the motivation that contributes to its formation and the intentional action that the intention generates; and this motivation may be the source of the motivational component of the intention. Moreover, intention may play a crucial cognitive role in the initiation and guidance of intentional action. For example, it may incorporate a representation of what is intended that helps to guide one's movements.[12]

I conclude this section with a point about strict akratic action. If intentions always mediate between reasons and intentional actions, then the here-and-now intentions defeated in instances of strict akratic action are replaced by competing intentions. The latter are the intentions that generate the strict akratic actions. Again, we may explain the agent's acting on these intentions rather than on their competitors by explaining why he was most motivated at the time of action to perform the actions in question.

4. Reasons-Explanations and Character

We occasionally refer to an agent's character in explaining his intentional actions. Young Mike may eat all the chocolate-chip cookies 'because he is selfish,' while Michele loans Richard fifty dollars 'because she is kind.' Characterological explanations of intentional actions need not compete with reasons-explanations. For example, Davidson's thesis that we explain (or "rationalize," in his technical sense) an action by constructing the "primary reason" why the agent performed the action (1963) is quite compatible with the idea that we can explain, in part, the agent's having the primary reason that he had, and, therefore, his acting as he did, by identifying a pertinent characterological feature of the agent. In Aristotle, the two sorts of explanation are nicely fused. He holds that when an agent performs an intentional action that is expressive of his character, his character helps to explain his having the occurrent intrinsic desire(s) on which he acts.[13]

Although *akrasia* and its opposite are traits of character,[14] I have made little of them *qua traits* in explaining continent and incontinent action. My reasons for this are twofold. First, as I have explained (Ch. 4.3), continent and incontinent actions are by no means limited, respectively, to continent and incontinent agents. Second, and much more importantly, characterological explanations are best regarded as promissory notes. In the earlier statements about Mike and Michele, we identify what we regard as salient explanatory items; but, for many purposes, we have not adequately explained their intentional behavior until we have enabled our audience to understand in some detail how the traits cited figure in the actions at issue. Presumably, Michele's generosity is not such that she would give just anyone a loan. Nor, we may suppose, is Mike's selfishness such that he would have devoured the cookies even if he had been convincingly threatened with a week's suspension of his television-watching privileges for doing so. When traits enter into the etiology of intentional behavior they do so in a causal context in which beliefs and desires are at work. Mike's selfishness and Michele's generosity are plausibly regarded as explaining their respective actions only via their influence on other psychological items—for example, the total motivational bases of Mike's urge to eat the cookies and Michele's desire to loan Richard the money. We can redeem the promissory notes by constructing adequate explanations of their respective actions that incorporate these additional items.

'Weak-willed' and 'strong-willed' (or 'self-controlled') are not treated in ordinary parlance as purely descriptive terms. They are also given an explanatory function. We say, for example, that Ann was able to resist temptation *because* she is strong-willed, whereas Andy gives in to peer pressure against his better judgment because he is weak-willed. One of the advantages of the modified belief-desire explanatory framework that I have been developing is that it helps us to see *how* the traits of *akrasia* and self-control can have explanatory import. Self-control, as I argued in Chapter 4, involves both motivation to act as one judges best and, typically, a collection of skills and powers of resistance. We have seen how this motivation and exercises of these skills and powers may influence one's motivational condition at the time of action and, therefore, one's intentional behavior. Through an exercise of self-control, as we saw in Chapter 5, an agent may intervene in his own motivational processes, generating a motivational balance favorable to continent action. The derivative account in Chapter 4 of *akrasia* (the trait) similarly prepares the way for an understanding of the bearing of this trait upon particular instances of akratic action.

5. Conclusion

In this chapter I have attempted to show both that the occurrence of incontinent and continent actions does not force a radical rejection of traditional belief-desire models of action-explanation and that it does call for substantial revision of the traditional models. Reasons-explanations are inadequate in instances of motivational conflict. They provide only one stage of an adequate explanation. A second stage is also required, one in which the agent's acting on the reasons that he does is explained. In constructing the second-stage explanation, we may usefully appeal to members of a range of psychological items examined in preceding chapters, items such as the total motivational base of a desire and exercises or nonexercises of self-control. The primary purpose of the present chapter has been, not to break new ground, but rather to examine the implications of results already obtained for a traditional approach to the explanation of intentional action and to modify that approach accordingly.

8

Akratic Belief

Although *akrasia* is typically treated as a strictly practical or 'actional' matter, its influence extends to belief as well. That it does should not be surprising. It has been recognized since antiquity that a person's motivational condition can have a powerful bearing upon what he does or does not believe: Sophocles's *Oedipus Rex* is a magnificent study of a species of this phenomenon. And some research on cognitive dissonance certainly seems to confirm this time-honored view.[1] Moreover, motivated doxastic failures are often supposed to be centrally involved in self-deception; for example, the smoker who continues to believe, in the face of strong evidence to the contrary, that smoking has no causal bearing on lung cancer. In some such cases, a charge of *akrasia* may be in order: Perhaps a *stronger* person would have acknowledged the unpleasant truth of the matter.

In this chapter I characterize a central species of incontinent believing and explain how it is possible. *Akrasia* is exhibited in a variety of ways in the practical or 'actional' sphere; but in the full-blown and most challenging case of the phenomenon, the akratic agent performs an intentional, free action contrary to a decisive better judgment that he both consciously holds at the time of action and consciously believes to be at odds with his performing the action at issue. This is what I have called *strict* incontinent action. What I am after in this chapter is an account of a comparable, full-blown variety of incontinent believing and an explanation of its possibility.

1. Strict Incontinent Belief

We say that incontinent action manifests the agent's weakness of will. Perhaps 'weakness' strikes us as too severe a charge in some instances of incontinent action. But in acting incontinently an agent shows at least that he is not perfectly self-controlled at the time. A perfectly self-controlled agent would not permit himself to be mastered by motivation that is at odds with his decisive better judgment. Presumably, we want to say something similar about incontinent *believing*. If it is *incontinent* believing, it should manifest some imperfection in the believer's self-control. This is not to suggest that our beliefs are under our direct voluntary control, that is, that we believe at will. However, belief-acquisition and belief-retention are often subject to our *indirect* control—for example, our (partial) control over how we gather data in a particular case.

The most detailed analysis of incontinent believing that I have encountered fails precisely because it ignores the weakness to which 'incontinence' refers. This is the analysis developed by John Heil in his otherwise instructive paper, "Doxastic Incontinence."[2] For a formal statement of the account, the reader should consult Heil's paper (p. 65). The following passage provides a useful illustration of his view, namely, that to believe incontinently is to believe "*in the teeth of* the evidence" (Heil's italics):

> The incontinent believer is typified by the psychoanalytic patient who has acquired what might be termed an intellectual grasp of his plight, but whose outlook evidently remains unaffected. Such a person has failed somehow to integrate his appreciation of certain facts into his overall psychological state. He continues to harbour beliefs, desires and fears that he recognizes to be at odds with his better epistemic judgment. (p. 69)

I do not doubt that in some such cases beliefs that one recognizes to be at odds with one's better epistemic judgment are *incontinently* harbored. But must this always be so? Suppose that Fred, a psychoanalytic patient, judges that since the truth about certain aspects of his life may be very painful, he is, all things considered, better off holding the beliefs that he now has about these things than he would be if he instead believed the propositions that seem best supported by the evidence. Perhaps Fred is properly charged with epistemic irresponsibility (see Kornblith, 1983) for holding these beliefs; but does he hold them incontinently?

Consideration of an analogous case from the practical or 'actional' sphere should prove helpful. Suppose that Barney judges that the moral reasons for doing A are better than the moral reasons for doing B (both of which actions he knows to be open to him), but that he nevertheless intentionally does B (and does not do A). From this, we cannot infer that Barney has acted incontinently, for he may have judged that, all things considered, it was better to do B than A. Even if Barney places appreciable value on moral considerations, he presumably has nonmoral values as well; and in some cases he may take moral considerations to be evaluatively overridden by other considerations. Similarly, a person who has epistemic values—for example, a pro-attitude toward his having only epistemically warranted beliefs—may take these values to be overridden by others in certain cases. Consider, for example, the undergraduate who sincerely states in the final exam for his philosophy of religion course that although he is now convinced that the bulk of the evidence supports the claim that the Christian God does not exist, he still finds himself believing that there is such a God and, what is more, sincerely maintains that, all things considered, it is quite *rational* for him to hold this belief, given that the strong evidence against Christian theism is not entirely conclusive and that he would be unbearably unhappy as an atheist or an agnostic. Such a person believes against his better *epistemic* judgment but in accordance with his better *all-things-considered* judgment. Therefore, although he may, from an epistemic point of view, believe irresponsibly, he does not believe incontinently (on the assumption that the all-things-considered judgment is not itself incontinently held). This point applies to Fred as well. Neither exhibits a deficiency (or imperfection) in *self-control* in believing as he does (unless *akrasia* or the associated imperfection is manifested in the better judgment itself).

The preceding paragraph suggests that there is, for our purposes, an important difference between the judgment that, all things considered, one's doing A is better than one's doing B and the judgment that, given all that is relevant to the epistemic warrant of p and q, p is more warranted than q. A person who holds the latter judgment may consistently judge that, all things considered, his believing q is better than his believing p; but an agent who holds the former judgment cannot consistently hold that, all things considered, his doing B is better than his doing A. The explanation is that considerations of epistemic warrant constitute only a species of value, a species that can be evaluatively overridden, in the believer's opinion, by nonepistemic values (cf. Ch. 4.2).

Heil has, I think, identified an important variety of epistemically irresponsible believing, namely, believing "in the teeth of the evidence," against one's epistemic better judgment. However, such believing is not incontinent if, in the agent's (nonakratically held) opinion, his pertinent epistemic values are evaluatively overridden by nonepistemic values of his. In that event, he is no more guilty of incontinence than is someone who, in accordance with his all-things-considered better judgment, acts against his better moral judgment.

Two further points should be made in this connection. The first concerns responsibility. Suppose that Betty believes that p is false even though she judges not only that there is much more epistemic warrant for

p than for not-p but also that, all things considered, her believing p would be better than her believing not-p. Suppose further, however, that she believes not-p during t only because a mad scientist, bypassing Betty's own belief-forming mechanisms, directly implanted this belief in her in such a way that no amount of self-control would enable her to dislodge it during t. Here again we do not have doxastic incontinence; for Betty's holding the pertinent belief during t is not, given the details of the story, due to any weakness (or associated imperfection) on her part. Nor even is this case one of epistemic irresponsibility.

This is, to be sure, a highly contrived case; but it does have a point. We need, in a characterization of doxastic incontinence, to pin the responsibility for the crucial belief (at least in significant part) on the believer. Incontinent *action,* traditionally conceived, is *free* action; and the preceding case points to the necessity of finding a doxastic analogue. An attempt to construct and defend an account of the analogue—what I shall call "free* belief"—would take us too far afield, but a gloss on the notion is in order. As I shall use the term, the *freedom** of a belief during a period of time is a function of the degree and kind of control that the believer or his doxastic mechanisms had, or were capable of having, in the etiology of his holding the belief during the period in question.

The second point is about motivation. The incontinent agent is defeated by motivation which opposes his better judgment. Standard analyses identify incontinent action as intentional action and therefore do not need to specify as well that it is motivated; for all intentional action is motivated. But the 'motivatedness' of incontinent action is one of its defining features. This is true as well of incontinent believing. *How* it is motivated will be discussed in some detail below. *That* it is motivated is a purely conceptual matter. To *be* incontinent (in the pertinent sense) is, by definition, to be deficient in one's capacity to contain or restrain one's desires, feelings, and the like; and incontinent 'behavior,' whether actional or doxastic, is a manifestation of this deficiency, or at least of an associated imperfection.

The following characterization of strict incontinent belief, modeled after the account of strict incontinent action in Chapter 1, accommodates the preceding points and avoids the problems with Heil's analysis:

> In believing that p during t, S exhibits strict doxastic incontinence if and only if the belief is motivated and free* and, during t, S consciously holds a judgment to the effect that there is good and sufficient reason for his not believing that p.

By "a judgment to the effect . . ." I mean a judgment that *settles* for S the matter of whether it is, all things considered, better to believe, or not to believe, that *p*. My analysis does not suggest that the judgment violated in strict doxastic incontinence must always, or even usually, be based in part on nonevidential considerations. Indeed, I would surmise that in typical instances of strict incontinent believing the subject takes evidential considerations alone to provide good and sufficient reason for his not believing *p*. However, in cases in which the subject "believes in the teeth of the evidence" but takes considerations of epistemic or evidential warrant to be overridden by other considerations, my analysis, unlike Heil's, does not entail that the subject believes incontinently. For, in such cases the subject does not consciously hold a judgment to the effect that there is good and *sufficient* reason for his not believing that *p*. I do not wish to deny that a believer's ranking nonepistemic considerations over epistemic ones in a particular case may itself exhibit incontinence. However, doxastic incontinence of this sort is beyond the scope of this chapter and the above analysis. My concern here, again, is with a single *species* of incontinent believing.

Two points should be clarified before this section is brought to an end. First, nothing that I have said depends upon the supposition that it is sometimes *rational* to believe in the teeth of the evidence. Nor do I pretend to have a formula for weighing epistemic against nonepistemic considerations. It is sufficient for my purposes that we can sometimes *take* our believing in the teeth of the evidence to be rational (or best, all things considered).[3] Second, although we expect agents to decide or intend to perform actions of certain types on the basis of their decisive practical better judgments, I am not suggesting that people decide or intend to *believe* certain propositions on the basis of their judgments about what it is best or better to believe (though they may occasionally decide to *get themselves* to believe certain things). Believing is not a kind of action. This point is plainly compatible, however, with its being the case that our judgments about evidence have an influence upon what we believe; and even judgments about what it is best, *practically speaking*, to believe may be efficacious—for example, the person convinced by Pascal's pragmatic argument for belief in God may, by conscientiously following the suggested program, bring it about that he holds theistic beliefs.

2. The Possibility of Strict Incontinent Belief

I turn now to the question of the *possibility* of strict incontinent believing. I shall start by addressing a general reservation that some readers may have. It may be suggested that '*S* consciously holds a judgment that there is good and sufficient reason for his not believing that *p' entails* '*S* does not believe that *p*', and that strict incontinent believing consequently is impossible. The underlying assumption would seem to be this: That to judge that there is good and sufficient reason for believing that *p is* to believe that *p* and, similarly, that to judge that there is good and sufficient reason for not believing that *p* precludes one's believing that *p*.[4] The assumption paints an attractive picture no doubt, but one that is overly optimistic about human rationality. Heil quite correctly observes (1984, p. 69) that psychoanalytic patients sometimes harbor not only fears that they recognize to be unwarranted, but beliefs as well. And, in any case, it would be presumptuous to rule this possibility out a priori.

In attempting to explain the possibility of full-blown doxastic incontinence, it will be useful to distinguish between two cases of the phenomenon. First, there is the case in which the agent's judgment that there is good and sufficient reason for his not believing *p* is based on evidential or epistemic considerations alone.[5] I will call this *narrow incontinent believing*. This is to be contrasted with the case in which the judgment is based on both epistemic and nonepistemic considerations, what I will call *broad incontinent believing*. The *judgment* is the same in both cases. It is a decisive better judgment. The difference between broad and narrow incontinent believing lies in the scope of the considerations on which decisive better judgments are based.

That narrow incontinent believing is possible seems clear. Some cases of self-deception are instances of this sort of incontinence. Consider the stock example of the woman who judges, solely on evidential grounds, that there is good and sufficient reason for her believing that her husband is having an affair (and for her not believing that he is not having an affair) but who nevertheless believes, owing in part to her wanting it to be the case that he has been faithful to her, that he has not been so engaged.

Broad incontinent believing may be more perplexing, but it too seems quite possible. Consider, for example, the insecure, jealous husband whose initial suspicion that his wife is having an affair develops into a genuine belief, even though he knows that his evidence that she is being unfaithful is quite weak, that he has much better evidence that she is not having an affair, and that he would be much better off not having the belief in question.

In some instances of incontinent believing, both broad and narrow, an explanation of the possibility of the phenomenon is not far to seek. Brief consideration of an explanation of the possibility of strict akratic *action* should prove useful. The better judgments against which akratic agents act are often formed on the basis of their *evaluations* of their reasons for action. But, as we have seen, the motivational force of a reason may not be in alignment with the agent's evaluation of that reason. Thus, one who judges it best, all things considered, to do an A, may be more motivated to perform, and consequently perform, some competing action, B.

The condition of at least some incontinent believers is quite similar. It is on the basis of his *evaluation* of (or evaluative attitudes toward) epistemic considerations that the person who exhibits narrow doxastic incontinence judges there to be good and sufficient reason for his not believing that p; but items that he takes to provide only weak evidence for p may, owing to his conative condition, have a great deal of salience at the time at which he forms or acquires a belief about the matter. Because of the attractiveness of what they suggest, the bulk of his attention may be drawn to these items, and his apprehension of competing items may be quite pale by comparison.[6] Since he consciously holds the judgment that there is good and sufficient reason for his not believing that p, he is in no position sincerely to justify to us his believing that p; indeed, our pressing him for justification may well make it difficult for him to retain the belief, if we manage to shift the focus of his attention to his reasons for not believing that p. But when he forms or acquires the belief that p, it presumably is not a concern for justification that is guiding him.

At least some cases of broad incontinent believing admit of the same sort of explanation. Suppose, for example, that Wilma judges not only that the evidence that her twelve-year-old son, Basil, has been experimenting with narcotics is very strong and much stronger than the contrary evidence but also that her believing that he has been doing so is much better supported by nonepistemic considerations than is her not believing this. She thinks that even if the epistemic evidence were significantly weaker, it would be best, practically speaking, for her to believe that Basil has been taking drugs, since she fears that in the absence of this belief it would be very easy for her to fail to give him guidance that he may well need. To be sure, Wilma wants it to be false that her beloved Basil has been using drugs, and she recognizes that believing that he has been doing so would be very painful for her; but she judges that the pain is outweighed by other practical considerations. Undoubtedly, many more details can be added to the story of Wilma's finally coming, on the basis of epistemic and nonepistemic considerations, to hold the judgment that there is good and sufficient reason for her not believing that Basil is innocent of drug use. However, let us suppose now, for the sake of brevity, that she does come to hold this judgment but that she nevertheless believes that he has not been using drugs.

Here again the salience of evidential items may properly enter into the explanation of incontinent believing. Because she very much wants it to be the case that Basil has not been experimenting with drugs, Wilma's attention may be drawn at crucial junctures to items suggestive of innocence: "Basil has always been a good little boy. Only a few weeks ago he was happily playing in the sand with his little brother's toy trucks in just the way that he played with his own toys a few short months ago. Can a boy like this be a drug user? He is only a *child*!" Wilma's decisive better judgment implies that she should not let herself be swayed by reflections of this sort after having given the evidential items involved due consideration in arriving at her overall epistemic judgment. But it is not hard to understand how, when fondly entertaining a vivid image of her beloved young son playing innocently and happily in the sand, Wilma may not be on her guard against self-deception.

Of course, if this is to be a case of strict incontinent believing, Wilma must satisfy the free* belief condition. Now, Wilma's story *can* be told in such a way that the pertinent belief is unfree*: One can suppose that her attention is *irresistibly* drawn to items suggestive of innocence and that the influence of these items upon her is such as to preclude her having any control whatsoever over what she believes about the matter at hand. However, it surely is not necessary to tell the story in this way. We may coherently suppose that it was within Wilma's power to take measures which would have resulted in her not being unduly swayed by emotively charged images of an innocent Basil. Such measures might include, for example, forcefully reminding herself at appropriate moments of her low assessment of the evidential merit of the considerations in question while forcing herself to recall, with suitable vividness, memories supportive of the opposite hypothesis.

The previously mentioned example of the insecure, jealous husband seems, at least initially, more problematic. In the case of Wilma, there is on the side of incontinent believing what we might call, with David Pears (1984, p. 42), a "desirable goal." Although Wilma judges that, all things (epistemic and otherwise) considered, it is best not to believe that Basil is innocent of drug use, there is still something substantial to be said, from her own point of view, for her believing that he is innocent. There is something significant to be gained by doxastic incontinence, even if this would result (in Wilma's own opinion) in a greater loss. But what does our jealous husband have to gain as a result of believing that his wife has been unfaithful? If we are at a loss for an answer to this question, we may be hard put to see what *motivates* his belief. And if we cannot get a grip on the motivational issue, can we understand his holding the belief in question? Furthermore, if the belief is not motivated, we do not have incontinence after all.

Pears (1984, p. 44) has suggested that in cases of the sort in question there is a "wish" for an "ulterior goal," namely, "the elimination of a rival." To be sure, the agent does not construct for himself a practical syllogism that starts with a wish to eliminate rivals for his wife's affection and that concludes—via a "minor premise" to the effect that his believing that his wife is having an affair would increase his chances of detecting and eliminating rivals—with a desire or decision to form the belief in question. But a subconscious analogue is quite possible; and the postulation of a goal-directed process of this sort does help to make intelligible our jealous husband's acquiring the belief in question.

It may seem that this explanatory retreat to the subconscious makes it difficult to interpret the case of our jealous husband as an instance of full-blown doxastic incontinence. If a subconscious process is operative here, one might think that matters are wholly beyond the agent's control, so that our jealous husband's infidelity-belief is unfree*. Indeed, Pears himself seems to suggest as much. He claims that when the wish for the ulterior goal is present, "nature takes over . . . and sets up an emotional program that *ensures* its achievement" (p. 44, my emphasis).

This, however, is a stronger line than is called for or even plausible in many cases. Jealousy need not turn an agent into an automaton. A jealous husband may know that he is disposed to make unwarranted inferences where his wife's fidelity is concerned and attempt to short-circuit the subconscious process in situations in which it seems to him likely to take effect if left unchecked. People attempt in a variety of ways to resist *acting* contrary to their better judgment. And a jealous man, upon first entertaining the suspicion that his wife is having an affair, might try to circumvent the doxastic pull of subconscious forces by going, for example, to the woman at once for reassurance, or by relating to friends his suspicion and the flimsy grounds on which it rests in order to generate salient support for the fidelity-hypothesis. If the subconscious "emotional program" is in fact such as to "ensure" the formation of the unwarranted belief, the belief would seem not to be free*—in which case a necessary condition of full-blown doxastic incontinence is not satisfied. But the suggestion is surely implausible that *no one* who holds a belief on the basis of the subconscious process that Pears describes had it within his power to take reasonable measures such that, if they had been taken, the process would have been short-circuited.

Two possible sources of confusion should be removed. First, although

I have appealed to Pears's suggestion as a helpful explanatory hypothesis, I certainly do not mean to be claiming that in all cases in which jealousy leads a person, via a subconscious process, to form the pertinent infidelity-belief, a wish to eliminate rivals does the motivational work. This work, I should think, may be done by a variety of desires, including certain self-destructive wishes that have nothing at all to do with the elimination of rivals. What is important for our purposes is that we have some way of making sense of cases of the sort in question and that it be sufficiently determinate to permit us to investigate the freedom* of the generated beliefs. Second, I have not taken a position on the extent and potency of the influence of motivation on belief, a subject of considerable controversy in psychological circles.[7] My analysis does commit me to the view that strict incontinent belief is motivated belief. But it is admitted on all sides that motivation has some influence on belief,[8] and I have said nothing about the *prevalence* of doxastic incontinence. If the relatively "cold" attribution theories are correct (see, e.g., Nisbett & Ross, 1980), there is much less doxastic incontinence than some motivation theorists may think; but disputes about the magnitude of the phenomenon affect neither my analysis of strict incontinent believing nor my explanation of its possibility.

3. Conclusion

Although there is substantial overlap between incontinent believing and self-deception, I have said little about the latter. Self-deception is discussed at length in the following two chapters. Here I shall make only one general observation about its relationship to incontinent believing. It is this: A person's being self-deceived in believing that *p* is neither a necessary nor a sufficient condition of his incontinently believing that *p*. As self-deception is typically (and, I think, correctly) conceived, the following points (among others) are true: (1) S is self-deceived in believing that *p* only if *p* is *false*; (2) nonepistemic considerations in favor of holding, or not holding, *p* are irrelevant to the truth of the claim that S is self-deceived in believing that *p*. In contrast, one may incontinently believe what is true, and (as I have shown) nonepistemic considerations of the sort in question are quite relevant to the truth of a charge of incontinent believing. The latter point opens up interesting possibilities that cannot be treated in detail in this chapter. First, cases are conceivable in which one is self-deceived in believing that *p* but does not *incontinently* believe that *p*—for example, a case in which S (nonakratically) takes the strong evidence that her husband is having an affair to be outweighed by nonepistemic considerations and ends up believing, falsely, but in accordance with her all-things-considered better judgment, that Mr. *S* is not having an affair. There is also the converse possibility, cases in which one incontinently believes that *p* but is not *self-deceived* in believing that *p*. An obvious example, given (1) above, is the case of an incontinently held *true* belief. But one can imagine examples to the same effect in which *p* is false—for example, a case in which *S* judges (non-self-deceptively) that his evidence for *p* (which proposition turns out to be false) is better than his evidence for not-*p*, judges (nonakratically) that he nevertheless has good and sufficient reason to believe that not-*p*, and yet incontinently believes that *p*, having been defeated by his attraction to (apparent) truth. Surely, a charge of self-deception is inappropriate here, since *S* believes in accordance with what he non-self-deceptively takes to be the better evidence.

Much remains to be said about doxastic incontinence. In my attempt to come to grips with the full-blown case, I have left the bulk of the phenomenal terrain unexplored.[9] However, I shall be satisfied if I have given an adequate account of strict incontinent believing and contributed to our understanding of its possibility. Strict incontinent believing is possible for roughly the reason that strict incontinent action is. The evaluations that give rise to *practical* decisive better judgments need neither fix nor precisely record motivational strength. Consequently, an agent's overall motivation can be at odds with his better judgment, with the result that he acts incontinently. Similarly, the assessments or evaluations that ground decisive better judgments about matters of *belief* need neither fully determine nor exactly gauge the causal power of belief-influencing items. This opens the door to the possibility of a mismatch between the determinants of belief (e.g., salience) and one's better judgment, with the result that one believes incontinently.[10]

I conclude with a comment on the irrationality of incontinent believing. Incontinent believing, like incontinent action, is subjectively irrational; for it is contrary to the agent's own decisive better judgment. Davidson's paradox of irrationality challenges us to explain these phenomena without rendering them rational. We have already seen how to do this with akratic action (Ch. 6). The same general strategy is applicable to akratic belief. Akratic beliefs are irrational for the reason just specified. And instances of akratic believing are explained by the etiologies of particular mismatches between pertinent determinants of belief and believers' decisive better judgments. In locating the causes of an akratic belief, we do not render the belief subjectively rational; for, the belief is caused contrary to the agent's decisive better judgment. Nor do we "compromise our ability to diagnose irrationality by withdrawing the background of rationality needed to justify any diagnosis at all" (Davidson, 1982, p. 303). The necessary background is still there. What justifies the diagnosis are the grounds for asserting that the belief in question is free* and contrary to the agent's better judgment.[11]

9

Self-Deception: The Paradox of Belief

Although incontinent believing has received scant attention in the literature, quite the reverse is true of self-deception. A great many attempts have been made in recent years to purge self-deception of paradox. Ironically, these efforts often make the phenomenon much more difficult to understand than we have reason to believe it to be. This chapter and the next address two interrelated paradoxes. The first—which is often regarded as *the* paradox of self-deception—is directly concerned with *what* the self-deceived person believes and with the possibility of his believing what he (apparently) does. The second, examined in Chapter 10, focuses on the *process* or *activity* of self-deception. The former paradox in particular raises some thorny questions about the nature of belief and about 'standard' conceptions of belief. For example, does the ordinary folk-psychological concept of belief permit an agent simultaneously to believe (consciously) that *p* is true and to believe (consciously) that *p* is false? If so, is this a vice or a virtue of the concept? Unfortunately, an extended excursion into the theory of belief is beyond the scope of this book. I shall not do for the philosophy of belief what I have tried to do for the philosophy of action. My aim is to clarify the nature and etiology of self-deception in the course of resolving the paradoxes to be examined.

What I shall call the paradox of belief may be formulated as follows for the purposes of introduction:

> For any *A* and *B*, when *A* deceives *B* into believing that *p*, *A* knows or truly believes that not-*p* while causing *B* to believe that *p*. So when *A* deceives *A* (i.e., himself) into believing that *p*, he knows or truly believes that not-*p* while causing himself to believe that *p*. Thus, *A* must simultaneously believe that not-*p* and believe that *p*. But how is this possible?[1]

The purpose of the present chapter is to show that this paradox can be resolved, and self-deception successfully described and explained, without importing problematic hypotheses such as half-belief, the multiple self, and 'knowing in one's heart.' The bulk of this chapter is addressed to what I shall call "ordinary self-deception," the sort that seems to occur with the greatest frequency in both real and fictional cases. What we learn about the common cases may, as we shall see in Section 4, be fruitfully applied to atypical ones.

1. A Little Background

Raphael Demos, in an influential article, provides us with the following description of self-deception:

> Self-deception exists, I will say, when a person lies to himself, that is to say, persuades himself to believe what he knows is not so. In short, self-deception entails that B believes both p and not-p at the same time. (1960, p. 588)

Demos makes it quite clear that he is restricting the meaning of 'self-deception' to a special case—indeed, the *strongest* case. However, subsequent writers often assume that this description, or something quite similar, captures the *general* idea of self-deception. Once this assumption is made, one may proceed in either of two ways. It may be supposed (1) that many cases ordinarily counted as self-deception are not properly so counted, since they do not involve lying to oneself; or (2) that any case generally described as self-deception must involve some such lying, even though it may seem not to. On either alternative, self-deception as a whole, as opposed to a special case of it, is made to seem paradoxical. And on the second alternative, as we shall see, paradox is generated in cases that are describable and explicable in quite unparadoxical ways.

The conception of self-deception as lying to oneself is fueled by the idea that interpersonal deception necessarily involves lying to another. If deceiving someone else is getting him to believe something that one knows (or correctly believes) is false, it is natural to understand self-deception as getting *oneself* to believe something that one knows (or correctly believes) is false. One approach to resolving the paradox is to reject the underlying account of interpersonal deception, which is often taken for granted, as it is, for example, by Jeffrey Foss: "One thing that is not always recognized about deception is that knowledge is a prerequisite: to deceive another, one must bring it about that the other believes what one knows to be false" (1980, p. 241).[2] Although knowledge or true belief may be a prerequisite of *intentional* deception—which is, admittedly, the central case of deception—that is not true of *all* deception. When we say that a person is *deceived* about something, *X*, we often mean simply that he is in error with respect to *X*, or that he holds a false belief concerning *X*. And there is a corresponding natural use of the verb 'deceive' in which to say that *A* deceived *B* with respect to *p* is simply to say (roughly) that *A* caused *B* to be deceived with respect to *p*—something which is typically done by inducing a false belief that *p* in *B*.[3] But surely *A* may induce a false belief that *p* in *B*, and thus deceive him in this sense, without knowing, or even believing, that *p* is false. Indeed, *A* may believe that *p* is true, and he may have intended to communicate this to *B* by telling him that *p*. This is not a case of *intentional* deceiving, but it is a case of deceiving nonetheless.

The last point is an important one; for, as I shall argue, the vast majority of cases of self-deception are not cases of *intentional* deceiving. If I am right about this, to base one's conception of self-deception on the model of intentional interpersonal deception is to misconstrue this vast majority of cases—that is, *ordinary* self-deception.[4] When self-deception is thus misconstrued, it is not surprising that philosophers should feel a need to appeal to such problematic hypotheses as the multiple self and half-belief in attempting to explain it.

At the same time, the suggestion that self-deception should be modeled after *un*intentional interpersonal deception runs the risk of oversimplifying matters. Unintentional interpersonal deception may be quite accidental. But *self*-deception seems to be *motivated* by desires or fears of the agent-patient. Self-deception, as we shall see, is not accidental; and this, I think, is part of the reason that so many philosophers have been disposed to conceive of it on the model of the intentional deception of another.

I shall show, however, that the nonaccidentality of self-deception does not imply that the agent must intentionally deceive himself. To be sure, self-deceivers often do engage in intentional behavior with the result that they become deceived with respect to *p*; but I shall argue that they rarely act with the *intention of deceiving themselves*. Unless there are unconscious intentions, this would involve consciously aiming at getting oneself to believe (or think, sincerely avow, etc.) something that one consciously knows or believes to be false. And although this is possible (e.g., I might hire a hypnotist to induce in me the false belief that my business is prospering), it also seems to be rather distant from common cases of self-deception generally treated in the literature on the topic. Does it typically happen that the man who, in the face of strong evidence to the contrary, falsely believes that his wife is not having an affair, or the woman who will not admit, even to herself, that her son is guilty of the crime of which he has rightly been convicted, at one time had the intention of 'getting myself to believe what I now know (or believe) to be false'? The correct answer, as I shall suggest, is 'No.' What goes on in these cases is usually more subtle—and much less problematic.

Self-deception may be helpfully compared to akratic action in this connection. When an agent acts incontinently he acts intentionally; but that he act incontinently typically is not part of his intention. He does not *aim* at acting incontinently; this is not part of the action-plan that he wants to put into effect. Although, against his better judgment, he intentionally eats the sweet before him, he is not (at least characteristically) intending at the time to act incontinently. If, similarly, the self-deceiver engages in intentional behavior that contributes to his entering a state of self-deception, perhaps he may do this without intending to deceive himself. But if he deceives himself without intending to do so, might he not deceive himself into believing that *p* is false without (first) believing that *p* is true?

2. Entering Self-Deception in Acquiring a Belief

In the present section I characterize a central range within a class of cases describable as "entering self-deception in acquiring the belief that *p*" and argue that self-deception, thus characterized, does not entail the simultaneous holding of contradictory beliefs. I select *belief* in preference to other doxastic conditions because self-deception is most commonly described in terms of belief; but I am confident that characterizations similar to mine can be constructed for other doxastic conditions (e.g., thinking that *p*, being disposed sincerely to avow that *p*, and failing to believe that not *p*). I concentrate on *entering* a condition of self-deception because descriptions of the so-called paradox of self-deception are generally concerned with the generation of this condition, as opposed to a person's being, or remaining, in self-deception. Sometimes, of course, one may enter self-deception, not in *acquiring* a belief, but in *retaining* one. This possibility is examined in the following section.

It is important to distinguish between the literal meaning derived from prefixing 'self' to 'deception' and the meaning that 'self-deception' is commonly used to communicate. If Smith unintentionally misreads a word in a newspaper item that he is reading to Jones, thereby causing him to have a false belief about a recent development, Smith has caused Jones to be deceived about the matter and is appropriately said to have deceived Jones (albeit unintentionally) about it. However, if Jones, due to unmotivated carelessness, misreads a clearly printed word in a news article, thereby causing himself to have a false belief (and, hence, to be deceived), neither the deceiving of himself, nor the condition of deception which he has produced in himself, is the sort of thing which we ordinarily call self-deception. This is because the common notion of self-deception makes essential reference to a *desiderative* element. Self-deception is commonly conceived of as something that occurs because (in part) the agent-patient *wants* something (to be the case).[5] It is often said that what the self-deceiver wants is to *believe* the proposition with respect to which he is self-deceived; but, in general, if he wants to believe that *p* this is because he wants it to be the case that *p*.[6] For example, the person who wants to believe that she is not dying of cancer, or that her husband is not having an affair, typically wants not to be dying of cancer or wants it to be the case that her husband is not having an affair. (What the deceiver wants to be the case may, of course, be wanted either for its own sake or for the sake of something else to which he takes it to be importantly related. For example, the woman who wants it to be the case that her husband is not having an affair may want this only because she wants it to be true that he loves her and believes that love entails fidelity.)

The following are, I suggest, some common ways in which a person's wanting that *p* may contribute self-deceptively to his believing that *p*. (Other 'strategies' are discussed in the following chapter.)

FOUR WAYS OF SELF-DECEPTION

1. *Negative Misinterpretation:* *S*'s desiring that *p* may lead *S* to misinterpret as not counting against *p* (or as not counting strongly against *p*) data which, in the absence of the desire that *p*, he would, if the occasion arose, easily recognize to count (or to count strongly) against *p*. Consider, for example, a man who has just been informed that an article of his was not accepted for publication. He hopes that it was *wrongly* rejected, and he reads through the comments offered. He decides that the reviewers misunderstood a certain crucial but complex point, that their objections consequently miss the mark, and that the paper should have been accepted. However, as it turns out, the reviewers' criticisms were entirely justified; and when, a few weeks later, he rereads his paper and the comments in a more impartial frame of mind, it is clear to him that this is so.

2. *Positive Misinterpretation:* *S*'s desiring that *p* may lead *S* to interpret as supporting *p* data which count against *p*, and which, in the absence of this desire, *S* would easily recognize to count against *p* (if he considered the data). Suppose, for example, that Sid is very fond of Roz, a young woman with whom he often eats lunch. If he wants it to be the case that

Roz loves him, he may interpret her refusing to go out on dates with
him and her reminding him that she is very much in love with her steady
boyfriend, Tim, as an effort on her part to 'play hard to get' in order to
encourage Sid to continue to pursue her.

3. *Selective Focusing/Attending:* S's desiring that p may lead him both to
fail to focus his attention on evidence that counts against p and to focus
instead on evidence suggestive of p. Attentional behavior may be either
intentional or unintentional. S may tell himself that it is a waste of time
to consider his evidence that his wife is having an affair, since she just
is not the sort of person who would do such a thing; and he may
intentionally act accordingly. Or, because of the unpleasantness of such
thoughts, he may find his attention shifting whenever the issue suggests
itself to him. Failure to focus on contrary evidence, like negative
misinterpretation, may contribute negatively to S's acquiring the belief
that p; for it may be the case, other things being equal, that if S had
focused his attention on his evidence for not-p, he would not have
acquired the belief that p. Selective focusing on supporting evidence
may contribute positively to S's coming to believe that p.

4. *Selective Evidence-Gathering:* S's desiring that p may lead him both to
overlook easily obtained evidence for not-p and to find evidence for p
which is much less accessible. Consider, for example, the historian of
philosophy who holds a certain philosophical position, who wants it to
be the case that her favorite philosopher did so too, and who
consequently scours the texts for evidence that he did while consulting
commentaries that she thinks will provide support for the favored
interpretation. Our historian may easily miss rather obvious evidence to
the contrary, even though she succeeds in finding obscure evidence for
her favored interpretation. Such one-sided evidence gathering may
contribute both positively and negatively to the acquisition of the false
belief that p. Consequently, one might wish to analyze selective
evidence gathering as a combination of 'hypersensitivity' to evidence
(and sources of evidence) for the desired state of affairs and 'blindness'—of which there are, of course, degrees—to contrary evidence
(and sources thereof).[7]

   In each of the numbered items (1–4) above, there is a desire-
influenced inappropriate treatment of data. The subject's desire that p leads
him to fail to appreciate the gravity of some evidence that he has that not-p,
to misconstrue the import of such evidence, to focus selectively on
evidence supportive of p, or to fail to locate readily available evidence that
not-p, while seeking evidence that p. If this manipulation of data leads in

turn to the acquisition of the false belief that p, then we *may* have an instance of self-deception. But we do not yet have sufficient conditions of entering self-deception; for we must first eliminate inappropriate causal chains—chains involving manipulative mind readers, mad scientists, belief-producing blows on the head, and the like.

However interesting such chains may be, we need not exercise ourselves over them here. What we are after is a characterization of a certain central range of cases of entering self-deception. And, in general, the more external forces contribute to the subject's entering self-deception, and the more accidental the connection between the subject's wanting that p and his becoming deceived that p, the less central the case. I shall propose therefore that the following is a list of characteristic and jointly sufficient conditions of a central case of S's entering self-deception in acquiring the belief that p:

CONDITIONS—CHARACTERISTIC AND SUFFICIENT—
FOR SELF-DECEPTION

1. The belief that p which S acquires is false.
2. S's desiring that p leads S to manipulate (i.e., to treat inappropriately) a datum or data relevant, or at least seemingly relevant, to the truth value of p.
3. This manipulation is a cause of S's acquiring the belief that p.
4. If, in the causal chain between desire and manipulation or in that between manipulation and belief-acquisition, there are any accidental intermediaries (links), or intermediaries intentionally introduced by another agent, these intermediaries do not make S (significantly) less responsible for acquiring the belief that p than he would otherwise have been.[8]

Several observations are in order here. First, we must distinguish between entering self-deception *in* acquiring the belief that p, and entering self-deception *as a* (partial) *result of* acquiring the belief that p. Imagine that S acquires a true belief that p, but mistakes p to imply r, which further proposition is false. Imagine also that S believes that r on the basis in part of the mistaken inference, and that he is self-deceived in believing r. In this case, S's acquiring the belief that p contributed to his entering a condition of self-deception, so that he entered self-deception as a partial *result* of acquiring the belief that p; but he did not enter self-deception *in* acquiring the belief that p. In a case which makes a related point, S acquires a *true* belief that p on the basis of evidence, e, which does not warrant the belief that p. If S enters (or is in) a condition of self-deception here, he is self-deceived in acquiring the belief that *p on the basis of e*, but *not* in acquiring the belief that *p simpliciter*.

The phrase "in acquiring the belief that *p*" is here to be understood in its strictest sense—what is meant is '*in-acquiring-the-belief-that-p simpliciter*.' I take it that, in this sense of the phrase, one cannot enter a condition of self-deception in acquiring the belief that *p* unless *p* is false. Hence, condition (1). (If *p* is true, *S* plainly is not *deceived in* believing that *p*. Nor, consequently, is he self-deceived in believing it.)

Whereas conditions (2) and (3) are concerned with the self-deceiver's distinctive contribution to his being deceived, the function of condition (4) is to give us a relatively pure range of cases of self-deception. Perhaps a person may enter self-deception in acquiring the belief that *p* when condition (4) is not satisfied; but if we are going to ask whether there is anything paradoxical about ordinary self-deception, we would do well to consider the purer, and hence clearer, cases.

The question 'What is self-deception?' is similar, in an interesting respect, to the question 'What is knowledge?' The latter question has often been formulated as follows: 'What must be added to true belief to yield knowledge?' A parallel formulation of the former question, at least as it has often been understood, is a natural—namely, 'What must be added to false belief to yield a condition of self-deception?'[9] What I have suggested is that, in many ordinary cases at least, the answer is to be found in conditions (2) and (3) and some further condition ruling out inappropriate causal chains.

The chief virtue of this characterization (conditions 1–4) is that it does not commit us to supposing that the self-deceived person, upon entering self-deception, is in the peculiar doxastic condition of believing that *p and* believing that not-*p*;[10] nor even must we suppose that he *once* believed that not-*p*. What generates the self-deceived person's belief that *p*, on my account, is a desire-influenced manipulation of data that are, or seem to be, relevant to the truth value of *p*. But the two varieties of misinterpretation depend at most upon the belief that certain bits of data seem to count against *p*, and the other two modes of manipulation identified above do not even depend upon this.[11] Part of what the self-deceiver does, in many cases, is to *prevent* himself from holding a certain true belief; and it is for this very reason that he does not believe that not-*p* while believing that *p*.

The central point here cannot be overemphasized. The self-deceiver's manipulation of data is motivated by wants; but it does not depend for its 'motivatedness' upon the subject's believing (or having believed) the negation of the proposition that he is self-deceived in believing. Because, for example, he takes a certain datum, *d*, to count against *p*, which proposition he wants to be the case, he may intentionally or unintentionally shift his attention away from d whenever he has thoughts of d; but to do this he need not believe that p is false.

One might suppose that the paradox does emerge at another level. It may be suggested, for example, that the person who positively or negatively misinterprets data, *intentionally misinterprets* the data, and that to do this he must believe that the data *do* count strongly against p, while both interpreting them *not* to count strongly against p and *believing* his interpretation. There is little reason, however, to suppose that this must be the case. Misinterpretation can often be explained on the weaker and unproblematic supposition that the agent recognizes or believes that the data *might be taken* to count strongly against p; or, given his emotional condition, he might simply see the data a certain way. In the same vein, we may wish to say, in some cases, that the agent intentionally interprets the data as he does—for example, that he self-consciously sets out to put a charitable construction upon the data, and intentionally does so. But this is not to say that he intentionally *misinterprets* the data, that is, that he misinterprets them with the intention of doing so. Even intentional misinterpretation, however, does not entail the paradox at issue. If an agent believes that his evidence about p supports p more strongly than not-p, there may be nothing to prevent him from attempting to construe the data as having the opposite result. By representing the data to himself in a certain way, he may even succeed in getting himself to believe that they do provide a better case for not-p than for p. But this does not entail his simultaneously holding the contradictory beliefs that the data support p more strongly than not-p and that they support not-p more strongly than p. Rather, his presenting the data to himself in a certain favored light, or his rehearsing an emotionally attractive construction of the data, may have the result that he both abandons his former belief about the weight of the data and forms the belief that the data warrant the belief that not-p.

It should be noticed that to explain a self-deceptive bit of data-manipulation by observing that S wanted it to be the case that p and believed that certain data counted, or might be taken to count, against (or for) p is not to explain by citing his *reason* for manipulating data. A want/belief pair constitutes a reason for action only when the belief-element is a belief to the effect that an action of a certain type is (or might be) conducive to achieving what is wanted. (E.g., my desire to purchase a salami and my belief that I may purchase one at Tony's constitute a reason for me to go to Tony's.) But the self-deceiver's belief that a certain datum counts against (or for) p, or that it might be taken to count against (or for) p, is not a belief about the conduciveness of some behavior to the achievement of the object of a desire. Intentional self-deceptive behavior—for example, an intentional shifting of one's attention away from q—is behavior engaged in for a reason. But the belief-element in the reason is not of the form 'datum d counts (or datum d might be taken to count) against p.' Rather, the self-deceiver who intentionally shifts his attention away from q wants to achieve something, and believes that he may do so by shifting his attention—for example, he wants to concentrate on his work and believes that he will do so only if he refrains from thinking about q. Similarly, the woman who intentionally takes an 'upbeat' approach in interpreting the data concerning her husband's fidelity may want to exercise the virtue of charity and believe that she may do so in this way.[12]

This is not to deny, of course, that self-deception may sometimes be served by self-deception. For example, the man who is self-deceived that p as a partial consequence of his intentionally refraining from thinking about d may have avoided thinking about d partly as a result of his believing, *owing to self-deception*, that he could best arrive at the truth about p after a good night's sleep. However, there is no need to suppose that the paradox at issue must emerge in this (or some other) prior self-deception. The agent's being self-deceived about how best to arrive at the truth may, for example, result from a motivated focusing on the sound rule of thumb that a well-rested person can think more clearly than a tired one. In short, the argument of this section applies to self-deception that functions in the service of further self-deception as well as to self-deception that does not.

Perhaps it will be objected that the characterization given in conditions 1 through 4 above fails precisely because the subject's being in the doxastic condition in question (i.e., believing that p while believing that not-p) *is* a characteristic of self-deception. We have already seen that the lexical reason for taking this view is a poor one. The only nonlexical reason that I have encountered does not seem significantly stronger. It is the suggestion that the behavior of self-deceived persons typically provides weighty evidence that they simultaneously hold contradictory beliefs. For example, one might suppose that the cancer patient who sincerely asserts that she will not die (of cancer), even though she has been informed independently by several specialists that she will die within one year, nevertheless does not make any serious long-term plans, and even looks into funeral arrangements. Now, I doubt that self-deceived persons *characteristically* engage in the type of conflicting (verbal and nonverbal) behavior imagined. (Indeed, our cancer patient may be influenced by a desire to live as one lives who has no serious worries, which desire might have the result that as long as she remains deceived she consistently lives

[acts] in just this way.) Even if I am wrong in so doubting, however, conflicting behavior itself does not provide strong evidence that self-deceived persons hold inconsistent beliefs. I believe today that I shall complete a draft of this chapter by Monday evening. Nevertheless, I have not requested that our extremely busy departmental typist set aside some time on Tuesday; and, if asked, I would probably say something to the effect that I will definitely have the draft ready for typing by the middle of the week. This does not indicate that, in addition to believing that I shall complete the draft by Monday evening, I also believe that I shall not, complete it by that time. Rather, I hold both the former belief and the belief that there is a significant chance (in the light of past experience) that I shall not be finished by that time. If the self-deceiver does engage in conflicting behavior, this may well be subject to a similar explanation. Although the self-deceived cancer patient believes and sincerely avows that she will not die of cancer, she may believe that the chance that she is wrong is significant enough to warrant looking into funeral arrangements.

One might still suggest that in *some* cases of self-deception a person's nonverbal behavior is *systematically* at odds with his assertions that *p*, and that in *these* cases there is every reason to suppose that, at one and the same time, the person both believes that *p* and believes that not-*p*. However, if a person *consistently* acts as one would act who believes that not-*p*, we have excellent reason to deny that he believes what he asserts. Such a case is analogous to that of the person who insists that, all things considered, it is better to do *A* than to do *B* and who yet, on the many occasions in which he has a choice between *A* and *B*, consistently and freely does *B*. Of such a person we say, not that he is incontinent, but that what he claims is not what he believes.

3. Entering Self-Deception in Retaining a Belief

It will prove useful to turn briefly to another, very common way of entering self-deception—namely, by *retaining* the belief that *p*.[13] Suppose that Sam has believed for many years that his wife, Sally, would never have an affair. In the past, his evidence for this belief was quite good. Sally obviously adored him; she never displayed a sexual interest in another man (in fact, she was a bit of a prude); she condemned extramarital sexual activity; she was secure, and happy with her family life; and so on. However, things recently began to change significantly. Sally is now arriving home late from work on the average of two nights a week; she frequently finds excuses to leave the house alone after dinner; and Sam has been informed by a close friend that Sally has been seen in the company of a certain Mr. Jones at a theater and local lounge. Nevertheless, Sam continues to believe that Sally would never have an affair. Unfortunately, he is wrong. Her relationship with Jones is by no means platonic.

If Sam is now self-deceived in believing that his wife would never have an affair, then he must have entered this condition. And his entering self-deception with respect to the proposition in question plainly does not fall within the scope of the characterization (conditions 1–4) above, since it is not in *acquiring* the belief that Sally would never have an affair that Sam enters self-deception, but rather in *retaining* this belief. However, a quite similar characterization is applicable, and may easily be constructed by the reader on the model given in conditions 1 through 4. More important for our purposes is the point that the types of data-manipulation which may generate self-deception by supporting the *retention* of a belief include the four types mentioned in the preceding section. Positive misinterpretation may be involved in the following way: Sam might reason that if his wife were having an affair, she would not be so obvious about it as to accompany her lover to places which she knows to be frequented by Sam's friends, and that her behavior, consequently, is evidence that she is *not* having an affair. Or he might negatively misinterpret the data, and even solicit Sally's aid in doing so by asking her for an 'explanation' of the data or by suggesting for her approval some innocuous hypothesis about her behavior. That there is scope in this case for selective focusing is obvious and not at all in need of comment. And even selective evidence-gathering, which may seem most appropriate to C, is capable of playing an important role. For example, Sam may set out to conduct an impartial investigation of the matter, but, due to the pertinent desire, locate less accessible evidence that she is not having an affair while overlooking more readily attainable support for the contrary conclusion.

It should also be noted that the case just described—a typical example of self-deception—is easily explained in these ways without supposing that Sam is in the paradoxical doxastic condition of believing that not-p while believing that p. Rather than appeal to hypotheses of multiple selves, unconscious knowledge, and the like, we may simply observe that there is nothing in the description of the case, nor in a plausible explication of it, that warrants the supposition that Sam holds contradictory beliefs.

4. Intentional Self-Deception

The 'ordinary' self-deception that I have been considering may profitably be contrasted with a straightforward case of intentional self-deception.

Attention to the latter should make it clearer just how different ordinary self-deception is from its intentional counterpart. But I shall also argue that the case to be examined is at most superficially paradoxical, and that there is no good reason to suppose that it involves the subject's being in the peculiar doxastic condition of believing that *p* while believing that not-*p*. I conclude the section with some brief remarks about lying to oneself.

Imagine that Guido believes, mainly on the basis of observed evil, that the Christian God does not exist. He thinks, however, that the existence of God would give his life some purpose or meaning, something which he very much wants; and he believes that the next best thing to living a purposeful, meaningful life is to *believe* that one is. Guido consequently decides to figure out a way of deceiving himself into believing that God exists, so that he may believe that his life has purpose and meaning, and he settles upon a Pascalian program. Let us suppose, finally, that the Christian God does not exist.

If Guido is not constantly focusing on what he is aiming at, I see no good reason to think that he cannot succeed in deceiving himself. After a while, he might find that he enjoys his religious activities; and he may begin to think that he was never really convinced about atheism, and that there is a significant chance that the world's evils are compatible with God's existence. As more time passes, he may become very pleased with himself for having hit upon this plan of 'deceiving himself' (which, of course, he would no longer describe in this way); for, he might think, if he had not done this, he would never have seen the light. He might even suspect that the Almighty had a hand in his decision.

Although this is an atypical case of self-deception, there is no need to suppose that Guido simultaneously believes that *p* is true and believes that *p* is false. Withdrawing his assent from the proposition 'God does not exist' would seem naturally to precede his forming that belief that God does exist. (This is not to say, however, that the supposition that self-deception is *always* intentional does not generate paradox, or at least the need for problematic notions in analyzing the phenomenon. For example, the supposition that there is *intentional* self-deception in our case of the man who, owing to a failure to focus his attention on the data, believes that his wife is not having an affair leads naturally to the further suppositions that he does believe, albeit unconsciously, that his wife is having an affair, and that the [alleged] intention of deceiving himself is therefore to be located at the unconscious level.)

The case of Guido is a case of intentional self-deception; but Guido does not lie to himself, at least in a strict sense of 'lie.' Now, the concept of lying to oneself is not itself problematic. When a stuntman prepares himself for a feat which he knows to be exceedingly dangerous, he may tell himself that there is nothing to fear, with the hope or intention of inducing in himself, if only for the crucial moment, the belief that this is so. The concept becomes more difficult when *success* is built into it. If the stuntman's lie is successful, he forms the belief that there is nothing to fear, even though the lie is told with knowledge that fear *is* warranted. This is not yet to say, however, that he simultaneously believes that p and believes that not-p. When A lies successfully to B, B may not believe the lie *immediately* upon being lied to—he may pause to assess the plausibility of what A has told him. Similarly, the stuntman may not form the belief that there is nothing to fear until some time after he has told himself this. So he may have *abandoned* the relevant true belief in the meantime. What must be added to the concept of successful reflexive lying in order to generate the paradox is that the liar believes the lie *at the moment* at which he lies to himself. How this modified concept can be instantiated is a tantalizing question, and one might be tempted to appeal to such interesting hypotheses as multiple selves or levels of consciousness in attempting to answer it. But we should pause to ask another question: Is there good reason to believe that the concept ever *is* instantiated? If not, then no matter how convincing one's answer to the theoretical question, we lack adequate grounds for thinking that, in answering it, one has explained how some actual phenomenon has occurred.

5. Related Phenomena

The literature on self-deception includes a variety of attempts to distinguish self-deception from such related phenomena as wishful thinking. Where such distinctions are properly drawn, we should certainly expect an adequate analysis of self-deception to permit us to make them. However, there is a tendency to draw these distinctions in such a way as to generate a conception of self-deception which is overly narrow.

Terence Penelhum has argued that if a person does not "know the evidence" against his belief, "we have not self-deception but ignorance" (1964, p. 88; cf. Szabados, 1974, p. 55). However, this depends upon what generates the failure to know (or have) the evidence. Suppose that S has some evidence against his false belief that p, that this evidence is not strong enough to warrant his withdrawing his assent from p, and that, owing to selective evidence gathering (influenced, of course, by the desire that p), he remains ignorant of additional evidence against p, although strong evidence is readily available to him. His ignorance of this data, rather than showing that he is not self-deceived, appears to *contribute* to his self-deception. We may suppose that he is deceived *because* he is ignorant—that is, that if he were not ignorant of the remaining evidence, he would not now be deceived. And since *he* is responsible for this ignorance, and responsible for it through behavior that seems straightforwardly self-deceptive, there is no good reason to think that his ignorance *precludes* self-deception.

Wishful thinking is the phenomenon most often distinguished from self-deception. Bela Szabados, in a paper devoted to locating the distinction, suggests that both the self-deceiver and the wishful thinker hold a false belief, and that both are influenced by a desire or motive of some sort, but that whereas "the self-deceiver fulfills *one* of the conditions for knowledge"—"he has good grounds for thinking that" the believed proposition is false—"the wishful thinker does not have such grounds" (1973, p.205; cf. Szabados 1974, p.61 and 1985, pp.148f.). Now I am not sure that there is just one type of phenomenon to which ordinary speakers of English typically apply the words 'wishful thinking,' and it is not clear to me how one should go about attempting to determine what wishful thinking is. A literal-minded person might talk about wishfully *thinking* that *p*, and observe that one might do this by supposing or imagining for a moment that *p* is true, without *believing* that it is. But, for the purposes of this chapter, I am willing to accept the stipulation that what the wishful thinker wishfully 'does' is to believe falsely that *p*. However, even if this stipulation is correct, it does not follow that beliefs which one is self-deceived in holding can be only nonwishfully held. If there is a distinction between wishful thinking and self-deception, it may simply be that wishful thinking (given the stipulation above) is a species of a genus denoted by the term 'self-deception.' If, for example, Szabados is right in what he says about contrary evidence, it may just be that wishful thinking is a form of self-deception in which, owing to some desire-influenced behavior of an appropriate sort, the self-deceiver lacks good grounds for rejecting the proposition that he is self-deceived in believing. It is true that 'wishful thinking,' unlike 'self-deception' (or, even worse, 'self-deceit'), has a harmless ring upon the ear, one that may bring to mind images of youthful idealism or puppy love. But imagine that it were called instead 'wishful false believing,' which name is quite appropriate if Szabados is right in his explication of the "thinking" involved.

Some instances of self-deception are also cases of strict akratic believing, as I explained in the preceding chapter. Others involve *akrasia* of one form or another. Many instances occupying the intersection of self-deception and strict akratic belief are relatively strong cases of self-deception. The person who is guilty of 'narrow' strict incontinent belief, unlike most of the agents in examples of self-deception presented in this chapter, believes that the evidence constitutes good and sufficient reason for his not believing that p, the proposition that he is self-deceived in believing. This belief about evidence may be held by many 'broad' incontinent believers as well. I concentrated in the present chapter on the weaker (and more common) cases of self-deception in refuting the thesis that self-deception necessarily involves the agent's sinultaneously believing p and believing not-p; for the falsity of this thesis is more easily seen in these cases. But I have also shown that even in instances of intentional self-deception the agent need not be in this paradoxical doxastic condition. And in Chapter 8 I argued that an agent may hold that there is good and sufficient reason for his believing that p without believing that p.

6. Conclusion

On the account developed and defended in this chapter, the person who enters self-deception typically does not do so by getting himself to believe something that he knows or believes to be false. Thus, the paradox described in Section 1 is resolved, at least for ordinary cases of self-deception. We have seen as well that even atypical, intentional self-deception need not be paradoxical. This is not to say, however, that self-deception is not a troublesome phenomenon. What should bother us about it is roughly what should bother us about akratic action. In both cases there is (typically) a display of desire-influenced irrationality.[14] The persons who acts incontinently in doing A, acts against his better judgment due to a contrary desire; and the self-deceived person, again due to desire, typically *believes* against his 'better evidence,' or against better evidence which he would have had, or could easily have acquired, if it were not for the desire in question.[15] That both types of irrationality occur is, to my mind, obvious. Exactly *how* they occur is not; but surely one important consideration is that the causal influence of our desires is not wholly under our control. I have given some indication of the ways in which our desires may lead us to believe against our 'better evidence.' And if I am right, we may leave the focal puzzles of the present chapter behind us in seeking to understand ordinary self-deception, and give our attention to the influence of desire on belief-formation and belief-retention.

  One final point is in order. We have noticed that just as the incontinent agent typically does not act with the *intention* of behaving incontinently, we typically do not enter self-deception as a result of an *intention* to deceive ourselves. But in neither case does the absence of the intention remove the person from the arena of blame. We think it right to blame people for their incontinent actions; and one is often properly blamed both for unintentional deceivings (when, e.g., one should have been more careful to get the facts straight, or to express them clearly) and for *being* deceived or taken in—even when the person deceived, or the person by whom one is deceived, is oneself.

10

Strategies of Self-Deception and the Strategy Paradox

The point of departure of the present chapter is what I shall call the *strategy paradox* of self-deception. In general, *A* cannot successfully employ a deceptive strategy against *B* if *B* knows *A*'s intention and plan. This seems plausible as well when *A* and *B* are the same person. A potential self-deceiver's knowledge of his intention and strategy would seem typically to render them ineffective. On the other hand, the suggestion that self-deceivers typically successfully execute their self-deceptive strategies *without* knowing what they are up to may seem absurd; for, an agent's effective execution of his plans seems generally to depend on his cognizance of them and their goals. So how, in general, can an agent deceive himself by employing a self-deceptive strategy?

This paradox is patterned to some degree after the doxastic paradox of self-deception examined in the preceding chapter. The central difference for present purposes is that the focus now is on, not the simultaneous holding of two beliefs whose propositional contents are mutually contradictory, but rather the task, project, or activity of deceiving oneself. Though the doxastic paradox has occupied center stage in the literature on self-deception, its companion paradox has been a source of theoretical perplexity[1] and merits separate treatment.

My formulation of the strategy paradox will suggest a straightforward resolution to Freudians and others who are attracted to the idea that human beings are (partially) composed of subagents capable of intentional behavior. The resolution, of course, is this: One mental subsystem (the deceiver) employs the strategy on another mental subsystem (the deceived) without the latter knowing, or even suspecting, what the former is doing. There is a standard objection: This is not *self*-deception, but the deception of one entity by another (e.g., Foss 1980, p.239; Sorensen 1985, p.66).

138

However, I shall not take this line of attack. Rather, I shall criticize arguments for the thesis that self-deception depends upon the existence of mental subagents, and I shall defend a resolution of the strategy paradox that does not involve the postulation of entities of this sort.

The reader of the preceding chapter may already have surmised what shape my resolution will take. There is an obvious problem—though not an insoluble one—with the idea that an agent may effectively employ a self-deceptive strategy with the intention of deceiving himself. If he knows what he is up to, how can his project succeed? Can an intentional project of this sort be anything short of self-defeating? However, if the argument of the preceding chapter is successful, people who deceive themselves typically do not do so *with the intention* of deceiving themselves. Nevertheless, self-deception is *strategic* in this sense: When we deceive ourselves, we generally do so by engaging in potentially self-deceptive behavior such as positive or negative misinterpretation, selective focusing, or selective evidence-gathering. Behaviors of this sort are, in a broad sense of the term, *strategies* of self-deception. But if they are engaged in without the intention of deceiving oneself, if they are not guided or monitored by that intention, they might not undermine themselves. This is the possibility that I shall explore here.

The strategy paradox, as I said, is my point of departure; resolving it is not my only major concern in this chapter. I also address two related questions. What can motivate the employment of particular strategies of self-deception? And how do these strategies work? In answering these questions—particularly the latter—I draw upon some experimental work in psychology.

At the end of the preceding chapter, I suggested that to understand self-deception we must attend to the influence of motivation upon the formation and retention of beliefs. Thus, the present chapter. I shall concentrate again on belief-formation; but the central points made below are easily applied to the retention of beliefs as well.

1. Mental Partitioning?

In Chapter 6 I had occasion to comment briefly on the 'functional theory' of mental partitioning recently developed by David Pears (1984, Ch.5).[2] This theory yields a straightforward resolution of the strategy paradox by dividing the agent's mind into two systems, only one of which is aware that the strategy is being employed. Earlier I argued that seeking a general explanation of akratic action in this theory (which Pears does *not* do) is an exercise in overkill. It will become clear in subsequent sections that an attempt to resolve the strategy paradox by appealing to Pearsian partitioning faces the same problem. The primary purpose of the present section is to explain how Pears's functional theory of mental systems may be applied to the paradox and to give the reader some sense of the difficulty of the task that the theory is intended to accomplish.

According to Pears's functional theory of systems:

> There is a schism whenever there is irrationality that the person is competent to avoid. . . . For if someone is competent to avoid a piece of irrationality, the cautionary belief will be somewhere within him, and, if it does not intervene and stop the irrationality, it will be assigned to a sub-system automatically by the functional criterion (1984, pp.69f.; cf. pp.72, 84).

The "cautionary belief" is a belief to the effect that, given one's evidence, it would be irrational to believe that p (pp.68, 69, 83). "The presence of the cautionary belief somewhere within the person follows from the assumption that he is competent to avoid the particular piece of irrationality" (p.72). And its placement exclusively in a subsystem in a case in which it fails to "stop the irrationality" is entailed by Pears's principle of partitioning, namely, that a mental element is assigned "exclusively to a sub-system if and only if it failed to interact in a rational way with an element in the main system which it ought to interact in a rational way" (p.105, cf. pp.97f.).[3]

A fundamental problem with this tidy model lies in the supposition that S is competent to avoid a particular bit of irrationality only if he has the pertinent "cautionary belief." Once it is supposed that the cautionary belief is present in all cases of irrationality that the agent is competent to avoid, a partitioning hypothesis does become attractive. How, one might ask, could an agent believe that it is irrational to believe that p and yet believe that p, unless these beliefs are somehow kept out of contact with one another? (For one answer, see Ch. 8.2 above.) However, the competence to avoid irrationality does *not* depend upon the presence of the cautionary belief. For example, Sid, in the Sid/Roz case of Chapter 9.2, may have been competent to avoid deceiving himself into believing that Roz loved him even though (we may suppose) he lacked the cautionary belief that it would be irrational to believe that Roz loved him. For, we may suppose, he was capable of seeing that his interpretation of the data was strongly biased and of rejecting his interpretation accordingly.

If he was capable of seeing this, why didn't he see it? This is reminiscent of a familiar question about the agent of an akratic action: If he was able to act in accordance with his better judgment, why did he not do so? Plausible answers to the latter question should, by now, be equally familiar. And the former question may properly be given a similar response. It was, we may suppose, within Sid's power to ask himself whether his interpretation of Roz's behavior toward him was unduly influenced by his desire for her love, to test his favored interpretation on trusted friends, and the like. And measures such as these may have been effective in preventing self-deception. He may have been so fascinated by the prospect of being loved by Roz that he *did* not take these measures. But this does not entail that he was *unable* to take them, any more than my having become so engrossed in the composition of this section that I lost track of the time and was consequently late for a meeting entails that I was unable to keep track of the time and to arrive at the meeting at the appointed hour.

Can Pears's functional theory be reconstructed to resolve the strategy paradox without postulating in all cases the existence of a cautionary belief? On Pears's view, the subsystem at work in cases of avoidable motivated irrational belief is "built around" the desire that the main system "form the irrational belief" (1984, p.87). Moreover, it is "aware of the main system's problem, which is that it has evidence pointing to an unwelcome conclusion. Also, if the solution of the problem is at all complicated, it must be aware of the weaknesses of the main system, in order to be able to adjust its strategy to them" (p.89). These claims about the awareness and nuclear desire of the subsystem suggest a way of distinguishing between subsystem and main system that does not hinge on the presence of a cautionary belief. The subsystem—"an internally rational centre of agency" (p.104, cf. p.87) that is "organized like a person"—has a *plan* that the main system does not have, namely, a strategy for getting the main system to form the favored belief.

If the main system is not aware of this plan or strategy, we have a sketch of a solution to the strategy paradox. An agent can successfully employ a strategy to deceive himself in roughly the same way that one agent can successfully employ a strategy to deceive another; for, in the intrapersonal case, the strategy is housed in, and executed by, one internally rational center of agency, and the favored belief is formed by another, unsuspecting system within the agent.

I shall reject this solution in the following section after examining a certain class of strategies of self-deception. Before I turn to these issues, something should be said about what Pears is trying to accomplish in his functional theory of systems and about the difficulty of the task.

Pears's aim is to provide a perfectly general psychological explanation of the formation of motivated irrational beliefs that the subject was competent to avoid forming. He attempts to achieve this universality, as he says, *by definition* (p.84). "A system's boundary is simply defined as a line across which some element in a person's psyche fails to produce its normal rational effect on the elements that control his daily life." On Pears's view, there must be such a boundary in all cases of irrationality of the sort in question; for, if there were not, the cautionary belief would have produced its normal effect—doxastic rationality.

Where, then, does the *explanation* of doxastic irrationality lie? Not, as Pears observes, in the "main system." For, all that his functional theory "tells us about the main system is that the irrationality occurred there, because the cautionary belief did not intervene effectively" (p.85). Nor does it lie in some hypothetical "psychological features of the frontier between the two systems." For, their separation consists only in the cautionary belief's failing to perform its normal function (p.87). There is, Pears says, "only one possible remaining source of the explanatory power of the functional theory and that is the sub-system itself." Ironically, the explanation that it yields is a *reasons-explanation:* The subsystem "wants the main system to form the irrational belief and it is aware that it will not form it, if the cautionary belief is allowed to intervene. So with perfect rationality it stops its intervention."

This explanation is intended to be taken quite literally. We could try to treat it as a figurative statement of the idea that there is something nonagential in the agent that renders his cautionary belief ineffective. But on Pears's view, at least against the background of a causal model of psychological events, it is true by definition that *something* renders a pertinent cautionary belief ineffective in an instance of (avoidable) motivated irrational belief. The crucial question is: *What* renders the cautionary belief ineffective? And Pears's answer is the subjectively rational behavior of the subsystem. "The essential point" of Pears's functional theory, as he emphasizes, "is that the sub-system is an internally rational centre of agency" (p.104). The subsystem *is* an agent that has, and acts for, reasons.

This is surely a drastic hypothesis. And only a very difficult question could have led Pears to embrace it. The question is this: *How* do an agent's desires result in his forming irrational beliefs that he is competent to avoid? Or rather, since Pears sets himself the task of finding a perfectly general psychological answer, it is this: What psychological element(s) mediate(s) between our desires and our avoidable irrational beliefs, when the former are causes of the latter?

Now, even if it were true that in any case of irrationality of this sort a cautionary belief is present and housed in an agential subsystem that renders it ineffective, Pears would have given only a very sketchy answer to the questions just articulated. Explaining doxastic irrationality in Pears's fashion is rather like explaining how one football team held another scoreless by saying that the former strategically rendered all of the latter's scoring attempts ineffective. The football fan wants much more than this. He wants to be told *how* team *A* rendered team *B*'s attempts ineffective. And one might start to construct an answer by identifying the strategies (defenses) that *A* employed in particular situations.

One might similarly attempt to flesh out Pears's explanation of motivated doxastic irrationality by identifying major strategies employed by his internally rational, agential subsystems. But this suggests another explanatory approach. Might not one *start* by identifying strategies of motivated doxastic irrationality and then ask what must be true about the psychological condition of the people who successfully employ them? One who takes this approach *might* find that there is no need to postulate Pearsian subsystems to explain the effective employment of these strategies.

In fact, this is close to Pears's own approach. He examines strategies of motivated irrational belief-formation first and then turns to the functional theory of systems. Pears explicitly claims that one of the general strategies that he identifies can only be ascribed to "a sub-system within the person" (p.63). And he commits himself to the view that "there is a schism whenever there is irrationality that the person is competent to avoid, even if it is a low degree of irrationality" (p.69). The issue of strategies is examined in detail in the following sections.

2. Internal Biasing Strategies: The Paradox Resolved

Strategies of self-deception are divisible into two general types: those constituted by the manipulation of data that one already has; and those that consist in the agent's controlling (to some degree) which data he acquires. I shall refer to them respectively as *internal-biasing* and *input-control* strategies.[4]

Two of the strategies identified in the preceding chapter fall squarely under the first heading. They are positive and negative misinterpretation. Selective focusing or attending is also a strategy of the first main type, when the agent is selectively focusing on, or attending to, data that he already has. However, when one only skims articles defending a certain political program that one despises, one may, as a result of one's level of attention, simply not encounter certain pertinent data. In such a case, one's attentional activity is a form of input-control; and, in some instances, the activity may contribute to self-deception.

Input-control strategies are divisible into two major subspecies. First, there are the strategies that operate upon data already present in the world, for example, selective evidence-gathering and (sometimes) selective focusing or attending. Second, there are strategies that control the input of data by *generating* data. An important strategy of this sort is what I shall call "acting as if." It is discussed in Section 4.

Another set of distinctions will also prove useful here. In any case of the employment of a self-deceptive strategy, we must distinguish among the following: (1) the nonintentional employment of the strategy (e.g., nonintentionally focusing selectively on data supportive of *p*); (2) the intentional employment of the strategy (e.g., intentionally focusing selectively on data supportive of *p*); and (3) the intentional employment of the strategy with the intention of deceiving oneself (e.g., intentionally focusing on data supportive of *p* with the intention of deceiving oneself into believing that *p*).

Now, Pears maintains that internal-biasing strategies can only be ascribed to a subsystem (p.63). Even if this is true, it does not follow that the strategy must be assigned to a Pearsian subsystem—that is, an internally rational subagent that has, and acts for, reasons. In the present section I shall argue that weaker hypotheses can account for the effective manipulation or biasing of data that the person already has. I shall start by summarizing some results of recent work on the etiology of 'cold' or unmotivated irrational belief and then show how they may be applied to the explanation of the *motivated* biasing of information that a subject already has. The upshot is a resolution of the strategy paradox as it applies specifically to internal-biasing strategies. Input-control strategies are examined in the following two sections.

Richard Nisbett and Lee Ross (1980) have identified a number of common sources of unmotivated irrational belief. Four are described below. These are the more illuminating for present purposes.

SOME SOURCES OF UNMOTIVATED IRRATIONAL BELIEF

1. *Vividness of Information:* The vividness of a datum for an individual is often a function of his interests, the concreteness of the datum, its "imagery-provoking" power, or its sensory, temporal, or spatial proximity (Nisbett & Ross, p.45). Vivid data are more likely to be recognized, attended to, and recalled than more pallid data. As a result, vivid data tend to have a disproportional influence on the formation and retention of beliefs.[5]

2. *The Availability Heuristic:* When people make judgments about the frequency, likelihood, or causation of an event, "they often may be

influenced by the relative availability of the objects or events, that is, their accessibility in the processes of perception, memory, or construction from imagination" (Nisbett & Ross, p.18). Thus, for example, a subject may mistakenly believe that the number of English words beginning with '*r*' is significantly higher than the number having '*r*' in the third position, because he finds it much easier to produce words on the basis of a search for their first letter (see Tversky & Kahnemann, 1973). Similarly, attempts to locate the cause(s) of an event are significantly influenced by manipulations that focus one's attention on a potential cause (Nisbett & Ross, p.22; Taylor & Fiske, 1975, 1978). "By altering actors' and observers' perspectives through video tape replays, mirrors, or other methods, one can correspondingly alter the actors' and observers' causal assessments" (Nisbett & Ross, p.22).[6]

3. *The Confirmation Bias:* When testing a hypothesis, people tend to search, in memory and in the world, more often for confirming than for disconfirming instances and to recognize the former more readily (Nisbett & Ross, pp.181f.).[7] This is true even when the hypothesis is only a tentative one (as opposed, e.g., to a belief of one's that one is testing). The implications of this tendency for the retention and formation of beliefs are obvious.

4. *Tendency to Search for Causal Explanations:* People tend to search for causal explanations of events (Nisbett & Ross, pp.183–186).[8] On a plausible view of the macroscopic workings of the world, this is as it should be. But given (1) and (2) above, the causal explanations upon which we so easily hit in ordinary life may often be illfounded; and, given (3), one is likely to endorse and retain one's first hypothesis much more often than one ought. Furthermore, ill-founded causal explanations can influence future inferences.[9]

It requires little imagination to see how the points just made may function in explanations of particular *motivated* irrational beliefs. For example, data may be rendered more vivid as a consequence of the apparent support that they offer for a proposition that the subject wishes to be true. And since vivid data are more likely to be recalled, they tend to be more 'available.' Similarly, motivation, via its influence on vividness, can affect which hypotheses—causal or otherwise—occur to us first. To be sure, Nisbett and Ross, like many of the psychologists whose work they cite in support of their conclusions, maintain that the influence of motivation on doxastic irrationality is not nearly as pervasive as some (e.g., some dissonance theorists) would have us believe.[10] But they do admit that "many inferential errors . . . can be traced to motivational or emotional causes" (1980, p.228).

Let us return now to Pears's contention that strategies of manipulating or biasing information that is already "in the mind" can be ascribed only to a subsystem. Again, three of the strategies mentioned in the preceding chapter fall into this category: positive and negative misinterpretation and (sometimes) selective focusing. I shall argue that a 'normal' agent (as opposed to a Pearsian subagent) may engage effectively in any of these activities.

I begin with selective focusing. Suppose that, as a result of his selectively focusing on evidence supportive of p, S comes to hold the irrational belief that p. Must we ascribe the selective focusing to a Pearsian subsystem? Surely not; for the focusing may not even be intentional. Perhaps, because S wants it to be the case that p, certain evidence that he has for p is much more vivid or salient for him than his opposing evidence, with the result that his attention is drawn to the former at the expense of the latter.

Suppose instead that S's selective attending *is* intentional. Perhaps, partially because he wants it to be true that his deceased father loved him, S finds his memories of a seemingly loving father very pleasant to entertain while also finding reflection on memories of a self-absorbed, uninterested father quite unpleasant. He may decide consequently to ignore the latter and to focus on the former when he finds himself thinking about his father or their relationship. In this way, he may gradually undercut the impact of the negative memorial evidence while increasing the salience of the evidence for the favored hypothesis. And he may consequently come to hold the (epistemically) irrational belief that his father did love him. But notice that it is S himself, and not an agential subsystem, that is intentionally focusing his attention on the pleasant memories. Again, there is no need to suppose that a Pearsian subsystem is at work.

Consider next a case in which negative misinterpretation plays a central role in S's deceiving himself about p. Tony, a high-school baseball player, is feeling a bit low because his friend Timmy was elected to the all-star team while he was not. He would like it to be true that he is as good a player as Timmy and he finds himself wondering whether this is so. He knows that Timmy's batting statistics for the year are significantly better. Timmy batted .325, hit 12 homeruns, and knocked in 40 runs, whereas Tony's figures were, respectively, .301, 8, and 32. But he decides that his midseason slump and a few bad breaks (e.g., the umpire in the Bobcats' game robbed him of a three-run homer by calling it foul) account for the difference. At the same time, he ignores Timmy's bad luck and the latter's terrible slump early in the season. Moreover, though Timmy's fielding percentage is slightly better than Tony's, Tony convinces himself that this is due to his playing a more difficult position than Timmy. (They play left and right field, respectively.) Finally, although Tony readily admits that Timmy had always been the better player in previous seasons, he judges (not necessarily irrationally) that the present season is the crucial one for deciding the issue. Thus, he comes to believe that he is every bit as good a player as Timmy.

Tony's self-deception may be rendered intelligible without the assistance of the strong hypothesis that a Pearsian subsystem generated the irrational belief in a 'main system.' The strategy that Tony employs in negatively misinterpreting the significance of the difference between his statistics and Timmy's has two main components. (1) He finds an explanation of the gap between his figures and Timmy's that seemingly has nothing to do with his (Tony's) proficiency as a ballplayer.[11] (2) He ignores the fact that central mitigating elements in the explanation—Tony's slump and bad luck—have very similar counterparts in the case of Timmy. (If it were not for the latter's slump, his statistics would have been significantly more impressive than they were.) The Pearsian hypothesis is required only if the successful employment of this two-pronged strategy somehow depends upon its not having the same agent and patient. It is *possible* that there is a subagent that wants some other system in Tony to believe that Tony is as good as Timmy and consequently intentionally causes that system to find (1)'s explanation and to ignore (2)'s fact. But we may suppose instead—rather more conservatively—that Tony's wish leads *him* to find the explanation and to ignore the fact. Because he wants it to be the case that he is as good a ballplayer as Timmy, the hypothesis that he is may be more salient for Tony. And certain 'supporting' data—for example, his own slump and bad breaks—are likely to be more vivid in memory simply because his initial, direct experience of them, given his interest in being a good ball player, was much more vivid than his experience of Timmy's slump and misfortunes. Moreover, if Tony's hypothesis seems plausible to him, given the data that he considers, he may be satisfied that it is correct and consequently not proceed to search for data that would similarly enhance his assessment of Timmy's proficiency.[12] Of course, Tony's wish may be a contributing cause not only of his locating and entertaining the favored hypothesis but also of the perceived plausibility of that hypothesis.

This is not to say that Tony's irrational belief was inevitable—that he could not have avoided forming this belief. One might suppose that when mechanisms of 'cold' irrational belief work in conjunction with motivational elements, the doxastic agent is at the mercy of forces beyond his control. However, this is to take the image of combined forces too seriously. Indeed, I suspect that when motivation activates a cold mechanism, the ordinary agent is more likely to detect bias in his thinking than he would be if motivation were not involved; and detection facilitates control. The popular psychology of the industrialized Western world certainly owes a great deal more to Freud than to the attribution theorists; and for members of that world, a thought-biasing 'wish' is likely to be more salient than, for example, a 'cold' failure to attend to base-rate information.

Rather than trouble the reader with yet another story about motivated irrational belief—this time involving positive misinterpretation—I shall turn to a more general issue. A non-Pearsian account of the functioning of positive misinterpretation in a particular case may easily be constructed along the lines just sketched.

How should the strategy paradox be resolved if we do not resort to a Pearsian partitioning hypothesis? A central theme in the preceding chapter suggests one approach, and the suggestion is reinforced by some of the points just made. I argued in Chapter 9 that when we deceive ourselves we typically do not do so intentionally. If this is right, and if self-deceptive strategies are effectively used in these typical cases, it is a mistake to attempt to understand their effective use on the model of the effective use of strategies in ordinary cases of interpersonal deception. For in standard cases of interpersonal deception, the agent employs deceptive strategies *with the intention* of deceiving the patient. To deceive oneself by means of a self-deceptive strategy (e.g., selective focusing or positive misinterpretation), one need not employ the strategy with the intention of deceiving oneself. As we have just seen, internal-biasing strategies of self-deception need not be guided by this intention to result in the agent's holding a favored belief. Pears's fundamental mistake was to suppose that this sort of guidance is required. Self-deceptive strategies may exploit cold mechanisms of irrational belief-formation, mechanisms that do not depend upon intentional guidance for their effectiveness.

So how, in general, can an agent deceive himself by employing a deceptive strategy?[13] This is the question with which I opened this chapter. We can answer it, if we can answer the following three questions:

1. How can S's employing X result in his believing that p?
2. How can S's desiring that p motivate him to employ X?
3. How can S's employment of X, motivated in the manner that it is, fail to be self-defeating?

In the case of the internal-biasing strategies just discussed, answers are readily accessible. First, S's biased interpretation or selective attention to data may exploit sources of cold irrational belief-formation. They can have a significant impact, for example, upon the availability and vividness of data. And the former strategy is well-suited to exploit the 'confirmation bias': Biased misinterpretation may suggest a favored hypothesis, thereby promoting a biased search for confirmatory data and further misinterpretation. Second, S's desiring that p may motivate biased interpretation or selective attending in a variety of ways. Because S desires that p, certain data that support p may be more salient for S and dominate his attentional field.[14] Alternatively, S's desiring that p may affect the hedonic quality of thoughts about confirmatory and disconfirmatory data, with the result that he decides to focus on the former in preference to the latter. Or S's desire that p may lead him to identify, entertain, and 'test' the hypothesis that p or hypotheses supportive of p.

Finally, although we have seen that even the *intentional* project of deceiving oneself need not be self-defeating, the point that most self-deception is nonintentional makes it easier to see how, in general, the employment of a self-deceptive strategy may fail to undermine itself. When an agent is, for example, manipulating the availability of data with the intention of deceiving himself into believing that p is true, we expect him to realize that the resulting evidential base has been shaped specifically to make it look as though p were true. And it is difficult to see how, given this realization, the data could have a significant impact upon his belief-formation processes at the time. However, when the agent does not intend to deceive himself, this problem does not arise. Even the agent who, for hedonic reasons, *intentionally* focuses selectively on data supportive of a favored hypothesis need have no realization whatever that he is shaping an evidential base for a favored belief; and cold mechanisms of belief-formation may eventually generate a predictable result.[15]

3. Some Input-Control Strategies

In the present section I examine some input-control strategies of self-deception and show how the strategy paradox may be resolved in their case. Again, input-control strategies are divisible into two main types: those that operate on data already present in the world, and those that generate data. The former are sufficiently similar to the internal-biasing strategies just discussed as not to require extended treatment. I briefly indicate how the three questions formulated above about the efficacy and motivation of a self-deceptive strategy may plausibly be answered in the case of selective evidence-gathering and of selective focusing upon the world. In the following section, I turn to data-generating strategies.

It is no mystery how, as a result of one's selectively focusing upon, or gathering, evidence supportive of p, one may come to believe that p. Belief-formation is strongly influenced by the 'availability' of data, that is, their accessibility in perception, memory, or imagination (see Nisbett & Ross, 1980, p.18); and selective focusing and evidence-gathering are likely to have a significant impact on availability. Nor is it difficult to understand how a nonintentional employment of these strategies might be motivated by a desire that p. Nonintentional selective focusing or evidence-gathering is sometimes due to the enhanced salience that certain data (or sources of data) supportive of p have as a result of one's desiring that p. And motivation may lead via social routes to nonintentional selective exposure to data. For example, the seventeen-year-old boy who wants it to be true that he is an important person but lacks the respect of his peers, may find the company of younger adolescents more congenial. And his (hedonically motivated) choice of companions may result in selective exposure to data supportive of the hypothesis that he is an important individual.

Intentional instances of selective focusing or evidence-gathering may be motivated in a variety of ways. In the preceding section, I suggested that one's desiring that p may affect the hedonic quality of attention to pertinent memories, with the result that one decides to focus only on the more pleasant memories. The same point may be made about selective attention to 'external' data. For example, the father who wants it to be true that his new urban environment does not pose a great threat to the welfare of his young children may find it very unpleasant to attend to graphic information about serious local violence and consequently decide to abandon his practice of watching local television news programs. Consider, in a similar vein, a woman who has just been offered a very attractive position in a major university. She wants it to be true that the move would be beneficial not only for her but for her family as well. And her desire influences her adoption of the following decision procedure: First she will seek out important evidence for the favored hypothesis and then she will gather contrary evidence for purposes of comparison. However, after taking the first step, she is so impressed by the evidence—for example, the active cultural scene, better schools for the children—that she intentionally makes only a cursory second-stage effort, and consequently has only a faint appreciation of the costs involved. (Her children, who now walk to school, will need to spend about ninety minutes a day riding buses; though she will receive a modest raise in salary, her family's cost of living will rise by twenty-five percent; the crime rate is astronomical compared to that of her small college town; there is a distinct possibility, in light of recent events, that she will leave her tenured appointment only to be denied tenure a few years hence at the university; etc.)

This brings us to the question about the failure of selective evidence-gathering and focusing to undermine themselves in particular cases. Again, my position is that self-deception is typically nonintentional; and I have no wish to contend that these input-control strategies are capable of promoting intentional self-deception. What I do claim is that by intentionally or nonintentionally engaging in these strategies, one may nonintentionally deceive oneself. And the explanation of the non-self-defeatingness of these strategies in specific instances is the same as that advanced concerning external-biasing strategies in the preceding section. When an agent biases the input of data with the intention of deceiving himself, the self-conscious nature of the project—while he is so engaged—would tend to strip the biased data-base of its power to generate belief. But when there is no such intention, this problem does not arise, and the mechanisms of cold irrational belief-formation may function smoothly.

Notice, finally, that if the argument in this section is successful, there is no need to suppose that selective focusing (upon external data) and selective evidence-gathering can lead to self-deception only if the mind is partitioned along Pearsian lines. The *same* agent may both engage in these activities and be deceived by them.

4. 'Acting as if' and the Cold Water Experiment

One way to exercise control over data-input is to generate data for ourselves. The present section examines a data-generating strategy that I shall call 'acting as if.' An agent's acting as if *p* were the case can generate data supportive of *p* both in a relatively direct, intrapersonal fashion and via a more circuitous social route. We often make inferences about ourselves on the basis of our observation of our own behavior, and by acting as if *p* were the case (e.g., as if one were courageous or kind) one may add to the evidential base. Moreover, by acting as if *p*, an agent may influence others' perceptions and treatment of him, thereby generating for himself social data supportive of *p*. The agent who consistently comports himself confidently in public is likely to be perceived and treated as a confident individual by others who observe his behavior, even if he is not. And their treatment of him may provide him with salient evidence that he is a confident person.

Rather than embark upon a general investigation of 'acting as if' and its operation as an intrapersonal and social strategy of self-deception, I shall focus on an illuminating experimental study recently conducted by George Quattrone and Amos Tversky (1984). In the first part of the discussion my target is a question about agents' beliefs about what they are doing when they are acting as if. Later in the section I turn specifically to the issue of 'acting as if' as a strategy of self-deception.

The bare bones of Quattrone and Tversky's experimental design, which is really quite elegant, are as follows. Thirty-eight undergraduate subjects were first required "to submerge their forearm into a chest of circulating cold water until they could no longer tolerate it" (p.240). They then pedaled an exercycle for one minute. Next came a brief "rest period" during which the subjects were given a "mini-lecture on psychophysics." In the course of the lecture subjects were led to believe that people have either of two different "cardiovascular complexes, referred to as Type 1 and Type 2 hearts" and that shorter and longer life expectancies were associated, respectively, with "increasing degrees" of Type 1 and Type 2 hearts (p.241). Subjects were then assigned randomly to either of two groups. Half "were informed that a Type 1 [unhealthy] heart would increase tolerance to cold water after exercise, whereas a Type 2 [healthy] heart would decrease tolerance" (p.240). The rest were told the opposite (i.e., a Type 1 heart would decrease tolerance to cold water and a Type 2 heart would increase tolerance). Finally, participants were subjected again to the "cold-pressor" trial, after which they completed a brief questionnaire. On the questionnaire, they were asked "to infer whether they were Type 1 or 2" and to answer the following question: "Did you purposely try to alter the amount of time you kept your hand in the water after exercise?" They were also asked "which type of heart had a longer life expectancy, which type they would prefer to be, and which type was able to tolerate cold water longer after exercise than before exercise" (p.241).

The experiment was designed to test the following three hypotheses (p.240):

1. Subjects would shift their tolerance threshold in the direction correlated with health and longevity . . .

2. By and large, subjects will deny that they purposefully tried to shift their tolerance . . .

3. Those subjects who do admit that they had purposefully tried to shift their tolerance would be less likely to infer that they had the preferred Type 2 heart than would subjects who deny the attempt to shift.

Each of these hypotheses received considerable confirmation. First, subjects who were told that decreased tolerance was diagnostic of a healthy heart "showed significantly less tolerance" on the second trial, "whereas subjects in the increase condition showed significantly more tolerance" the second time around (p.242). Twenty-seven of the thirty-eight subjects showed the predicted shift. Second, only nine subjects indicated that they had tried to shift their tolerance. Third, only two of the nine (22%) who admitted this inferred that they had a Type 2 (or 'healthy') heart, whereas twenty of the twenty-nine "deniers" (69%) inferred that they had a Type 2 heart.

How are these data to be explained? It seems clear that many of the subjects did try to "shift their tolerance" in the second trial, and a potential motive is obvious. Assuming that most of the twenty-nine "deniers" were *sincerely* denying having tried to do this, what explains their doxastic condition?[16] Quattrone and Tversky contend that the subjects deceive themselves, and they construe self-deception, following Gur and Sackheim (1979), as a condition in which: (1) the subject "simultaneously holds two contradictory beliefs," one of which he is not aware that he holds; and (2) "the lack of awareness is motivated" (p.239). The subject, they claim, believes both that he "purposefully engaged in the behavior to make a favorable diagnosis" and that he did not do this; and, we are told, his "lack of awareness . . . regarding the former belief is motivated by [his] desire to accept the diagnosis implied by [his] behavior."

I have already challenged the conception of self-deception that Quattrone and Tversky borrow from Gur and Sackheim (Ch.9). What I want to argue now is that the results of the cold water experiment do not warrant the claim that subjects engaged in self-deception of this sort. In particular, I shall contest the contention that "deniers" believed that they "purposefully engaged in the behavior to make a favorable diagnosis."

Quattrone and Tversky do not say why they suppose that deniers had the belief in question. They do not claim that deniers had this belief at the level of awareness *while* they were trying to shift their tolerance and then, in the apparently brief period before filling out the questionnaire, rendered themselves unaware of this belief. Rather, they seem to hold that the deniers were never aware of the belief. The subjects simply "*fail to realize* that they purposefully selected the action in order to make the diagnosis" (p.240, my emphasis). Now, what is to prevent us from supposing that the deniers were effectively motivated to shift their tolerance without believing, at any level, that this is what they were doing? The idea that belief is a byproduct of 'purposeful' action—that whenever one engages in purposeful action one is aware of one's purpose and activity and consequently believes that one is acting for that purpose—is irrelevant here; for the experimenters' supposition, if I am not mistaken, is that the deniers were not aware of what they were doing. And, in any case, we shall see shortly that the byproduct thesis is false. Perhaps, then, Quattrone and Tversky are tacitly assuming that whenever an agent purposefully A-s the belief that he is A-ing for some specified purpose guides his action or in some way helps to explain his behavior. But this is a mistake. It is enough, in the present case, that the agents are more motivated to generate favorable diagnostic evidence than they are not to do so and that they believe (to some degree) that their pulling their hands out of the water earlier/later would constitute such evidence. The motivation and belief can result in purposeful action without their believing, at any level, that they are "purposefully engaged in the behavior to make a favorable diagnosis."

The following cases illustrate the general point that an agent can A for a purpose, P, without believing that he is A-ing for that purpose:

Case 10.1

A weary young mother has a suppressed wish to retaliate against her six-month-old son for waking her up at all hours, and she is well aware that when he cries at night he finds her presence very comforting. The wish and belief in fact explain her effective decision to let him cry for twenty minutes before entering his room, but she does not believe, at any level, that she is retaliating against him. Rather, she thinks that her purpose is simply to train him to fall back asleep on his own.

Case 10.2

A man who is upset by his wife's new career and increasing independence has an unacknowledged wish to make her as unhappy as he is. He realizes that his having an affair would hurt his wife. And this wish and realization go a long way toward explaining the affair that he has just initiated. However, he does not believe, at any level, that he is having the affair to make his wife unhappy. He believes instead that his behavior is due to the extra time that he now has, his need for affection, the attractiveness of the young woman with whom he is involved, and so on.

Case 10.3

A five-year-old is angry with his parents for making him go to kindergarten, and he wishes to repay them for the harm that they have done him. He realizes that they would find bed-wetting quite troubling. And the wish and belief lead him to begin wetting his bed. However, he does not think that he is doing this purposely.

Case 10.4

A woman who is desirous of her parents' love believes that they would love her if she were a successful physician. Consequently, she enrolls in medical school. But she does not believe, at any level, that her desire for her parents' love is in some way responsible for her decision to enroll.

In each of these cases a desire/belief pair results in purposeful action without the agent's believing that he is engaging in the action for the sake of the desired object. To be sure, I *stipulate* that the agents do not have the beliefs in question. My point is that this stipulation does not render the cases incoherent. An agent may *A* in order to *B* without believing that this is what he is doing. My suggestion about the sincere deniers in the cold water experiment is that they similarly do not believe, at any level, that they are attempting to shift their tolerance for diagnostic purposes, nor even that they are attempting to shift their tolerance at all.

I should emphasize that this suggestion in no way depends on the supposition that the sincere deniers are unaware of their motivation to shift their tolerance. Indeed, it seems to me likely that many of them are aware of this motivation. However, from the suppositions (1) that some motivation, *M*, that *S* has for *A*-ing results in his *A*-ing and (2) that *S* is aware that he has this motivation for *A*-ing, it certainly does not follow that *S* is aware (or even believes unconsciously) that he *is A*-ing (in this case, purposely shifting his tolerance). Nor, a fortiori, does it follow that he believes, consciously or otherwise, that he is *A*-ing for reasons having to do with *M*. The agent may believe that *M* has no influence whatever on his behavior, while not holding the converse belief. (Compare Case 10.4 above. The woman may know that her desire for her parents' love provides her with motivation to enroll in medical school without also believing that this motivation is partially responsible for her decision to enroll.)

Now, there is evidence that Quattrone and Tversky's sincere deniers do not have the beliefs at issue—namely, their sincere reports. And there is no evidence that they do have these beliefs. If the beliefs were required, at least at the level of unawareness, to explain their actions, we would have good reason to hold that they had these beliefs. But the beliefs are not required for this purpose. They do not play an indispensable explanatory role. Indeed, it is unclear how the belief that one is "purposefully engaged in the behavior to make a favorable diagnosis" *can* explain one's engaging in this behavior. The *pertinent* belief is this, that holding one's hand in the water for a longer/shorter time than on the first trial would contribute to a favorable diagnosis. But this belief may guide an agent's behavior without his believing that it is—that is, without his believing that he is keeping his hand in the water for a longer/shorter time in order to provide a basis for the desired diagnosis. Moreover, it is unclear what reason we have to suppose that the beliefs postulated by Quattrone and Tversky are required as byproducts of the agents' activity, since it seems evident that agents can engage in purposeful behavior without identifying their purpose. (In this case, they may take their hands out of the water when they do for the diagnostic purpose of shifting their tolerance without realizing that this is why they are removing their hands from the water at the time in question.)[17] To be sure, the subjects' sincere reports are not evidence that they do not have the beliefs at the level of unawareness; for, if they were unaware of these beliefs, the beliefs would be unreportable. But since the beliefs play no explanatory role, and need not arise as byproducts of the agents' behavior, they ought not be postulated.

Quattrone and Tversky reasonably suspect that (many of) the sincere deniers are *self-deceived* in believing that they did not purposefully try to shift their tolerance. They adopt Gur and Sackheim's characterization of self-deception and then interpret their results accordingly. But suppose that they had adopted an alternative account of self-deception, for example, one that approximates my statement in Chapter 9.3 of characteristic and jointly sufficient conditions of a central case of S's entering self-deception in acquiring the belief that p. They could then have held the following: (1) sincere deniers, owing to a desire to live a long, healthy life, were motivated to infer that they had a Type 2 heart; (2) this motivation (in conjunction with a belief that an upward/downward shift in tolerance would constitute evidence for the favored proposition) led them to try to shift their tolerance; (3) this motivation also led them to believe that they were not purposefully shifting their tolerance (and not to believe the opposite). This is compatible with their results and does not involve the unwarranted assumption that the subjects had the true belief (at the level of unawareness) that they purposefully shifted their tolerance.

The question remains *how* the subjects' motivation led them to believe that they did not try to shift their tolerance. One plausible suggestion is anticipated by Quattrone and Tversky:

> The physiological mechanism of pain may have facilitated self-deception in this experiment. Most people believe that heart responses and pain thresholds are ordinarily not under an individual's voluntary control. This widespread belief would protect the assertion that the shift could not have been on purpose, for how does one "pull the strings"? (p.243)

Of course, if the false belief that one did not try to shift one's tolerance is *unmotivated*, one is not self-deceived in holding this belief on my account (and many other accounts) of self-deception. But the inference from the belief about ordinary uncontrollability to the belief that one did not try to alter the amount of time one left one's hand in the water need not be completely cold. For example, a sincere denier's motivation may have rendered the "uncontrollability" belief so salient that it defeated internal cues to the contrary in the belief-forming process. Moreover, the agent may have been capable of recognizing that he was trying to shift his tolerance. (Some experimental subjects did recognize this, of course.)

Thus far, I have not directly addressed the issue of 'acting as if' as a strategy of self-deception. It is not the sincere deniers' acting as if they had Type 2 hearts that leads them to be self-deceived in believing that they did not try to shift their tolerance. *This* belief has another source. But their acting as if may lead them to be self-deceived about another matter. Suppose that some of the sincere deniers who infer from their behavior that they have healthy hearts in fact do not. These subjects have been taken in by their own behavior.

There is a great deal of experimental evidence that we often make inferences about ourselves on the basis of our observation of our own behavior.[18] What I want to suggest now is that this cold tendency may be exploited by motivation in instances of self-deception. The preceding discussion proves quite useful in this connection. For although an agent's believing (consciously) that he is acting as if p in order to provide himself with evidence that p would tend to undermine the project, we have seen that an agent can be ignorant of what is motivating him to act as if. In fact, this meets the most difficult challenge involved in understanding how acting as if can lead to self-deception. For there is nothing mysterious about our tendency to form beliefs—including false beliefs—about ourselves on the basis of our observation of our own behavior; and it is not difficult to see why someone may be motivated to act as if p by a desire that p.

Here are some examples of motivation to act as if: (1) An agent believes that he can cultivate in himself the trait of kindness (or self-confidence, courage, etc.) by acting as if he were already possessed of the trait. Given this belief, if he wants to become a kind person, he has a reason to act as if he were kind. (2) A person who values a trait or attitude that he believes he lacks may take pleasure in actions of his that are associated with the trait, however infrequent they may be, because they indicate to him that he is making some progress. He may consequently have hedonic motivation to act as if he had the trait or attitude in question. (3) A person who is dissatisfied with a situation that he thinks would be difficult to correct—for example, the unhappy state of his marriage—may act as if he is content in order to make his situation more bearable, or to make it easier to postpone coming to a decision on the matter.[19]

Consider the following case. Jack, a high-school sophomore, would love to be in love. He has a steady girlfriend, Jill, whose company he enjoys very much, but it would be an exaggeration to say that he loves her. Nevertheless, Jack's fascination with the idea of being in love leads him to treat Jill as if he loved her. He constantly phones her, sends her cute little gifts and letters, expresses a deep concern for her happiness and welfare, and so on. And he infers from his behavior that he does love Jill.

In this case, Jack exercises control over data-input by generating data for himself. He does not intend to deceive himself into believing that he is in love with Jill, but this is what he does. He is taken in by his own behavior, behavior motivated by a desire that the favored hypothesis be true. Though the most readily available data support this hypothesis, someone who knows Jack well (e.g., his mother) and is familiar with the fascination that the idea of being in love holds for him may well believe that Jack is merely quite fond of Jill. Indeed, if Jack himself were made to consider the latter hypothesis, he might come to the same conclusion.

As I mentioned earlier, one can also generate 'social' evidence for a favored hypothesis by acting as if the hypothesis were true. In the preceding example, for instance, many of those who observe Jack's behavior, including Jill, might conclude that he is in love; and their subsequent treatment of Jack may provide him with additional evidence that he loves Jill. They may, for example, express to him their wish that they loved someone as much as he loves Jill. What I have called the social strategy of acting as if does not raise any new problems, and I shall not give it separate treatment.

5. Conclusion

This chapter had two interrelated goals: to resolve the strategy paradox and to illuminate the *process* of self-deception. The second was the more fundamental of the two, since the resolution offered hinged upon the discussion of the etiology of beliefs that agents are self-deceived in holding. However, it would have been a mistake to give the etiological investigation a purely subordinate role. Thus, I took matters further, especially in Section 4, than was necessary to resolve the paradox.

In developing the resolution advanced here, I rejected an alternative resolution involving the postulation of subagents capable of intentional behavior. My quarrel is not with the idea that the mind is composed of subsystems, but rather with the hypothesis that some of the subsystems are agents of intentional actions. This, I suggested, is a drastic hypothesis, and I argued that we can understand self-deception without it.

Part of the attraction of subagents is that their activities render self-deception and akratic action explicable on traditional belief-desire models of action-explanation. Even if the *person*[20] believes or acts irrationally, the etiology of the belief or action centrally involves the workings of a subagent that behaves rationally in light of its beliefs and desires. However, I argued earlier that a psychological model that gives beliefs and desires an important explanatory role may yield adequate explanations of irrational actions without relying on the hypothesis of intentional subagency. And in the present chapter I showed that strategies of self-deception do not depend for their efficacy upon intentional execution and monitoring by a subagent.

§

Conclusion

Much undoubtedly remains to be said about the problems and phenomena examined in this book and about their bearing upon other important philosophical issues. One promising research project is a full-scale investigation of the implications of motivated irrational behavior for our understanding of *rational* behavior. I have shown that standard belief-desire models of action-explanation cannot adequately explain subjectively rational, continent action performed in the face of competing motivation, and I sketched a model of action-explanation that accommodates both incontinent and continent action. But this may only scratch the surface. For example, motivated irrationality seems to raise serious difficulties for some traditional decision theories. Can the rationality of a decision be assessed solely in terms of the maximization of subjective expected utility, if our values or desires sometimes rest on irrational self-deception or akratic reasoning?

Another possibility worth investigating concerns autonomy. One approach to explicating the notion would be to ask what must be added to self-control, in the sense developed in Chapter 4, to yield autonomy. The autonomous or self-ruled agent would seem to be self-controlled in my sense. But even effective self-control, as we saw, is not sufficient for autonomy. The self-controlled agent whose subjectively rational decisive better judgments rest on values generated and maintained by brainwashing is, ultimately, heteronomous.

I am not suggesting that an attempt to understand irrational action and belief must be justified by its fruitfulness vis-à-vis other important philosophical issues. The suggestion seems to me patently false. Irrationality poses challenging and weighty theoretical problems in its own right. For this claim, my best argument is this book.

§

Notes

CHAPTER 1

1. Euripides may have had Socrates in mind here. See Guthrie (1971, p.258).

2. Grounds for the parenthetical qualification are found in Bratman (1984).

3. The issue of subjectively irrational action is complicated by the possibility of subjectively irrational judgments (see Ch.4). Suppose that an agent deceives himself into judging that, all things considered, it is best not to do B, but that he freely and intentionally does B. Is his doing B subjectively irrational even if, in the absence of self-deception, he would have judged his doing B best, all things considered? I am inclined to say that it is. It is irrational from the point of view of his own all-things-considered better judgment, even if it is not irrational from the perspective of the collection of his pertinent nonakratic values, desires, and beliefs as a whole.

4. I am assuming that he does not hold at t an overriding (or equally weighty) judgment that it would be better not to do A at t.

5. On action that is derivatively akratic, see Pears (1982a, 1982b); compare with Rorty (1980c).

6. It is sometimes held that, for Aristotle, the conclusion of a practical syllogism *is* the action. See Anscombe (1963, p.60); Grant (1885, Vol. 1., pp.265–268); Nussbaum (1978,pp.185–188,194f.,202–205,342–346); Wiggins (1978/79, p.262). I attempt to refute this interpretation in Mele (1984a).

7. Especially *Nicomachean Ethics* (hereafter, *NE*) VII.3 and *De Motu Animalium*, Ch.7.

8. See *De Motu Animalium* 701a20–22 and n.6 above.

9. The relationship between judging best and intending is discussed in Chapter 2 below.

10. Sometimes, for reasons of brevity, I shall refer to the evaluated items simply as wants or desires. The nouns 'want' and 'desire,' when so employed, denote the things wanted or desired, not the wanting or desiring of them.

11. In this book, I shall use the nouns 'want' and 'desire' in a broad, semitechnical sense that has considerable currency in the philosophical literature on action. As I shall use these terms, to say that S has a desire or a want to A is to say that he has some motivation to A, the propositional content of which makes essential reference to his (prospective) A-ing. I shall use the verbs 'want' and 'desire' in a correspondingly broad sense. My usage does not

capture some of the niceties of standard English; but the distinctions that are blurred can be articulated by differentiating among types of desires or wants in my broad sense. We may distinguish between appetitive and nonappetitive wants, between wants that are felt urges and wants that are not, and so on.

12. An *intentionalistic* psychological model of action-explanation is a psychological model that gives important explanatory roles to intentional states (e.g., beliefs and desires). Many of the psychological notions with which I shall be working are central elements in so-called 'folk-psychology.' There is no place in this book for an extended effort to meet recent sweeping criticisms of folk psychology (e.g., Stich, 1983; Churchland, 1981). However, much of this book constitutes an indirect argument for the conceptual richness and explanatory power of a philosophically and experimentally refined intentionalistic psychology. Such a psychology, as we shall see, provides the basis for clear, detailed, and persuasive resolutions of difficult problems about akratic behavior, self-control, and self-deception. We shall also see, in passing, that folk-psychological notions (e.g., motivation and belief) are alive and flourishing in empirical psychology. For an instructive rebuttal of Stich and Churchland, see Horgan and Woodward, 1985.

13. For arguments to the contrary (about some similar cases), see Bratman (1984) and compare with Harman (1976).

14. The expression 'X is motivated to A' often means, of course, that X has some motivation to A. I shall use the expression in both senses and distinguish them only when disambiguation is crucial.

15. See Mischel (1968). See also Hunt (1965); Mischel (1973); Vernon (1964).

CHAPTER 2

1. See also Pears (1984, Ch.9).

2. See Davidson (1985a, p.202).

3. Let us say that A and B are competing actions for an agent at a time if and only if he can do either, but not both, at that time.

4. Not every action against a here-and-now intention need be an akratic action. If one can act incontinently against a here-and-now intention, perhaps one can also act continently against an *akratic* here-and-now intention.

5. Compare with Alston (1977). A variety of self-control strategies are usefully discussed in Thoreson and Mahoney (1974), Ainslie (1982), and Elster (1984).

6. On the bearing of the agent's modes of picturing alternatives on his subsequent actions, see, for example, Mischel & Mischel (1977) and Ch.6.3 below. I do not suggest that this picturing technique, nor any of the techniques mentioned here, will always be efficacious.

7. From my (1984e).

8. We may suppose that Alex does not just *find* his hand stopping, but rather that he stops its motion out of a desire not to harm himself and a belief that he will harm himself if he executes his present plan.

9. See my comments in Section 1 about a similar identification of better judgment with intention.

10. It is worth mentioning that if Fred came to believe that he could prevent himself from eating the pie only by killing himself, we would expect him, upon taking this new datum

into account, to judge it best all things considered to eat the pie. Presumably, satisfying his desire for the pie would be better than killing himself.

CHAPTER 3

1. This formulation excludes causal accounts of intentional action on which (havings of) reasons are not held to be causes of action (e.g., Skinner, 1953). My concern is with what might be termed, more strictly, traditional philosophical causal theories of action. A similar formulation of a *CTA* is found in Stoutland (1980, p.351).

2. Recent instructive attempts to resolve the problem include Brand (1984, Ch.1), Searle, (1983, pp.107–111,135–140), and Thalberg (1984). For an as yet unresolved difficulty posed by a certain species of waywardness, see Mele (1986c).

3. What Davidson does say is that *P1* and *P2* "derive their force" from a "very persuasive" and promising view of action (*WWP*, p. 102). Many philosophers have not been convinced. For some recent criticisms of *P2* in particular, see Audi (1979, p.190); Pears (1982a, pp.40–43); Taylor (1980, pp.499–505); Watson (1977, pp.319–321).

4. Davidson reaffirms the point in his (1985a p.206):

> . . . I am committed to the view that an agent is incontinent only if he fails to reason from a conditional 'all things considered' judgment that a certain course of action is best to the unconditional conclusion that that course of action is best. . . . [S]uch a failure is just what I defined to be a case of incontinence, and what I argued was possible. . . .

> I find it strange . . . to think of an incontinent intention or action as an error in belief, since I think of evaluative judgments as conative propositional attitudes. So to fail to reason to the right 'conclusion' means, in practical reasoning, to fail to form attitudes in a rational, coherent way. Among those attitudes are intentions. Failure to form an intention in accord with the principle of continence is, I still think, all too possible.

5. The idea that *akrasia* may be manifested in a failure to form a certain intention is defended in Audi (1979, p.181) and in Rorty (1980c).

6. In Section 4, I shall reject the idea that unconditional judgments *are* intentions (cf.Ch.2.1). But in the present case the agent both unconditionally judges that it is best to prick his finger here and now and intends to do so.

7. One who is bothered by talk of desires growing stronger or weaker may wish instead to speak of a desire for *x* being supplanted by a stronger or weaker desire for *x*. This does not affect my point.

8. Compare Santas (1966).

9. 'Wanting more' in the evaluative sense does *involve* motivation; for, as I have characterized the notion, what are evaluated are objects of wants having motivational force.

10. This issue is examined at length in Chapter 6.

11. Is there an exception? The assertion that all 'reasons-explanations' here come to an end is false if and only if there is a case in which it is *for a reason* that an agent acts on his reason for doing *x* instead of on his reason for performing the action that he judged best, all things considered. In such a case, the agent intends the following, that he act on his reason for doing *x* instead of his reason for doing the action judged best. That is, he intends to

perform the action of 'acting for such and such a reason instead of for the reason that such and such an action is best.' (This *may* be the sort of case that Dostoevsky is trying to develop in his *Notes from Underground*.) However, it seems to me likely that what happens in such a case is that although the agent might describe himself, say, as 'affirming my human freedom by acting on a lesser reason in preference to a greater one,' the reason on which he acts is in fact taken by him to be the greater, that is, he regards considerations of human freedom as overriding (cf. Dostoevsky, 1960, Sec.7). (The main point of the paragraph to which this note is appended does not, of course, depend upon the truth of this conjecture.)

12. For evidence of Davidson's inclusive understanding of reasons see, for example, *WWP*, p.111: "He does x for a reason r, but he has a reason r' that includes r and more, on the basis of which he judges some alternative y to be better than x."

13. For instance, a city dweller may think it best to rid himself of his fear of snakes by forcing himself to handle some. When he sees how anxious a confrontation with the feared reptiles makes him, he may justifiably judge that overcoming his fear of snakes is just not worth the trouble.

14. See, for example, Thoresen and Mahoney's survey (1974).

15. Watson tries to do this in his article (1977).

16. This is a Davidsonian line. For Davidson, "events related as cause and effect fall under strict deterministic laws" (1970b, p.81) and there are no strict psychological or psychophysical laws (pp.89–99). Nevertheless, "some mental events interact causally with physical events" (p.80). This is possible because all mental events, in Davidson's view, are physical events. When one event causes another, there is some physical description under which the events "instantiate a strict law" (p.99; Cf. Davidson, 1974).

CHAPTER 4

1. On the effectiveness of planning in self-control, see, for example, Ajzen (1985); Schifter and Ajzen (1985).

2. Brandt (1979, pp.111, 126f., 333ff.).

3. For an attempt to classify these modes, see Ainslie (1982, p. 744); compare Elster (1984, p.103).

4. See Janis and Mann (1977, pp.283f.).

5. Compare Aristotle, *NE* 1150a 9–14; Watson (1977, p.325).

6. See Chapter 1.1 for the distinction drawn in the last clause.

7. The reader who balks at this claim will find substantial support for it in Chapters 8, 9, and 10 below.

8. Pears (1984); Rorty (1983; 1980b). Compare Dennett (1978, Ch.16).

9. A specific version of this general account of self-deception is defended in Chapter 9 below. The general account is not universally accepted. See, for example, Audi (1982).

10. This list of commitment-types is not, of course, exhaustive. Nor, in speaking of doxastic self-control, do I mean to suggest that there are two distinct kinds of self-control, one concerned with beliefs and the other with actions. Rather, self-control functions in both the actional and the doxastic spheres.

11. If Sonny is responsible for his being in this condition, he may have exhibited self-control in getting himself into it. See Section 1 above.

12. On this broader notion of self-control, see, for example, Dennett (1984, Ch.3).

CHAPTER 5

1. Alston (1977) is an exception. On a related paradox, see Schiffer (1976).

2. The motivational terms in this chapter should be understood in their occurrent sense unless otherwise indicated.

3. Some cases of this sort also raise the paradox of downhill self-control, discussed in Section 4 below.

4. Compare with, for example, Brandt & Kim (1963, p.426), von Wright (1963, p.103), Goldman (1970, pp.50f., 105f.).

5. I have more to say about this in Chapter 6.3.

6. For a classical precedent, see Plato, *Republic* 440b.

7. My treatment of the paradoxes of self-control is similar in spirit to Alston's investigation of the issue. I go beyond Alston both in distinguishing among a number of related paradoxes of self-control and, more importantly, in explaining in some detail how the pertinent motivational features of the cases are possible. Even if we distinguish among levels of motivation in Alston's fashion and suppose, for example, that Ian desires to alter the balance of his lower-level motivation by uttering a self-command, we still want to understand *how* it is possible for his motivation to utter the command to be stronger than his motivation to get back to work. The suggestion that Dc and Dw are located in two different systems is useful; but the question how their having different systemic locations helps to explain their relative strengths remains to be answered. And when the answer is developed along my lines, we see that there is no need to place Dc and Dw in different Alstonian systems. The object of Dc—that is, Ian's uttering the self-command—need not be "designed" (or intended) to alter Ian's motivational condition in order to turn the trick; and if it is not so designed, Dc is not "higher-level" motivation, in Alston's sense.

CHAPTER 6

1. Davidson's model includes "overlapping territories" (1982, p.300). Thus two objects may simultaneously be both in different subdivisions and in the same subdivision.

2. A more exact definition of an *MCNR* would be relativistic in form: a mental event, E, is an *MCNR* relative to a mental item, M, if and only if E is a cause of, but not a reason for, M. If this is kept in mind, the looser formulation will not mislead.

3. This does not preclude their being found in the intersection of the two partitions. See Note 1 above.

4. At the end of his paper, Davidson mentions a related example to support his observation that the effective functioning of an *MCNR* is not a "sufficient condition for irrationality" (1982, p.305).

5. For a useful discussion of the effectiveness of a technique of this sort, see Cautela (1983).

6. Not all such cases are equally intelligible, of course. The degree of intelligibility depends upon the agent's assessment of his reason.

7. I suspect that Davidson is thinking that the desire to A is not a reason for something like the following complex event: doing A, given that one both judges it best not to A and holds that one should always act on one's better judgments. This fits his remark that irrationality arises because "the desire to [A] has entered into the decision to do it twice over" (1982, p.297). The desire enters as a reason for A-ing and again as a cause of—but not a reason for—something describable as follows: "S's A-ing even though he holds that he has better reason not to A and that he should act on his better judgments." Of course, locating an appropriate candidate for an effect of an $MCNR$ in a case of akratic action is a far cry from establishing Davidson's thesis.

8. Pears reports (1984, p.96n.) that Davidson has expressed agreement with his way of developing the principle of partitioning.

9. See Haight (1980, Ch.3) for an interesting philosophical investigation of the phenomenon.

10. Aristotle has *practical* thinking in mind here. See, e.g., Nussbaum (1978, p. 185).

11. Compare with Estes (1972).

12. See, for example, Miller and Karniol (1976); Patterson and Mischel (1976); Yates and Mischel (1979); Karniol and Miller (1983).

13. This is not to say that every instance of opting for the "less preferred" reward in Mischel's studies is akratic. Waiting itself is often aversive, and even a young child may rationally decide to sacrifice a more distant reward in order to put an end to his waiting. (On shifts in subjects' evaluations of reward objects during delay, see Karniol & Miller, 1983.)

14. We may also safely suppose, if need be, that Susan believes that it is best, all things considered, to act in accordance with her all-things-considered better judgments. Compare with Davidson (1982, p.297).

CHAPTER 7

1. For some $TBDM$-s see Audi (1979, 1980); Davidson (1980); Goldman (1970); Tuomela (1977).

2. See, for example, Anscombe (1963, p.9); Davidson (1980, p.264); Goldman (1970, p.76). In the limiting case, when S A-s for the sake of A-ing alone, his reason for A-ing is simply his desire to A (in the broad, technical sense of 'desire' that I have been employing).

3. Notice that, on Davidson's view, intentions mediate between reasons and actions even in cases of the second sort. When the intention is acquired simultaneously with the initiation of the action, the intention mediates between reasons and the "development" of the action.

For the view that intention (or a kind of intention) is the proximate (psychological) cause of intentional action, see also Alston (1974); Brand (1979, 1984); Goldman (1976); Ryan (1970); Sellars (1966, 1973).

4. Mele (1984a).

5. Mele (1984e).

6. Proponents include Alston (1974, p.95); Audi (1973); Davidson (1970); Davis (1984, p.50); Tuomela (1977, pp.132f.). The most carefully qualified version of the thesis that I have seen is in Audi (1973, pp.395f.). I attempt to refute this version in Mele (1984e).

7. See Davidson's $P1$-$P2$ (1970a, p.94) for one example. Recall that, for Davidson, a better judgment—that is, an unconditional judgment—is an intention.

8. What I have in mind here is an intentionalistic psychology, that is, one that gives important explanatory roles to intentional states (e.g., beliefs and desires).

9. I argue elsewhere (Mele, 1984e) that the possibility of an intention's being out of line with the balance of one's motivation is not restricted to cases in which the intention is formed on the basis of deliberation. (Brand attacks the *IMAT* in his recent book; but his objections trade upon a sense of 'desire' that is too narrow to capture the notion of motivation employed in the *IMAT*. See Brand (1984, pp.122f.).)

10. For a third aspect, the role of intentions in plans, see Bratman (1984).

11. See the references cited in Note 6 above. See also Beardsley (1978, p.180); Brand (1979, pp.146–149; 1984, Ch.9); and Harman (1976, p.436). Brand, Davidson (but not in 1963), and Harman all reject the idea that intention is *reducible* to a combination of belief and desire.

12. See, for example, Brand (1982; 1984, Ch.7); Goldman (1976); and Searle (1979; 1983, Ch.3).

13. See Mele (1984c, 1984d).

14. Again, these traits may typically be 'regional.'

CHAPTER 8

1. Festinger, in his pioneering book on cognitive dissonance (1957), advances the following two "basic" hypotheses:

1. "The existence of dissonance, being psychologically uncomfortable, will motivate the person to try to reduce the dissonance and achieve consonance."
2. "When dissonance is present, in addition to trying to reduce it, the person will actively avoid situations and information which would likely increase the dissonance." (p.3)

More recently, attempts have been made to explain the data without using motivational hypotheses (e.g., Bem 1965, 1967, 1972; Miller & Ross 1975), prompting numerous defenses of motivational hypotheses (e.g., Kelley & Michela 1980, Weary 1980, Gollwitzer et al. 1982). The debate continues to be quite lively. For a useful review of the literature on attribution theory, see Harvey and Weary (1984). See also Tetlock and Levi (1982).

2. Heil (1984). See also Rorty (1983); Pears (1984, Ch.4); Davidson (1985b).

3. Interesting arguments for a stronger view are advanced in Meiland (1980).

4. Compare with Gardiner (1970, p.230) and Fingarette (1969, p.25).

5. Here and hereafter I use "the agent's judgment that there is good and sufficient reason . . ." as shorthand for "a consciously held judgment of the agent to the effect that there is good and sufficient reason . . .".

6. The influence of salience on attention and belief-formation is examined in Chapter 10.2 below.

7. See Nisbett and Ross (1980, pp. 231–248).

8. See, for example, Nisbett and Ross (1980, p.228).

9. For a partial map, see Rorty (1983).

10. Of course, neither the action nor the belief will be incontinent in the strict sense unless the agent meets the freedom condition.

11. Notice that not all instances of self-deception need be similarly irrational.

CHAPTER 9

1. For other formulations, see Audi (1982, p.133); Bach (1981, p.351); Canfield and Gustavson (1962, p.32); Pugmire (1969, p.339); Siegler (1968, p.147); and the references in Note 10 below.

A related paradox about the doxastic condition of the self-deceived individual has also received attention. Typically, when *A* deceives *B*, *A* does not believe the falsehood that, as a result of *A*'s efforts, his victim does believe. If, analogously, the self-deceiver both does and does not believe that *p*, the state seems hopelessly paradoxical. Assuming (1) that it is strictly the same individual who, at one and the same time, both does and does not believe that *p* (i.e., barring certain kinds of partitioning) and (2) that 'believe' is being used univocally, the condition at issue is a blatant *logical* impossibility. The paradox of belief is weaker. If it is logically impossible for an individual simultaneously to believe consciously that *p* and to believe consciously that not-*p*, this will be due to a special feature of believing—namely, that it (unlike, e.g., desiring) is *exclusive*. However, that believing is exclusive is not *obviously* correct; and the stronger paradox in no way depends upon exclusivity of this sort.

On the stronger paradox, see de Sousa (1970, p.308); Hamlyn (1971); Rorty (1972, 1980); Foss (1980, p.237); Haight (1980, pp.14ff.); Sorensen (1985). The resolution of the belief paradox advanced below dissolves the stronger paradox as well.

2. Compare with Haight (1980, p.9); Martin (1985, p.16).

3. Compare with the second definition of 'deceive' in the *Compact Edition of the Oxford English Dictionary:* "To cause to believe what is false . . . ."

Two further lexical points are in order: (1) 'deception' refers both to the act of deceiving and to the condition or state of one who is deceived. 'Self-deception' may be understood accordingly as referring both to deceivings of oneself and to states or conditions of deception which one produces in oneself. (2) The verb 'deceive' has both a doxastic and a nondoxastic use. To deceive, in the doxastic sense of the word, is, roughly, to induce a false belief. In the nondoxastic sense, 'deceive' means 'betray' or 'deal treacherously with.' My concern here is with doxastic deceiving only. For a contrasting approach, see Hamlyn (1971).

4. Examples of this error are: Siegler's contention that a person is "in self-deception" only if "he knows (or believes) that *p*" and "he believes that not-*p* as a result of desire and fear" (1968, p.147); Amelie Rorty's claim that if *S* is self-deceived, then it is generally the case that "*S* believes *d*" and "*S* does not believe *d*" (1972, p.393); Audi's suggestion that "self-deception is, roughly, a state in which *S* unconsciously knows that *p*, but sincerely avows, or is disposed so to avow, not-*p*" (1976, p.381); Foss's assertion that "self-deception, like deception of another, has knowledge as a prerequisite: one deceives himself that *p* just in case he convinces himself that *p*, knowing *p* to be false" (1980, p.242); and Davidson's contention that "The self-deceiver must intend the 'deception'" (1985b, p.144).

For similar claims in the psychological literature on self-deception, see Gergen (1985, p.229); Joseph (1980, pp.767, 777); Quattrone and Tversky (1984, p.239); Sackheim and Gur (1985, p.1365); Snyder (1985, p.35).

5. Again, I construe 'want' broadly and make no distinction between wanting and desiring. (See Ch.1, n.11.)

6. On this point see Bach (1981, p.353) and Szabados (1974, p.68). The case of the jealous husband in the preceding chapter is an exception.

7. There is a substantial body of empirical literature on doxastic behavior of the kinds identified in Items 1–4. I shall draw upon it in Chapter 10, in an attempt to illuminate the

etiology of self-deception and to resolve what I shall call the "strategy paradox" of self-deception. Instructive philosophical work on mechanisms of self-deception includes Fingarette (1969); Bach (1981); and Pears (1984, Ch.4).

8. There is no need, I think, for a further condition excluding desires generated by deviant causal chains. Entering self-deception is a matter of *responding* in a certain way (or range of ways) to a desire that one has. It is the response that we must look for wayward causal chains, not in the generation of the desire that elicits the response.

9. There is, of course, a disanalogy. Although it is generally agreed that knowledge entails belief, one way of attempting to dissolve the "paradox of self-deception" is to deny that the person who is self-deceived that *p* believes that *p*. See, for example, Audi (1976, 1982, 1985) and Bach (1981).

10. For Demos, this is precisely the paradox, that is, that the self-deceived person "believes both *p* and not-*p* at the same time" (1960, p.588). Compare with Miri (1974, p.577); Paluch (1967, p.268); Penelhum (1964, p.88).

11. This is obvious in the case of one-sided evidence-gathering; and notice that selective focusing may sometimes be due simply to the pleasantness or unpleasantness of certain thoughts or to the desire-enhanced salience of certain data. I discuss these matters at length in Chapter 10.

12. In a case of intentional self-deception (see Sec. 10.4), one might intentionally *A* because one wants to believe that *p* and believes that *A*-ing is a means to this goal.

13. Richard Reilly (1976, p.393) seems to hold that this is the typical way of entering self-deception. In light of recent experimental work on belief perseverance, one should not be surprised if this were at least the most common way. See Nisbett and Ross (1980, pp.175–188) for a survey of the literature.

14. Strict incontinent action is *always* subjectively irrational in this sense, that the agent's free action is contrary to his own decisive better judgment. Some instances of self-deception may not be similarly irrational, as I suggested in Chapter 8.

15. This last clause does not represent a disanalogy. The better judgment against which the akratic agent acts is sometimes only the judgment that he would have made (given his values and the particular circumstances) if the contrary desire(s) had not interfered.

CHAPTER 10

1. See, for example, Champlin (1977); Fingarette (1969); Haight (1985); Hamlyn (1971); Pears (1974, 1984, Ch.5); Chanowitz and Langer (1985); Sartre (1943/1956, pp.47–54).

2. Pears's "reason for calling this theory 'functional'," as he observes, "is not the usual one, namely that the function of a belief makes it the belief that it is, but, rather, that its function governs its assignment to a system within the person" (p.69, n.3).

3. I am assuming that the failure to "stop the irrationality" is a failure "to interact in a rational way," as Pears intends the latter-quoted phrase to be understood.

4. Pears distinguishes between these two types of strategy and treats "acting as if something were so in order to generate the belief that it is so" as a third strategy (1984, p.61). I shall suggest later that the third strategy is a species of input-control.

5. For support, see Borgida and Nisbett (1977); Enzle et al. (1975); Tesser (1978); Walster (1966); Wason and Johnson-Laird (1965).

6. Compare with, for example, Arkin and Duval (1975); Regan and Totten (1975).

7. Compare with Snyder and Swann (1978); Swann and Read (1981); Wason and Johnson-Laird (1965).

8. Compare with Nisbett and Wilson (1977); Wilson and Nisbett (1978).

9. There is considerable evidence that an individual's self-schema or self-conception has a significant influence on encoding, recall, and interpretation of information as well as on the seeking and eliciting of information (see Markus, 1977; Kelley & Michela, 1980; Taylor & Crocker, 1980; Swann & Read, 1981). I have not included self-schemas in my list of common sources of unmotivated irrational belief because it is unclear to what extent their influence is unmotivated. Tetlock and Levi (1982) is an excellent review article. See also the references in Chapter 8, Note 1 above.

For a detailed study of the influence of *mood* on recall, attention, interpretation, prediction, evaluation, learning, and other forms of cognition, see Gilligan and Bower (1984).

10. For an attempt to identify the target of their criticisms, see Nisbett and Ross (1980, pp.234f.).

11. On "explaining away" of this sort, see Snyder (1985).

12. Compare David Kanouse's suggestion (1972, p.131):

> Individuals may exert more cognitive effort in seeking an adequate explanation when none has yet come to mind than they do in seeking for further (and possibly better) explanations when an adequate one is already available . . . [W]hen more than one satisfactory explanation is potentially available to an individual, which one he adopts may depend primarily on which of the various possible explanations is most *salient*.

13. The discussion of the case of Guido in Chapter 9.4 shows how this can happen in at least one type of *intentional* self-deception. But my concern here is with the more typical cases.

14. There is no vicious circularity here. Because S desires that p, certain data supportive of p may be much more salient for him than they would otherwise have been; and his focusing selectively upon them may render them even more vivid, thereby giving them greater weight in the process of belief-formation.

15. Again, it does not follow from this lack of realization that the irrational belief is inevitable. See the discussion of avoidability in Chapter 10.1.

16. Several features of the experiment were designed to reduce the likelihood that subjects would lie to impress the experimenters. (1) Subjects were told that only *shifts* in tolerance would be indicative of heart-type and that neither the experimenter present during the first trial nor the one administering the second trial would know the results of the other trial. (2) The experimenter at the second trial was presented as a secretary who "knew nothing of the study's hypotheses, description, or rationale" (p.24). (3) The questionnaires were filled out anonymously.

17. Subjects are invited to take their hands out of the water when they give their discomfort a rating of 10, thereby indicating that they have reached a point at which they "would rather not tolerate the cold any longer" (p.241). The point in the text may be formulated in terms of a rating report.

18. The central thesis of Daryl Bem's theory of self-perception, which has received substantial experimental support, is that

Individuals come to 'know' their own attitudes, emotions, and other internal states partially by inferring them from observations of their own overt behavior and/or the circumstances in which this behavior occurs. Thus, to the extent that internal cues are weak, ambiguous, or uninterpretable, the individual is functionally in the same position as an outside observer, an observer who must necessarily rely upon those same external cues to infer the individual's inner states. (Bem, 1972, p.2; cf. Bem & McConnell, 1970, p.23)

Bem is sometimes misconstrued as holding the much stronger position that inferences about oneself are made *solely* on the basis of one's observations of one's behavior and circumstances. See, for example, Quattrone and Tversky (1984, p.239).

19. On defensive procrastination, see Janis and Mann (1977, p.109).

20. Of course, the postulation of intentional subagency complicates the notion of personhood.

§

Bibliography

Ainslie, G. (1982). "A Behavioral Economic Approach to the Defense Mechanisms: Freud's Energy Theory Revisited." *Social Science Information* 21:735–780.

―――― (1975). "Specious Reward: A Behavioral Theory of Impulsiveness and Impulse Control." *Psychological Bulletin* 82:463–496.

Ainslie, G. & Haendel, V. (1983). "The Motives of the Will." In E. Gottheil et al., eds. *Etiologic Aspects of Alcohol and Drug Abuse* (Springfield, NJ: Thomas), pp. 119–140.

Ainslie, G. & Herrnstein, R. (1981). "Preference Reversal and Delayed Reinforcement." *Animal Learning and Behavior* 9:476–482.

Ajzen, I. (1985). "From Intentions to Actions: A Theory of Planned Behavior." In J. Kuhl & J. Beckman, eds. *Action Control: From Cognition to Behavior* (Heidelberg: Springer), pp. 11–39.

Alston, W. (1977). "Self-Intervention and the Structure of Motivation." In T. Mischel, ed. *The Self: Psychological and Philosophical Issues* (Oxford: Basil Blackwell), pp. 65–102.

―――― (1974). "Conceptual Prolegomena to a Psychological Theory of Intentional Action." In S. Brown, ed. *Philosophy of Psychology* (New York: Barnes & Noble), pp. 71–101.

Anscombe, G. (1963). *Intention.* 2nd ed. Ithaca: NY: Cornell University Press.

Aristotle. *Nicomachean Ethics.* In W. Ross, ed. *Works of Aristotle*, Vol. 9 (London: Oxford University Press, 1915).

―――― *De Motu Animalium.* In W. Ross, ed. *Works of Aristotle*, Vol. 5 (London: Oxford University Press, 1915).

Arkin, R. & Duval, S. (1975). "Focus of Attention and Causal Attributions of Actors and Observers." *Journal of Experimental Social Psychology* 11:427–438.

Audi, R. (1985). "Self-Deception and Rationality." In Martin, ed. *Self-Deception and Self-Understanding* (Lawrence, KA: University of Kansas Press), pp. 169–194.

_____ (1982). "Self-Deception, Action, and Will." *Erkenntnis* 18:133–158.

_____ (1980). "Wants and Intentions in the Explanation of Action." *Journal for the Theory of Social Behavior* 9:227–249.

_____ (1979). "Weakness of Will and Practical Judgment." *Nous* 13:173–196.

_____ (1976). "Epistemic Disavowals and Self-Deception." *The Personalist* 56:43–62.

_____ (1973). "Intending." *Journal of Philosophy* 70:387–402.

Bach, K. (1981). "An Analysis of Self-Deception." *Philosophy and Phenomenological Research* 41 1981:351–370.

Beardsley, M. (1978). "Intending." In A. Goldman & J. Kim, eds. *Values and Morals* (Dordrecht: Reidel), pp. 163–184.

Bem, D. (1972). "Self-Perception Theory." *Advances in Experimental Social Psychology* 6:1–62.

_____ (1967). "Self-Perception: An Alternative Interpretation of Cognitive Dissonance Phenomena." *Psychological Review* 74:183–200.

_____ (1965). "An Experimental Analysis of Self-Persuasion." *Journal of Experimental Social Psychology* 1:199–218.

Bem, D. & McConnell, H. (1970). "Testing the Self-Perception Explanation of Dissonance Phenomena: On the Salience of Premanipulation Attitudes." *Journal of Personality and Social Psychology* 14:23–31.

Berlyne, D. (1960). *Conflict, Arousal and Curiosity.* New York: McGraw-Hill.

Borgida, E. & Nisbett, R. (1977). "The Differential Impact of Abstract vs. Concrete Information on Decisions." *Journal of Applied Social Psychology* 7:258–271.

Brand, M. (1984). *Intending and Acting.* Cambridge, MA: MIT Press.

_____ (1982). "Cognition and Intention." *Erkenntnis* 18:165–187.

_____ (1979). "The Fundamental Question in Action Theory." *Nous* 13:131–151.

Brandt, R. (1979). *A Theory of the Good and the Right.* Oxford: Clarendon Press.

Brandt, R. & Kim, J. (1963). "Wants as Explanations of Actions." *Journal of Philosophy* 60:425–435.

Bratman, M. (1984). "Two Faces of Intention." *Philosophical Review* 93:375–405.

Canfield, J. & Gustavson, D. (1962). "Self-Deception." *Analysis* 23:32–36.

Castaneda, H. (1975). *Thinking and Doing.* Dordrecht: Reidel.

Cautela, J. (1983). "The Self-Control Triad." *Behavior Modification* 7:299–315.

Champlin, T. (1977). "Double Deception." *Mind* 85:100–102.

Chanowitz, B. & Langer, E. (1985). "Self-Protection and Self-Inception." In Martin, ed. *Self-Deception and Self-Understanding* (Lawrence, KA: University of Kansas Press), pp. 117–135.

Churchland, P. (1981). "Eliminative Materialism and Propopsitional Attitudes." *Journal of Philosophy* 78:67–90.

Davidson, D. (1985a). "Replies to Essays I–IX." In B. Vermazen & M. Hintikka, eds. *Essays on Davidson* (Oxford: Clarendon Press), pp. 195–219.

_____ (1985b). "Deception and Division." In E. LePore & B. McLaughlin, eds. *Actions and Events* (Oxford: Basil Blackwell), pp. 138–148.

_____ (1982). "Paradoxes of Irrationality." In R. Wolheim & J. Hopkins, eds. *Philosophical Essays on Freud* (Cambridge: Cambridge University Press), pp. 289–305.

_____ (1980). *Essays on Actions and Events*. Oxford: Clarendon Press.

_____ (1978). "Intending." In Y. Yovel, ed. *Philosophy of History and Action* (Dordrecht: Reidel), pp. 41–60. Reprinted in Davidson (1980).

_____ (1974). "Psychology as Philosophy." In S. Brown, ed. *Philosophy of Psychology* (New York: Barnes & Noble), pp. 41–52. Reprinted in Davidson (1980).

_____ (1973). "Freedom to Act." In T. Honderich, ed. *Essays on Freedom of Action* (London: Routledge & Kegan Paul), pp. 137–156. Reprinted in Davidson (1980).

_____ (1970a). "How is Weakness of the Will Possible?" In J. Feinberg, ed. *Moral Concepts* (Oxford: Clarendon Press), pp. 93–113. Reprinted in Davidson (1980).

_____ (1970b). "Mental Events." In L. Foster & J. Swanson, eds. *Experience and Theory* (Cambridge, MA: University of Massachusetts Press), pp. 79–101. Reprinted in Davidson (1980).

_____ (1963). "Actions, Reasons, and Causes." *Journal of Philosophy* 60:685–700. Reprinted in Davidson (1980).

Davis, W. (1984). "A Causal Theory of Intending." *American Philosophical Quarterly* 21:43–54.

Demos, R. (1960). "Lying to Oneself." *Journal of Philosophy* 57:588–595.

Dennett, D. (1984). *Elbow Room*. Cambridge, MA: MIT Press.

_____ (1978). *Brainstorms*. Montgomery, VT: Bradford Books.

Dostoevsky, F. *Notes from Underground*. R. Matlaw, trans. New York: Dutton, 1960.

Elster, J. (1984). *Ulysses and the Sirens*. Rev. Ed. Cambridge: Cambridge University Press.

_____ (1983). *Sour Grapes*. Cambridge: Cambridge University Press.

Enzle, M., Hansen, R., & Lowe, C. (1975). "Humanizing the Mixed-Motive Paradigm: Methodological Implications from Attribution Theory." *Simulation and Games* 6:151–165.

Estes, W. (1972). "Reinforcement in Human Behavior." *American Scientist* 60:723–729.

Festinger, L. (1957). *The Theory of Cognitive Dissonance*. Stanford, CA: Stanford University Press.

Fingarette, H. (1969). *Self-Deception*. London: Routledge & Kegan Paul.

Foss, J. (1980). "Rethinking Self-Deception," *American Philosophical Quarterly* 17:237–243.

Frankfurt, H. (1971). "Freedom of the Will and the Concept of a Person." *Journal of Philosophy* 68:5–20.

Gardiner, P. (1970). "Error, Faith, and Self-Deception." *Proceedings of the Aristotelian Society* 70:221–243.

Gergen, K. (1985). "The Ethnopsychology of Self-Deception." In Martin, ed. *Self-Deception and Self-Understanding* (Lawrence, KA: University of Kansas Press), pp. 228–243.

Gilligan, S. & Bower, G. (1984). "Cognitive Consequences of Emotional Arousal." In C. Izard, J. Kagan, & R. Zajonc. eds. *Emotions, Cognition, and Behavior* (Cambridge: Cambridge University Press), pp. 547–588.

Goldman, A. (1976). "The Volitional Theory Revisited." In M. Brand & D. Walton, eds. *Action Theory* (Dordrecht: Reidel), pp. 67–84.

————— (1970). *A Theory of Human Action*. Englewood Cliffs, NJ: Prentice-Hall.

Gollwitzer, P., Earle, W., & Stephan, W. (1982). "Affect as a Determinant of Egotism: Residual Excitation and Performance Attributions." *Journal of Personality and Social Psychology* 43:702–709.

Grant, A. (1885). *The Ethics of Aristotle*. London: Longmans, Green.

Gur, R. & Sackheim, H. (1979). "Self-Deception: A Concept in Search of a Phenomenon." *Journal of Personality and Social Psychology* 37:147–169.

Guthrie, W. (1971). *The Sophists*. Cambridge: Cambridge University Press.

Haight, M. (1985). "Tales from a Black Box." In Martin, ed. *Self-Deception and Self-Understanding* (Lawrence, KA: University of Kansas Press). pp. 244–260.

————— (1980). *A Study of Self Deception*. Sussex, Eng.: Harvester Press.

Hamlyn, D. (1971). "Self-Deception." *Proceedings of the Aristotelian Society* 45:45–60.

Hare, R. (1963). *Freedom and Reason*. Oxford: Oxford University Press.

Harman, G. (1976). "Practical Reasoning." *Review of Metaphysics* 79:431–463.

Harvey, J. & Weary, G. (1984). "Current Issues in Attribution Theory and Research." *Annual Review of Psychology* 35:427–459.

Heil, J. (1984). "Doxastic Incontinence." *Mind* 93:56–70.

Horgan, T. & Woodward, J. (1985). "Folk Psychology Is Here to Stay." *Philosophical Review* 94:197–226.

Hume, D. *A Treatise of Human Nature*. ed. L. A. Selby-Bigge. Oxford: Oxford University Press, 1888.

Hunt, J. (1965). "Traditional Personality Theory in the Light of Recent Evidence." *American Scientist* 53:80–96.

Jackson, F. (1984). "Weakness of Will." *Mind* 93:1–18.

Janis, I. & Mann, L. (1977). *Decision Making*. New York: Macmillan.

Joseph, R. (1980). "Awareness, the Origin of Thought, and the Role of Conscious Self-Deception in Resistance and Regression." *Psychological Reports* 46:767–781.

Kanouse, D. (1972). "Language, Labeling, and Attribution." In E. Jones et al., eds. *Attribution: Perceiving the Causes of Behavior* (Morristown, NJ: General Learning Press), pp. 121–135.

Karniol, R. & Miller, D. (1983). "Why Not Wait? A Cognitive Model of Self-Imposed Delay Termination." *Journal of Personality and Social Psychology* 45:935–942.

Kelley, H. & Michela, J. (1980). "Attribution Theory and Research." *Annual Review of Psychology* 31:457–501.

Kornblith, H. (1983). "Justified Belief and Epistemically Responsible Action." *Philosophical Review* 92:33–48.

Markus, H. (1977). "Self-Schemata and the Processing of Information about the Self." *Journal of Personality and Social Psychology* 35:63–78.

Martin, M., ed. (1985). *Self-Deception and Self-Understanding*. Lawrence, KA: University of Kansas Press.

Meiland, J. (1980). "What Ought We to Believe? Or the Ethics of Belief Revisited." *American Philosophical Quarterly* 17:15–24.

Mele, A. (1986a). "Incontinent Believing." *Philosophical Quarterly* 36:212–222.

———— (1986b). "Is Akratic Action Unfree?" *Philosophy and Phenomenological Research* 46:673–679.

———— (1986c). "Intentional Action and Wayward Causal Chains: The Problem of Tertiary Waywardness." *Philosophical Studies* 47:

———— (1985a). "Aristotle on *Akrasia, Eudaimonia*, and the Psychology of Action." *History of Philosophy Quarterly* 2:375–393.

———— (1985b). "Self-Control, Action, and Belief." *American Philosophical Quarterly* 22:169–175.

———— (1984a). "Aristotle on the Proximate Efficient Cause of Action." *Canadian Journal of Philosophy*, 10 (suppl):133–155.

———— (1984b). "Pears on *Akrasia*, and Defeated Intentions." *Philosophia* 14:145–152.

———— (1984c). "Aristotle on the Roles of Reason in Motivation and Justification." *Archiv für Geschichte der Philosophie* 66:124–147.

———— (1984d). "Aristotle's Wish." *Journal of the History of Philosophy* 22:139–156.

———— (1984e). "Intending and the Balance of Motivation." *Pacific Philosophical Quarterly* 66:370–376.

———— (1983a). "*Akrasia*, Reasons, and Causes." *Philosophical Studies* 44:345–368.

———— (1983b). "Self-Deception." *Philosophical Quarterly* 33:365–377.

———— (1981a). "Choice and Virtue in the *Nicomachean Ethics*." *Journal of the History of Philosophy* 19:405–423.

———— (1981b). "The Practical Syllogism and Deliberation in Aristotle's Causal Theory of Action." *The New Scholasticism* 55:281–316.

———— (1981c). "Aristotle on *Akrasia* and Knowledge." *The Modern Schoolman* 58:137–157.

Miller, D. & Karniol, R. (1976). "The Role of Rewards in Externally and Self-Imposed Delay of Gratification." *Journal of Personality and Social Psychology* 33:594–600.

Miller, D. & Ross, M. (1975). "Self-Serving Biases in the Attribution of Causality: Fact or Fiction?" *Psychological Bulletin* 82:213–235.

Miri, M. (1974). "Self-Deception." *Philosophy and Phenomenological Research* 34:576–585.

Mischel, W. (1973). "Toward a Cognitive Social Learning Reconceptualization of Personality." *Psychological Review* 80:252–283.

———— (1968). *Personality and Assessment.* New York: Wiley.

Mischel, W. & Baker, N. (1975). "Cognitive Appraisals and Transformations in Delay Behavior." *Journal of Personality and Social Psychology* 31:254–261.

Mischel, W. & Ebbesen, E. (1970). "Attention in Delay of Gratification." *Journal of Personality and Social Psychology* 16:329–337.

Mischel, W., Ebbesen, E., & Zeiss, A. (1972). "Cognitive and Attentional Mechanisms in Delay of Gratification." *Journal of Personality and Social Psychology* 21:204–218.

Mischel, W. & Mischel, H. (1977). "Self-Control and the Self." In T. Mischel, ed. *The Self: Psychological and Philosophical Issues* (Oxford: Blackwell), pp. 31–64.

Mischel, W. & Moore, B. (1980). "The Role of Ideation in Voluntary Delay for Symbolically Presented Rewards." *Cognitive Therapy and Research* 4:211–221.

———— (1973). "Effects of Attention to Symbolically-Presented Rewards on Self-Control." *Journal of Personality and Social Psychology* 28:172–179.

Moore, B., Mischel, W., & Zeiss, A. (1976). "Comparative Effects of the Reward Stimulus and its Cognitive Representation in Voluntary Delay." *Journal of Personality and Social Psychology* 34:419–424.

Mounce, H. (1971). "Self-Deception." *Proceedings of the Aristotelian Society* 45:61 72.

Navarick, D. & Fantino, E. (1976). "Self-Control and General Models of Choice." *Journal of Experimental Psychology: Animal Behavior Processes* 2:75–87.

Neely, W. (1974). "Freedom and Desire." *Philosophical Review* 83:32–54.

Nisbett, R. & Ross, L. (1980). *Human Inference: Strategies and Shortcomings of Social Judgment.* Englewood Cliffs, NJ: Prentice-Hall.

Nisbett, R. & Wilson, T. (1977). "The Halo Effect: Evidence for Unconscious Alteration of Judgments." *Journal of Personality and Social Psychology* 35:250–256.

Nussbaum, M. (1978). *Aristotle's De Motu Animalium.* Princeton: Princeton University Press.

Palmer, A. (1979). "Characterizing Self-Deception." *Mind* 88:45–58.

Paluch, S. (1967). "Self-Deception." *Inquiry* 10:268–278.

Patterson, C. & Mischel, W. (1976). "Effects of Temptation-Inhibiting and Task-Facilitating Plans on Self-Control." *Journal of Personality and Social Psychology* 33:209–217.

Pears, D. (1984). *Motivated Irrationality*. Oxford: Oxford University Press.

————— (1982a). "How Easy is Akrasia?" *Philosophia* 11:33–50.

————— (1982b). "Motivated Irrationality." *Proceedings of the Aristotelian Society* 56:157–178.

————— (1974). "Freud, Sartre, and Self-Deception." In R. Wolheim, ed. *Freud* (Garden City, NY: Anchor Books), pp. 97–112.

Penelhum, T. (1964). "Pleasure and Falsity." *American Philosophical Quarterly* 1:81–91.

Plato, *Phaedrus*. In B. Jowett, trans. *The Dialogues of Plato*. 4th ed. Vol. 3 (Oxford: Clarendon Press, 1953).

————— *Protagoras*. In B. Jowett, trans. *The Dialogues of Plato*. 4th ed. Vol. 1 (Oxford: Clarendon Press, 1953).

————— *Republic*. In B. Jowett, trans. *The Dialogues of Plato*. 4th ed. Vol. 2 (Oxford: Clarendon Press, 1953).

Pugmire, D. (1982). "Motivated Irrationality." *Proceedings of the Aristotelian Society* 56:179–196.

————— (1969). "'Strong' Self-Deception." *Inquiry* 12:339–346.

Quattrone, G. & Tversky, A. (1984). "Causal Versus Diagnostic Contingencies: On Self-Deception and on the Voter's Illusion." *Journal of Personality and Social Psychology* 46:237–248.

Rachlin, H. & Green, L. (1972). "Commitment, Choice, and Self-Control." *Journal of the Experimental Analysis of Behavior* 17:15–22.

Regan, D. & Totten, J. (1975). "Empathy and Attribution: Turning Observers into Actors." *Journal of Personality and Social Psychology* 32:850–856.

Reid, T. (1788). *Essays on the Active Powers of Man*. Edinburgh: Bell.

Reilly, R. (1976). "Self-Deception: Resolving the Epistemological Paradox." *The Personalist* 57:391–394.

Rorty, A. (1983). "Akratic Believers." *American Philosophical Quarterly* 20:175–183.

————— (1980a). "Akrasia and Conflict." *Inquiry* 22:193–212.

————— (1980b). "Self-Deception, Akrasia, and Irrationality." *Social Science Information* 19:905–922.

————— (1980c). "Where Does the Akratic Break Take Place?" *Australasian Journal of Philosophy* 58:333–346.

————— (1972). "Belief and Self-Deception." *Inquiry* 15:387–410.

Ryan, A. (1970). *Intentional Behavior: An Approach to Human Motivation*. New York: Ronald Press.

Sackheim H. & Gur R. (1985). "Voice Recognition and the Ontological Status of Self-Deception." *Journal of Personality and Social Psychology* 48:1365–1372.

Santas, G. (1966). "Plato's *Protagoras* and Explanations of Weakness." *Philosophical Review* 75:3–33.

Sartre, J. (1943/1956). *Being and Nothingness*. H. Barnes, trans. New York: Washington Square Press.

Schiffer, S. (1976). "A Paradox of Desire." *American Philosophical Quarterly* 13:195–203.

Schifter, D. & Ajzen, I. (1985). "Intention, Perceived Control, and Weight Loss: An Application of the Theory of Planned Behavior." *Journal of Personality and Social Psychology* 49:843–851.

Searle, J. (1983). *Intentionality*. Cambridge: Cambridge University Press.

———— (1979). "The Intentionality of Intention and Action." *Inquiry* 22: 253–280.

Sellars, W. (1973). "Action and Events." *Nous* 7:179–202.

———— (1966). "Thought and Action." In K. Lehrer, ed. *Freedom and Determinism* (New York: Random House), pp. 105–139.

Siegler, F. (1968). "An Analysis of Self-Deception." *Nous* 2:147–164.

Skinner, B. F. (1953). *Science and Human Behavior*. New York: Macmillan.

Snyder, C. (1985). "Collaborative Companions: The Relationship of Self-Deception and Excuse Making." In Martin, ed. *Self-Deception and Self-Understanding* (Lawrence, KA: University of Kansas Press), pp. 35–51.

Snyder, M. & Swann, W. (1978). "Behavioral Confirmation in Social Interaction: From Social Perception to Social Reality." *Journal of Experimental Social Psychology* 14:148–162.

Solnick, J., Kannenberg, C., Eckerman, D., Waller, M. (1980). "An Experimental Analysis of Impulsivity and Impulse Control in Humans." *Learning and Motivation* 11:61–77.

Sorensen, R. (1985). "Self-Deception and Scattered Events." *Mind* 94:64–69.

Sousa, R. de (1970). "Self-Deception." *Inquiry* 13:308–321.

Stich, S. (1983). *From Folk Psychology to Cognitive Science*. Cambridge, MA: MIT Press.

Stoutland, F. (1980). "Oblique Causation and Reasons for Action." *Synthese* 43:351–367.

Swann, W. & Read, S. (1981). "Self-Verification Processes: How We Sustain Our Self-Conceptions." *Journal of Experimental Social Psychology* 17:351–372.

Szabados, B. (1985). "The Self, its Passions, and Self-Deception." In Martin, ed. *Self-Deception and Self-Understanding* (Lawrence, KA: University of Kansas Press), pp. 143–168.

———— (1974). "Self-Deception." *Canadian Journal of Philosophy*. 4:51–68.

———— (1973). "Wishful Thinking and Self-Deception." *Analysis* 33:201–205.

Taylor, C. (1980). "Plato, Hare, and Davidson on Akrasia." *Mind* 89:499–518.

Taylor, S. & Crocker, J. (1980). "Schematic Bases of Social Information Processing." In E. Higgins et al., eds. *The Ontario Symposium on Personality and Social Psychology*, (Hillsdale, NJ: Erlbaum), 1:89–133.

Taylor, S. & Fiske, S. (1978). "Salience, Attention and Attribution: Top of the Head Phenomena." In L. Berkowitz, ed. *Advances in Experimental Social Psychology*, (New York: Academic Press), 11:250–288.

————— (1975). "Point of View and Perceptions of Causality." *Journal of Personality and Social Psychology* 32:439–445.

Tesser, A. (1978). "Self-Generated Attitude Change." In L. Berkowitz, ed. *Advances in Experimental Social Psychology*, (New York: Academic Press), 11:289–338.

Tetlock, D. & Levi, A. (1982). "Attribution Bias: On the Inconclusiveness of the Cognition-Motivation Debate." *Journal of Experimental Social Psychology* 18:68–88.

Thalberg, I. (1985). "Questions about Motivational Strength." In E. Lepore & B. Mclaughlin, eds. *Actions and Events* (Oxford: Basil Blackwell), pp. 88–103.

————— (1984). "Do Our Intentions Cause Our Intentional Actions?" *American Philosophical Quarterly* 21:249–260.

Thoresen, C. & Mahoney M. (1974). *Behavioral Self-Control*. New York: Holt, Rinehart & Winston.

Tuomela, R. (1977). *Human Action and its Explanation*. Dordrecht: Reidel.

Tversky, A. & Kahnemann, D. (1973). "Availability: A Heuristic for Judging Frequency and Probability." *Cognitive Psychology* 5:207–232.

Vernon, P. (1964). *Personality Assessment: A Critical Survey*. New York: Wiley.

Walster, E. (1966). "Assignment of Responsibility for an Accident." *Journal of Personality and Social Psychology* 3:73–79.

Wason, P. & Johnson-Laird, P. (1965). *Psychology of Reasoning: Structure and Content*. London: Batsford.

Watson, G. (1977). "Skepticism about Weakness of Will." *Philosphical Review* 86:316–339.

Weary, G. (1980). "Examination of Affect and Egotism as Mediators of Bias in Causal Attributions." *Journal of Personality and Social Psychology* 38:348–357.

Wiggins, D. (1978/79). "Weakness of Will, Commensurability, and the Objects of Deliberation and Desire." *Proceedings of the Aristotelian Society* 79:251–277.

Wilson, T. & Nisbett, R. (1978). "The Accuracy of Verbal Reports about the Effects of Stimuli on Evaluations and Behavior." *Social Psychology* 41:118–131.

Wright, G. von. (1963). *The Varieties of Goodness*. London: Routledge & Kegan-Paul.

Yates, B. & Mischel, W. (1979). "Young Childrens' Preferred Attentional Strategies for Delaying Gratification." *Journal of Personality and Social Psychology* 37: 286–300.

§

Index